Property of
Arkansas Library Commission
506½ Center St.
Little Rock, Arkansas

THE LIFE OF
EDGAR ALLAN POE

IN TWO VOLUMES

VOLUME II

Edgar Allan Poe.

THE LIFE OF
EDGAR ALLAN POE
PERSONAL AND LITERARY

WITH HIS CHIEF CORRESPONDENCE
WITH MEN OF LETTERS

BY

GEORGE E. WOODBERRY

VOLUME II

BIBLO and TANNEN
NEW YORK
1965

First published March 1909

Reprinted 1965 by
Biblo and Tannen Booksellers and Publishers, Inc.
63 Fourth Avenue New York, N.Y. 10003

Library of Congress Catalog Card Number: 65-23484

Printed in U.S.A. by
NOBLE OFFSET PRINTERS, INC.
NEW YORK 3, N. Y.

CONTENTS

ILLUSTRATIONS

THE LIFE OF EDGAR ALLAN POE

CHAPTER VIII

THE STYLUS

THE Prospectus of "The Stylus" was issued through the columns of the Philadelphia "Saturday Museum," March 4, 1843, which called attention to it in an editorial notice, together with a biography of Poe. It was shorter than that of the "Penn Magazine," but the identity of the two projects is avowed, and in the important parts describing the aims of the editors the same sentences formerly used are incorporated. The "*chief purpose*" is still declared to be to found a journal distinguished by "a sincere and fearless opinion," and it is announced as earnest of this intention that "an important feature of the work, and one which will be introduced in the opening number, will be a series of 'Critical and Biographical Sketches of American Writers,'" a plan that afterwards took many forms.

"The Stylus" was to be illustrated also, like the "Penn," and an agreement, signed January 31, 1843, had been entered into between Clarke and Poe on one side and F. O. C. Darley on the other, in accordance with which the latter was to furnish not less than three original designs per month to Clarke and Poe, at seven dollars each, until July 1, 1844, and was not to contribute similar designs for use in any other magazine during that period. The subjects were to be given by the editors; and the first work put into the artist's hands for this purpose was "The Gold Bug," for which he made and delivered some designs. Poe himself took the story to Mr. Darley, with whom he held pleasant relations. "He impressed me," writes the latter, "as a refined and very gentlemanly man; exceedingly neat in his person; interesting always, from the intellectual character of his mind, which appeared to me to be tinged with sadness. His manner was quiet and reserved; he rarely smiled. I remember his reading his 'Gold Bug' and 'Black Cat' to me before they were published. The form of his manuscript was peculiar: he wrote on half sheets of note paper, which he pasted together at the ends, making one continuous piece, which he rolled up tightly. As he read he dropped it upon the floor. It was very neatly written, and without corrections, apparently."[1] Several of these small rolls still exist.

Poe had also asked Thomas to write the biographical sketch of him for the "Museum," and himself furnished the memoranda. Thomas was obliged to decline: —

WASHINGTON, February 1, 1843.

MY DEAR POE, — You judged rightly I did not write to you [while] waiting "for some definite action of Congress on Smith's case." I feel most anxious (?) in the matter for you, my friend. About the biography. I duly received your notes, and determined at the earliest moment to take it in hand. Congress is now, you know, in session, and my labors at the department are terrible while it continues. There (?) I have set myself about writing out the notes, and there (?) I have been taken off. It would be a labor of love with me, Poe, as you know, and let who will do it now; some of these days I will do it better unless they do it d—d well. I could not do it until Congress adjourns, and not speedily then — I am so much occupied. I therefore think it best to send you the MS. as you request,

[1] Darley to the author, February 26, 1884.

but I do it with regret. I should be most glad to greet you in the capital. Come on if possible.

Yes, I saw the "Saturday Museum" in Mr. Robert Tyler's room, and happened to light upon the article in which we are mentioned. I read that portion of it to him, and shall take care that he is not misinformed on the subject. I remember Mr. Hirst.

Why the d—l did you not give me an inkling of what your good luck is. I was at a party last night, and came to the department rather dull, but when I opened your letter, and read, "In high spirits, Yours truly, E. A. Poe," I rose to "high spirits" myself. I assure you, Poe, that nothing gives me greater pleasure than to know that you are well and doing well.

Remember me most affectionately to your mother and lady and believe me truly your friend, F. W. Thomas.[1]

The desired biography was written by a young Philadelphia poet, H. B. Hirst, then an habitual associate of Poe, who breakfasted and went walking with him, and has been represented as a writer in whose work Poe's presence

[1] Griswold MSS.

is to be found. The life was written from Poe's memoranda, and a portrait was lithographed from a miniature; both were printed in the "Saturday Museum," of which it was also announced he was to be editor. He sent the paper [1] to Thomas, and others: —

PHILADELPHIA, February 25, 1843.

MY DEAR THOMAS, — Herewith I forward a "Saturday Museum" containing a Biography and caricature, both of myself. I am ugly enough, God knows, but not *quite* so bad as that. The biographer is H. W. Hirst of this city. I put into his hands your package, as returned, and he has taken the liberty of stating his indebtedness for memoranda to yourself — a slight extension of the truth for which I pray you to excuse him. He is a warm friend of yours, by the by — and a warm friend is a matter of moment at all times, but especially in this age of lukewarmness. *I* have also been guilty of an indiscretion in quoting from a private letter of yours to myself — I could not forego the temptation of letting the world know how well you thought of me.

[1] This was an advance copy, or else the issue of March 4 was a reprint from an earlier number.

On the outside of the paper you will see a Prospectus of "The Stylus" — my old "Penn" revived and remodelled under better auspices. I am anxious to hear your opinion of it. I have managed *at last* to secure, I think, the great object — a partner possessing ample capital, and, at the same time, so little self-esteem as to allow me entire control of the editorial conduct. He gives me, also, a half interest, and is to furnish funds for all the business operations — I agreeing to supply, for the first year, the literary matter. This will puzzle me no little, but I must do my best — write as much as possible myself, under my own name and pseudonyms, and hope for the casual aid of my friends, until the first stage of infancy is surpassed. The articles of copartnership have been signed and sealed for some weeks, and I should have written you before, informing you of my good luck, but that I was in hope of sending you, at the same time, a specimen sheet. Some little delay has occurred in getting it out on account of paper. In the mean time, all arrangements are progressing with spirit. We shall make the most magnificent magazine, as regards externals, ever seen. The finest paper, bold type, in single column, and superb wood-engravings in the manner of the French illustrated edition of "Gil Blas" by Gigoux, or "Robinson Crusoe" by Grandville.

There are three objects I would give a great deal to accomplish. Of the first I have some hope, but of the two last exceedingly little, unless you aid me. In the first place, I wish an article from yourself for my opening number; in the second, one from Mr. Rob Tyler; in the third, one from Judge Upshur. If I could get all this, I should be made, but I despair. Judge Upshur wrote some things for "The Messenger" during my editorship, and if I could get him interested in the scheme he *might*, by good management, be induced to give me an article, I care not how brief, or on what subject, *with his name*. It would be worth to me at least $500, and give me *caste* at once. I think him, as a reasoner, as a speaker, and as a writer, absolutely unsurpassed. I have the *very highest* opinion of his abilities. There is no man in America from whom I so strongly covet an article. Is it procurable?

In a few weeks, at farthest, I hope to take you by the hand. In the mean time write, and let me know how you come on. About a week since I enclosed an introductory letter to yourself in one to a friend of mine (Professor Wyatt) now in Washington. I presume you have seen him. He is much of a gentleman, and I think you will be pleased with him.

Virginia and Mrs. Clemm beg to be remembered. Truly your friend,

EDGAR A. POE.[1]

P. S. Smith not rejected yet! Ah, if I could only get the inspectorship, or something similar, *now* — how completely it would put me out of all difficulty.

Poe himself was shortly after sent to Washington to obtain subscriptions among his political friends, and, if possible, those of the President and Cabinet through his old acquaintance, Rob Tyler. He apparently also meant to lecture, and to look after his prospects of becoming an office-holder. The visit was unfortunate. On the evening of his arrival he began to drink. On the next day, March 11, he wrote to his partner: —

WASHINGTON, March 11, 1843.

MY DEAR SIR, — I write merely to inform you of my well-doing, for, so far, I have done nothing.

My friend Thomas, upon whom I depended,

[1] Griswold MSS.

is sick. I suppose he will be well in a few days. In the meantime I shall have to do the best I can.

I have not seen the President yet.

My expenses were more than I thought they would be, although I have economized in every respect, and this delay (Thomas being sick) puts me out sadly. *However*, all is going right. I have got the subscriptions of *all* the departments, President, &c. I believe that I am making a *sensation* which will tend to the benefit of the magazine.

Day after to-morrow I am to lecture. Rob Tyler is to give me an article, also Upshur. Send me $10 by mail as soon as you get this. I am grieved to ask you for money in this way, but you will find your account in it twice over.

Very truly yours, EDGAR A. POE.[1]

THOS. C. CLARKE, Esq.

The next day his friend Dow[2] wrote in his behalf: —

WASHINGTON, March 12, 1843.

DEAR SIR, — I deem it to be my bounden duty to write you this hurried letter in relation to our mutual friend E. A. P.

[1] Gill, p. 120.

[2] Then editor of the *Daily Madisonian*, a Tyler organ.

He arrived here a few days since. On the first evening he seemed somewhat excited, having been overpersuaded to take some port wine.

On the second day he kept pretty steady, but since then he has been, at intervals, quite unreliable.

He exposes himself here to those who may injure him very much with the President, and thus prevents us from doing for him what we wish to do and what we can do if he is himself again in Philadelphia. He does not understand the ways of politicians nor the manner of dealing with them to advantage. How should he?

Mr. Thomas is not well and cannot go home with Mr. P. My business and the health of my family will prevent me from so doing.

Under all the circumstances of the case, I think it advisable for you to come on and see him safely back to his home. Mrs. Poe is in a bad state of health, and I charge you, as you have a soul to be saved, to say not one word to her about him until he arrives with you. I shall expect you or an answer to this letter by return of mail.

Should you not come, we will see him on board the cars bound to Phila., but we fear he might be detained in Baltimore and not be out of harm's way.

I do this under a solemn responsibility. Mr. Poe has the highest order of intellect, and I cannot bear that he should be the sport of senseless creatures who, like oysters, keep sober, and gape and swallow everything.

I think your good judgment will tell you what course you ought to pursue in this matter, and I cannot think it will be necessary to let him know that I have written you this letter; but I cannot suffer him to injure himself here without giving you this warning.

Yours respectfully, J. E. Dow.[1]

To THOMAS C. CLARKE, Esq.,
Philadelphia, Pa.

Poe, however, was sent home by himself, and arrived at Philadelphia March 15, where he was met at the station by Mrs. Clemm. After going home he called on Clarke, and, the next day, wrote to his two friends: —

PHILADELPHIA, March 16, 1843.

MY DEAR THOMAS AND DOW, — I arrived here in perfect safety, and *sober*, about half-past four last evening — nothing occurring on the road of any consequence. I shaved and break-

[1] Gill, p. 121.

fasted in Baltimore, and lunched on the Susquehanna, and by the time I got to Philadelphia felt quite decent. Mrs. Clemm was expecting me at the car-office. I went immediately home, took a warm bath and supper, and then went to Clarke's. I never saw a man in my life more surprised to see another. He thought by Dow's epistle that I must not only be dead but buried, and would as soon have thought of seeing his great-great-great-grandmother. He received me, therefore, very cordially, and made light of the matter. I told him what had been agreed upon — that I was a little sick, and that Dow, knowing I had been, in times past, given to spreeing upon an extensive scale, had become unduly alarmed, &c., &c. — that when I found he had written, I thought it best to come home. He said my trip had improved me, and that he had never *seen me looking so well!* — and I don't believe I ever did. This morning I took medicine, and, as it is a snowy day will avail myself of the excuse to stay at home — so that by to-morrow I shall be *really* as well as ever. Virginia's health is about the same; but her distress of mind had been even more than I had anticipated. She desires her *kindest* remembrances to both of you — as also does Mrs. C.

Clarke, it appears, wrote to Dow, who must have received the letter this morning. Please reënclose the letter to me, here, so that I may know how to guide myself. And, Thomas, do write immediately as proposed. If *possible*, enclose a line from Rob Tyler — but I fear under the circumstances, it is not so. I blame no one but myself.

The letter which I looked for, and which I wished returned, is not on its way — reason, no money forthcoming — Lowell had not yet sent it. He is ill in New York, of ophthalmia. Immediately upon receipt of it, or before, I will forward the money you were both so kind as to lend, which is eight to Dow, and three and a half to Thomas. What a confounded business I have got myself into, attempting to write a letter to two people at once!

However, this is for Dow. My dear fellow, thank you a thousand times for your kindness and great forbearance, and don't say a word about the cloak turned inside out, or other peccadilloes of that nature. Also, express to your wife my deep regret for the vexation I must have occasioned her. Send me, also, if you can, the letter to Blythe. Call, also, at the barber's shop just above Fuller's and pay for me a levy which I believe I owe. And now, God bless you, for a nobler fellow never lived.

And this is for Thomas. My dear friend, forgive me my petulance and don't believe I think all I said. Believe me, I am very grateful to you for your many attentions and forbearances, and the time will never come when I shall forget either them or you. Remember me most kindly to Dr. Lacey — also to the Don, whose mustachios I do admire after all, and who has about the finest figure I ever beheld — also to Dr. Frailey. Please express my regret to Mr. Fuller for making such a fool of myself in his house, and say to him (if you think it necessary) that I should not have got half so drunk on his excellent port wine but for the rummy coffee with which I was forced to wash it down. I would be glad, too, if you would take an opportunity of saying to Mr. Rob Tyler that if he *can* look over matters and get me the inspectorship, I will join the Washingtonians forthwith. I am as serious as a judge — and much [more] so than many. I think it would be a feather in Mr. Tyler's cap to save from the perils of mint julep — and "Port wines" — a young man of whom all the world thinks so well and who thinks so remarkably well of himself.

And now, my dear friends, good-by, and believe me most truly yours,

EDGAR A. POE.

Upon getting here I found numerous letters of subscribers to my magazine — for which no canvass has yet been made. This was unexpected and cheering. Did you say, Dow, that Commodore Elliot had desired me to put down his name? Is it so, or did I dream it? At all events, when you see him, present my respects and thanks. Thomas, you will remember that Dr. Lacey wished me to put him down — but I don't know his first name — please let me have it.

[NOTE BY THOMAS: This letter explains itself. While his friends were trying to get Poe a place he came on to Washington in the way he mentions. He was soon quite sick, and while he was so Dow wrote to one of his friends in Philadelphia about him! Poor fellow. A place had been promised his friends for him, and in that state of suspense which is so trying to all men, and particularly to men of imagination, he presented himself in Washington certainly not in a way to advance his interests. I have seen a great deal of Poe, and it was his excessive and at times marked sociability [?] which forced him into his "frolics," rather than any mere morbid appetite for drink, but if he took but one glass of weak wine or beer or cider, the rubicon of the cup had been passed with him, and it almost always ended in excess and sickness. But he fought against the propensity as hard as ever Coleridge fought against it, and I am inclined to believe, after his sad experience and suffering, if he could have gotten office with a fixed salary, beyond the need of literary labour, that he would have redeemed himself, at least at this time. The accounts of his derelictions in this respect after I knew him were very much exaggerated. I have seen men who drank bottles of wine to Poe's wine-glasses who yet escaped all imputations of intemperance. His was one of those temperaments whose only safety is in total abstinence. He suffered terribly after any indiscretion. And, after all, what Byron said of Sheridan was truer of Poe: —

> . . . Ah, little do they know
> That what to them seemed vice might be but woe.

And, moreover, there is a great deal of heartache in the jestings of this letter. T.] [1]

Thomas soon replied: —

[1] Griswold MSS.

WASHINGTON, March 27, 1843.

MY DEAR FRIEND, — Yours of the 10th I duly received. I would have answered it immediately, but my desk got so behindhand during my illness, when you were here, that every moment of my time has been engaged in bringing it up.

Dow's epistle, I suppose, astounded your folks. He tells me that he mentions a conversation with me in it. Our friend Dow, you know, is an imaginative man, and he thought that you, as we say in the West, had "broken for high timber" I have had a hearty laugh at him for his fears. I am glad to learn that you are well.

I rejoice to know that your wife is better. I cannot leave the office at present to see Robert Tyler, as you suggest, to get a line from him. But this I can tell you, that the President yesterday asked me many questions about you, and spoke of you kindly. John Tyler, who was by, told the President that he wished he would give you an office in Philadelphia, and before he could reply a servant entered and called him out. John had heard of your frolic from a man who saw you in it, but I made light of the matter when he mentioned it to me, and he seemed to think nothing of it himself. He seems to feel a deep interest in you — Robert was not by. I feel satisfied that I can get you something from his pen for your Magazine. He lately made a speech here on St. Patrick's day, which has won for him great applause — you will find it in the "Intelligencer" of this morning. Read it and tell me what you think of it. I write in the greatest haste, and have not your letter by me, so reply to it from memory. Write as soon as you get this. Be of good cheer. I trust to see you an official yet.

In the greatest haste, yours truly,

F. W. THOMAS.[1]

While the affairs of the "Stylus" were faring thus, the "Pioneer" failed, in March, 1843. The contract bound Lowell and Carter to furnish the publishers five thousand copies on the twentieth of each month under a penalty of five hundred dollars in case of failure and the publishers to take that number at a certain price. The March number was eight days late, and the publishers, in the face of what was probably seen to be an unfortunate speculation, claimed the forfeit, but offered to waive it if the contract should be altered so as to require them to take only so many copies as they could sell. The result was that the editors were obliged to stop printing from a

[1] Griswold MSS.

lack of credit, and were left with a large indebtedness for manufacture as well as to contributors. Lowell wrote to Poe about it: —

BOSTON, March 24, 1843.

MY DEAR FRIEND, — I have neglected writing to you too long already, in the hope of being able to remit the money I owe you. When I shall have stated the facts, I think that you will excuse my want of punctuality. The magazine was started on my own responsibility, & I relied on the payments I should receive from my publishers to keep me even with my creditors until the Magazine should be firmly established. You may conceive my distress when the very first note given me by my publishers has been protested for nonpayment, & the magazine ruined. For I was unable to go on any farther, having already incurred a debt of $1800 or more.

I hope soon to make such arrangements as will enable me to borrow this sum — pay all my debts & leave [me] free to go [to] work & apply my earnings to getting the load off my shoulders. The loss of my eyes at this juncture (for I am as yet unable to use them to any extent) adds to my distress. I shall remit to you before long — meanwhile do write me on receipt of this & tell me that you forgive me for what truly is more my misfortune than my fault — & that you still regard me as ever

Your friend in all ways,

J. R. LOWELL.[1]

P. S. I hear you have become an Editor. Is it true? I hope so; if it were only to keep our criticism in a little better trim.

That Clarke had not been implacably offended by the untoward incident at Washington appears from Poe's reply, in which the project of the "Stylus" is announced to Lowell, who was himself ill with ophthalmia.

PHILADELPHIA, March 27, '43.

MY DEAR FRIEND, — I have just received yours of the 24th and am deeply grieved, first that you should have been so unfortunate, and, secondly, that you should have thought it necessary to offer me any apology for your misfortunes. As for the few dollars you owe me — give yourself not one moment's concern about *them.* I am poor, but must be very much poorer, indeed, when I even think of demanding them.

But I sincerely hope all is not so bad as you

[1] Griswold MSS.

suppose it, and that, when you come to look about you, you will be able to continue "The Pioneer." Its decease, just now, would be a most severe blow to the good cause — the cause of a Pure Taste. I have looked upon your Magazine, from its outset, as the best in America, and have lost no opportunity of expressing the opinion. Herewith I send a paper, "The Phil. Sat. Museum," in which I have said a few words on the topic.

I am *not* editing this paper, although an announcement was prematurely made to that effect; but have the privilege of inserting what I please editorially. On the first of July next I hope to issue the first number of "The Stylus," a new monthly, with some novel features. I send you, also, a paper containing the Prospectus. In a few weeks I hope to forward you a specimen sheet. I am anxious to get a poem from yourself for the opening number, but, until you recover your health, I fear that I should be wrong in making the request.

Believe me, my dear friend, that I sympathize with you *truly* in your affliction. When I heard that you had returned to Boston, I hoped you were entirely well, and your letter disappoints and grieves me.

When you find yourself in condition to write, I would be indebted to you if you could put me in the way of procuring a brief article (also for my opening number) from Mr. Hawthorne — whom I believe you know personally. Whatever you gave him, we should be happy to give. A part of my design is to illustrate, whatever is fairly susceptible of illustration, with finely executed wood-engravings — after the fashion of Gigoux's "Gil Blas" or Grandville's "Gulliver" — and I wish to get a tale from Mr. Hawthorne as early as possible (if I am so fortunate as to get one at all), that I may put the illustration in the hands of the artist.

You will see by the Prospectus that we intend to give a series of portraits of the American literati, with critical sketches. I would be glad if I could so arrange matters as to have you *first*, provided you yourself have no serious objection. Instead of the "full-length portraits" promised in the Prospectus (which will be modified in the specimen sheet), we shall have medallions about three inches in diameter. Could you put me in possession of any likeness of yourself? — or would you do me the same favor in regard to Mr. Hawthorne? — You perceive I proceed upon the ground that you are intimate with

Mr. H., and that making these inquiries would not subject you to trouble or inconvenience.

I confess that I am by no means so conversant with your own compositions (especially in prose) as I should be. Could you furnish me with some biographical and critical data, and tell me when or how I could be put in possession of your writings generally? — but I fear I am asking altogether too much.

If the 4th number of "The Pioneer" is printed, I would be obliged if you would send me an early copy through the P. O.

Please remember me to Mr. Carter, and believe me

Most sincerely your friend,

EDGAR A. POE.[1]

J. RUSSELL LOWELL, Esqre.

Lowell wrote to him, with regard to all these topics three letters: —

BOSTON, April 17, 1843.

MY DEAR FRIEND, — Hawthorne writes me that he shall be able to send an article in the course of a week or two. His terms are $5 a page, but probably, as your pages will "eat up" Copy with a less anaconda-like appetite than

[1] Lowell MSS.

the fine print magazines, your best plan would be to pay him so much by the article. His wife will make a drawing of his head or he will have a Daguerreotype taken, so that you can have a likeness of him.

As to my own effigies. Page has painted a head of me which is called very fine, & which is now Exhibiting (I believe) at the National Academy in New York. This might be Daguerreotyped — or I might have one taken from my head as it is now — namely in a more civilized condition — the portrait by Page having *very* long hair, not to mention a beard and some symptoms of moustache, & looking altogether, perhaps, too antique to be palatable to the gentle public. But you shall use your own judgment about that.

I write now in considerable confusion, being just on the eve of quitting the office which I occupy as "Attorney & Counsellor at Law." I have given up that interesting profession, & mean to devote myself wholly to letters. I shall live with my father at Cambridge in the house where I was born. I shall write again soon & send you a poem and some data for a biographical sketch. Take my best love in exchange for your ready sympathy & use me always

JAMES RUSSELL LOWELL

as you may have occasion as your affectionate friend. J. R. L.[1]

My address will be "Cambridge, Mass." in future. I do hope and trust that *your* magazine will succeed. Be very watchful of your publishers & agents. They must be driven as men drive swine, take your eyes off them for an instant & they bolt between your legs & leave you in the mire. J. R. L.

CAMBRIDGE, May 8, 1843.

MY DEAR FRIEND, — I have been delaying to write to you from day to day in the expectation that I should have received an article from Hawthorne to send with my letter. I am now domiciled in the country & have been doing nothing but ramble about, gardening, farming, tending an increasing flock of poultry & in short, being out of doors & in active exercise as much as possible in order to restore my eyes effectually.

I have got the idea of Hawthorne's article so fixed in my mind that I forgot that I did not send you a poem in my last. I have such a reluctance to go into the city that though I have been here nearly three weeks I have not even

[1] Griswold MSS.

brought out my MSS. yet. But I mean to do it in a day or two & shall then send you something which I hope will be to your liking. You must forgive my dilatoriness, my dear friend, the natural strength of which is increased by the pressure of my debts — a source of constantly annoying thought which prevents my doing almost anything as yet.

With regard to a sketch of my own life, my friend [Robert] Carter thinks that he can give it better than I — and perhaps he will send you one. Meanwhile I give a few dates. I was born Feby 22, 1819, in this house at Cambridge — entered Harvard College in 1834 & took my degree as Bachelor of Arts in regular course in 1838 — my master's degree in 1841. While in college I was one of the editors elected to edit the periodical then published by the undergraduates, & also to deliver the Class poem — a yearly performance which requires a poet every year who is created as easily by the class vote as a baronet or peer of the realm is in England. I was in the Law School under Judge Story for two years & upwards, took a degree of Bachelor of Laws by force of having my name on the books as a student — & published a volume of rather crude productions (in which there is more of everybody else than of myself) in January, 1841. On the Mother's side I am of Scotch descent.

I forgot to thank you for the biographical sketch of your own eventful life which you sent me. Your early poems display a maturity which astonished me & I recollect no individual (& I believe I have all the poetry that was ever written) whose early poems were anything like as good. Shelley is nearest, perhaps.

I have greater hopes of your "Stylus" than I had of my own magazine, for I think you understand editing vastly better than I shall for many years yet — & you have more of that quality — which is the Siamese twin brother of genius — industry — than I.

I shall write again shortly. Meanwhile, I am your affectionate & obliged friend

J. R. L.[1]

[No date. Postmark, BOSTON, May 16.]

MY DEAR FRIEND, — I send you this little poem with some fears that you will be disappointed therein. But it is on the whole the most likely to please of any that I could lay my hands on — my MSS. being trusted to fortune like the

[1] Griswold MSS.

Sybil's leaves, & perhaps, like hers, rising in value to my mind as they decrease in number. You must tell me frankly how you like what I sent & what you should like better. Will you give me your address more particularly so that in case I have a package to send you I can forward it by express?

With all truth & love I remain your friend,

J. R. L.[1]

A letter from Carter is of the nature of an appendix to all this correspondence: —

CAMBRIDGE, MASS., June 19, 1843.

MY DEAR SIR, — I send you with this letter a copy of the "Boston Notion," April 29, containing an abridgment which I made of the sketch of your life and writings which appeared in the "Phila. Sat. Museum." I was absent from the city when it was printed and did not see the proof; consequently it is full of atrocious errors. What has become of the "Stylus"? I trust that it has not been found prudent to relinquish the enterprise, though I fear that such is the case. It would give the friends of pure and elevated literature in this region great pleasure to learn that it is only temporarily delayed.

[1] Griswold MSS.

Mr. Lowell is in excellent health and his eyes have nearly recovered their usual strength. He has entirely abandoned his profession and is living at his father's house in the vicinity of this village. About a fortnight since he began to scribble vigorously and has within that period written about a thousand lines. You will see in the next "Democratic Review," or at least in the August no., his longest and . . . [margin cut] blank verse and is entitled "Prometheus." It contains nearly four hundred lines I think, and was written in seven or eight hours. At least, I left him one day at 11 A. M. and he had concluded to begin it immediately, and when I saw him again at about 8½ P. M. the same day he read to me upwards of two hundred and fifty lines and he had written besides before he began some stanzas of a long poem in ottava rima which has occupied him chiefly for the last two weeks. Graham has also a poem from him and there will be one in the next "New Mirror."

Within a week I have read for the first time, "Pym's Narrative." I lent it to a friend who lives in the house with me, and who is a lawyer, a graduate of Harvard, and a brother of Dr. O. W. Holmes, yet he is so completely deceived by the minute accuracy of some of the details, the remarks about the statements of the press, the names of people at New Bedford, &c. that, though an intelligent and shrewd man he will not be persuaded that it is a fictitious work, by any arguments drawn from the book itself, though . . . [margin cut] the latter part of the narrative. I dislike to tell him that I *know* it to be fictitious, for to test its truthfulness I gave it to him without remark and he has so committed himself by grave criticisms on its details that I dread to undeceive him. He has crossed the Atlantic twice and commented on an inaccuracy in the description of Pym's midnight voyage with his drunken friend. I have not the book in the house, and knowing nothing of the sea, did not clearly comprehend the objection, but I think it was upon setting a "jib" or some such thing upon a dismasted *sloop* — I know that the words "jib," "sloop," & "only one mast" occurred in his remarks.

To return to a safer subject — I am extremely desirous of knowing the name of your novel in two volumes alluded to in the "Museum" . . . and if it be not a secret, or one that can be confided to a stranger, would be obliged by its communication. And while I am in an inquisitive mood, let me beg of you to tell me whether the name of the author of Stanley is *Walter* or *Wm* Landor and whether he has recently or will soon publish anything. Also who is the author of "Zoe" and the "Aristocrat"?

My address is still "Boston, care of Rev. Dr. Lowell."

Truly & respectfully your friend [1]
[Signature cut out.]

At the same time Poe received from one of his Baltimore relatives, William Poe, a letter partly of congratulation and sympathy, partly of warning: —

BALTIMORE, June 15, 1843.

DEAR EDGAR, — I wrote you on the 15th ulto. since which time I have received nothing from you; mine was in answer to a letter received giving an account of your many recent reverses, and I fear it was in a style not relished by you, but in great sincerity of feeling for you and yours I wrote it, and the reason why I presumed to be so free in my expressions was in consequence of the great friendship I feel for you, and interest I take in your welfare, and therefore hoped to hear again from you, and of your wife's being better, and your recovery from the sickness and de-

[1] Griswold MSS.

spondency you were suffering when you last wrote. I still write from the same motives. I observed in the "Baltimore Sun" newspaper in an editorial that you have again lately been successful in having awarded to you a prize of $100 by the "Dollar Newspaper" for a tale called the "Gold Bug," which gave me much pleasure, and hope it came in time to relieve you from some of your pecuniary wants. Ought you ever to give up in despair when you have such resources as your well-stored mind to apply to? Let me entreat you then to persevere, for I hope the time is not far distant when a change will take place in your affairs and place you beyond want in this world.

Will you write to me freely, and let me know what are your prospects in getting out "The Stylus," and how your wife is, and Mrs. Clemm — how is she? It would give me pleasure to hear from her. There is one thing I am anxious to caution you against and which has been a great enemy to our family, — I hope, however, in your case, it may prove unnecessary, — "a too free use of the Bottle." Too many, and especially literary characters, have sought to drown their sorrows and disappointments by this means, but in vain, and only, when it has been too late, discovered it to be a deeper source of misery. But enough of this, say you, and so say I: therefore, hoping this may find you in better spirits and better prospects of future happiness, I subscribe myself, Yours affectionately,

WILLIAM POE.[1]

But the "Stylus" had been abandoned. He wrote of its demise to Lowell: —

PHILADELPHIA, June 20, 1843.

MY DEAR FRIEND, — I owe you fifty apologies for not having written you before — but sickness and domestic affliction will suffice for all.

I received your poem, which you undervalue, and which I think truly beautiful — as, indeed, I do all you have ever written — but alas! my Magazine scheme has exploded — or, at least, I have been deprived, through the imbecility, or rather through the idiocy of my partner, of all means of prosecuting it for the present. Under better auspices I may resume it next year.

What am I to do with the poem? I have handed it to Griswold, subject to your disposition. (See next page.)

My address is 234 North Seventh St., above

[1] Griswold MSS.

Spring Garden, West Side. Should you ever pay a visit to Philadelphia, you will remember that there is no one in America whom I would rather hold by the hand than yourself.

With the sincerest friendship I am yours,

EDGAR A. POE.[1]

But Poe was sick and poor. On June 11 he had written to Griswold:—

DEAR GRISWOLD, — Can you not send me $5? I am sick and Virginia is almost gone. Come and see me. Peterson says you suspect me of a curious anonymous letter. I did not write it, but bring it along with you when you make the visit you promised to Mrs. Clemm. I will try to fix that matter soon. Could you do anything with my *note?* Yours truly,

E. A. P.[2]

It was probably in response to this letter that Griswold called upon him at his home, in the outskirts, to which the family had removed from their earlier dwelling-place, in the spring of 1842, probably for the sake of Virginia's health, as the situation was more in the country.[3] Griswold gave a description of it:—

[1] Lowell MSS. [2] Griswold, xx.

[3] On settling in Philadelphia, Poe took lodgings in Arch

"When once he sent for me to visit him, during a period of illness caused by protracted and anxious watching at the side of his sick wife, I was impressed by the singular neatness and the air of refinement in his home. It was in a small house, in one of the pleasant and silent neighborhoods far from the centre of the town, and though slightly and cheaply furnished everything in it was so tasteful and so fitly disposed that it seemed altogether suitable for a man of genius. For this and for most of the comforts he enjoyed, in his brightest as in his darkest years, he was chiefly indebted to his mother-in-law, who loved him with more than maternal devotion and constancy." [1]

To this same period of unusual poverty and suffering Mayne Reid's characterization of Mrs. Clemm probably belongs: —

"She was the ever-vigilant guardian of the home, watching it against the silent but continuous sap of necessity, that appeared every day to

Street, and in September, 1839 (Poe to Brooks, Stoddard, lxxxvi), removed to a small house probably on Coates Street, North Fairmount Park, where he was living in 1842 (*City Directory*, 1843); by May of that year (*supra*, i, 326) he again removed to Seventh Street above Spring Garden (*City Directory*, 1844).

[1] Griswold, xxxiv.

be approaching closer and nearer. She was the sole servant, keeping everything clean; the sole messenger, doing the errands, making pilgrimages between the poet and his publishers, frequently bringing back such chilling responses as 'The article not accepted,' or 'The check not to be given until such and such a day,' — often too late for his necessities. And she was also the messenger to the market; from it bringing back not 'the delicacies of the season,' but only such commodities as were called for by the dire exigencies of hunger."[1]

He remembered the house as "a lean-to of three rooms (there may have been a garret with a closet), of painted plank construction, supported against the gable of the more pretentious dwelling," — the latter being a four story red-brick mansion of a wealthy Quaker. But Mr. T. C. Clarke, whose family visited the Poes more or less frequently, describes it as a cottage set back from the street amid luxuriant grape and other vines, and ornamented in winter with flowers. It was a small, humble home with a plot of grass by the side, a porch with a rose-bush and vine, and low eaves; and at times one room was

[1] *Onward*, quoted in the *Brooklyn Daily Eagle*, March 30, 1869.

rented to a boarder.[1] There Clarke especially remembered Virginia, slowly wasting away in consumption, but "wearing on her beautiful countenance the smile of resignation, and the warm, even cheerful look with which she ever greeted her friends." [2] The appearance of the house, however, and the simple hospitality enjoyed in it, must have varied materially; its contents were known to the pawnbroker; and it is said that the family now became the object of charity.

During these trying months Poe won the one-hundred-dollar prize from "The Dollar Newspaper," edited by Joseph Sailer, for the story of "The Gold Bug," originally intended for the "Stylus" and now recovered from Graham by exchanging a critical article for it. This, the most widely circulated of his tales, was published in two parts: the first June 21, 1843, and the second (together with the first, which was reprinted) a week later. On July 12 it was published again with two other prize tales in a supplement. A charge that it was plagiarized from Miss Sherburne's "Imogene, or The Pirate's Treasure," was made in "The Spirit of the Times," and was widely circulated, but a

[1] Mrs. Weiss, p. 94.

[2] Gill, p. 101.

refutation was quickly attempted in "The Dollar Newspaper," July 19. The only other stories of Poe's published during this year were "The Tell-Tale Heart" in the "Pioneer," the third of the tales of conscience, and "The Black Cat" in the "United States Saturday Post" (as the old "Saturday Evening Post" was now called), August 19, and "Morning on the Wissahiccon," a quiet landscape sketch of the environs of Philadelphia (evidently "The Elk," mentioned hereafter), contributed to Willis's annual, "The Opal," for 1844. In criticism he published in the "Pioneer" "Notes upon English Verse," a purely metrical discussion, which he afterwards remoulded into the "Rationale of Verse"; and in "Graham's" four critical notices: "Flaccus," a satirical review of one Thomas Ward, which he afterwards regarded as in his best manner, and "William Ellery Channing," perhaps the most contemptuous notice he ever seriously wrote, — these being the second and third of the series "Our Amateur Poets"; "Fitz-Greene Halleck," being No. viii of "Our Contributors"; and Cooper's "Wyandotte," a perfunctory performance. He also published, in the "Pioneer," "Lenore," a greatly revised version of his old "Pæan," and in "Graham's"

THE GOLD BUG

the fine poem entitled "The Conqueror Worm." In the fall an edition of his "Tales," in parts, was undertaken, but only one issue is known.[1]

Poe still interested himself from time to time in the solution of cryptographs, an occupation which the following letter to Tomlin, the Tennessee poet and postmaster, who had taken the greatest interest in the "Stylus," with its sidelights upon other topics, sufficiently illustrates: —

PHILA., August 28, 1843.

MY DEAR SIR, — I have just rec[d] your letter, enclosing one in hieroglyphical writing from Mr. Meek, and hasten to reply, since *you* desire it; although, some months ago, I was obliged to make a vow that I would engage in the solution of no more cryptographs. The reason of my making this vow will be readily understood. Much curiosity was excited throughout the country by my solutions of these cyphers, and a great number of persons felt a desire to test my powers individually — so that I was at one time absolutely overwhelmed; and this placed me in a dilemma; for I had either to devote my whole time to the solu-

[1] *The Prose Romances of Edgar A. Poe. No. 1. The Murders of the Rue Morgue* and *The Man that was Used Up.* 1843, 8vo, pp. 40, paper. Philadelphia: George B. Zieber & Co.

tions, or the correspondents would suppose me a mere boaster, incapable of fulfilling my promises. I had no alternative but to solve all; but to each correspondent I made known my intentions to solve no more. You will hardly believe me when I tell you that I have lost, in time, which to me is money, more than a thousand dollars, in solving ciphers, with no other object in view than that just mentioned. A really difficult cipher requires vast labor and the most patient thought in its solution. Mr. Meek's letter is very simple indeed, and merely shows that he misapprehends the whole matter. It runs thus: —

[Here follows the solution.]

This is the whole of Mr. Meek's letter — but he is mistaken in supposing that I "pride myself" upon my solutions of ciphers. I feel little pride about anything.

It is very true, as he says, that cypher writing is "no great difficulty if the signs represent invariably the same letters and are divided into separate words." But the fact is, that most of the criptographs sent to me (Dr. Frailey's for instance) were *not* divided into words, and moreover, the signs *never* represented the same letter twice.

But here is an infallible mode of showing Mr.

Meek that he knows nothing about the matter. He says cipher writing "is no great difficulty if the signs represent invariably the same letters and are divided into separate words." This is true; and yet, little as this difficulty is, he cannot surmount it. Send him, as if from yourself, these few words, in which the conditions stated by him are rigidly preserved. I will answer for it, he cannot decipher them for his life. They are taken at random from a well-known work now lying beside me:—

[Here follows Poe's cryptograph.]

And now, my dear friend, have you forgotten that I asked you, some time since, to render me an important favor? You can surely have no scruples in a case of this kind. I have reason to believe that I have been maligned by some envious scoundrel in this city, who has written you a letter respecting myself. I believe I know the villain's name. It is Wilmer. In Philadelphia no one speaks to him. He is avoided by all as a reprobate of the lowest class. Feeling a deep pity for him, I endeavoured to befriend him, and you remember that I rendered myself liable to some censure by writing a review of his filthy pamphlet called the "Quacks of Helicon." He has returned my good offices by slander behind my back. *All* here are anxious to have him convicted — for there is scarcely a gentleman in Phila[a] whom he has not libelled, through the gross malignity of his nature. Now, I ask you, as a friend and as a man of noble feelings, to send me his letter to you. It is your *duty* to do this — and I am sure, upon reflection, you will so regard it.

I await your answer impatiently.

Your friend, E. A. POE.[1]

Tomlin answered and sent the desired enclosure:—

JACKSON, TENNESSEE, September 10, 1843.

DEAR SIR,—My friendship for you, and nothing else, has prevailed on me to enclose you the letter of L. A. Wilmer, Esquire. But I much fear that in doing it I have violated somewhat the rules that govern correspondence in such matters. Believing, however, that your great good sense will but protect my honor in this transaction, I remain with affectionate regard,

Yours ever, JNO. TOMLIN.

PHILADELPHIA, May 20, 1843.

DEAR SIR, — . . . Literary affairs are at a very low ebb in this city at present.

[1] Poe to John Tomlin, Esq., MS.

Edgar A. Poe (you know him by character, no doubt, if not personally) has become one of the strangest of our literati. He and I are old friends, have known each other from boyhood, and it gives me inexpressible pain to notice the vagaries to which he has lately become subject. Poor fellow! he is not a teetotaller by any means, and I fear he is going headlong to destruction, moral, physical, and intellectual. . . .

Your obliged and sincere friend,

L. A. WILMER.[1]

Wilmer, after Poe's death, was one of his most faithful defenders. Scandal, however, was busy with Poe's name, and found its way into print in one of the city papers, in an article of which Poe suspected Griswold to be the author. There is a tradition that he visited Saratoga this summer, as the guest of a wealthy Philadelphia lady, and also in the previous summer; but little is now recollected of the incident.[2]

After the fall came, the main information concerning Poe is derived from his letters to Lowell: —

[1] Griswold MSS.

[2] Mrs. Weiss, p. 195. The same story reappears in the tradition concerning the composition of "The Raven."

PHILADELPHIA, September 13, 1843.

MY DEAR FRIEND, — Since I last wrote you I have suffered much from domestic and pecuniary trouble, and, at one period, had nearly succumbed. I mention this by way of apology to the request I am forced to make — that you would send me, if possible, $10 — which, I believe, is the amount you owe me for contribution. You cannot imagine how sincerely I grieve that any necessity can urge me to ask this of you — but I ask it in the hope that you are now in much better position than myself, and can spare me the sum without inconvenience.

I hope ere long to have the pleasure of conversing with you personally. There is no man living with whom I have so much desire to become acquainted.

Truly your friend,

EDGAR A. POE.[1]

J. R. LOWELL, Esqre.

PHILADELPHIA, October 19, 1843.

MY DEAR FRIEND, — I was upon the point of fulfilling a long neglected duty and replying to Mr. Carter's letter, enclosing $5, when I received yours of the 13th, remitting $5 more. Believe me

[1] Lowell MSS.

I am sincerely grateful to you both for your uniform kindness and consideration.

You say nothing of your health — but Mr. C. speaks of its perfect restoration, and I see, by your very MS., that you are well again, body and mind. I need not say that I am rejoiced at this — for you must know and feel that I am. When I thought of the possible loss of your eyesight, I grieved as if some dreadful misfortune were about happening to myself.

I shall look with much anxiety for your promised volume. Will it include your "Year's Life," and other poems already published? I hope that it may; for these have not yet been fairly placed before the eye of the world. I am seeking an opportunity to do you justice in a review, and may find it in "Graham," when your book appears. No poet in America has done so much. I have maintained this upon all occasions. Mr. Longfellow has genius, but by no means equals you in the true spirit. He is moreover so prone to imitation that I know not how to understand him at times. I am in doubt whether he should not be termed an arrant plagiarist. You have read his "Spanish Student"? I have written quite a long notice of it for Graham's December number. The play is a poor composition, with some fine poetical passages. His "Hymn to the Night," with some strange blemishes, is glorious. — How much I should like to interchange opinions with you upon poems and poets in general! I fancy that we should agree, usually, in results, while differing, frequently, about principles. The day may come when we can discuss everything at leisure, in person.

You say that your long poem has taught you a useful lesson, — "that you are unfit to write narrative — unless in a dramatic form." It is not you that are unfit for the task — but the task for you — for any poet. Poetry must eschew narrative — except, as you say, dramatically. I mean to say that the *true* poetry — the highest poetry — must eschew it. The Iliad is *not* the highest. The connecting links of a narrative — the frequent passages which have to serve the purpose of binding together the parts of the story, are necessarily prose, from their very explanatory nature. To color them — to gloss over their prosaic nature — (for this is the most which can be done) requires great skill. Thus Byron, who was no artist, is always driven, in his narrative, to fragmentary passages, eked out with asterisks. Moore succeeds better than any one. His "Alciphron" is wonderful in the force, grace, and nature of its purely narrative passages: — but pardon me for prosing.

I send you the paper with my life and portrait. The former is true in general — the latter particularly false. It does not convey the faintest idea of my person. No one of my family recognized it. But this is a point of little importance. You will see, upon the back of the biography, an announcement that I was to assume the editorship of the "Museum." This was unauthorized. I never did edit it. The review of "Graham's Magazine" was written by H. B. Hirst — a young poet of this city. Who is to write your life for "Graham"? It is a pity that so many of these biographies were entrusted to Mr. Griswold. He certainly lacks independence, or judgment, or both.

I have tried in vain to get a copy of your "Year's Life" in Philadelphia. If you have one, and could spare it, I would be much obliged.

Do write me again when you have leisure, and believe me,

Your most sincere friend,

EDGAR A. POE.[1]

J. R. LOWELL, Esqre.

[1] Lowell MSS.

At some time during the summer Poe is said to have made his début as a lecturer in the "Egyptian Hall," Baltimore. He appeared in Philadelphia in the same rôle, November 25, and made a favorable impression. His subject was "The Poets and Poetry of America"; and while the lecture was largely compiled from his former book reviews, it was especially distinguished by an attack, which seems to have been unusually severe, on Griswold's volume. At some time before this date there had appeared in the "Saturday Museum" an anonymous review of the third edition of Griswold's work, in which that reverend gentleman was held up to public ridicule in the most scoffing and bitter style, and contrasted with Poe by name, much to the latter's praise and to his own degradation. This mingled expression of pique, wrath, and scorn, with its flaunting self-commendation, is indubitably Poe's own work. Poe afterwards explained the attack to Griswold, which he described as "some absurd jokes at your expense," as being due to "——'s false imputation of that beastly article to you," referring to the scandalous publication of the summer in a Philadelphia paper. The flagellation Griswold received in the lecture, which does not seem to have displeased his literary associates, caused an open breach between himself and Poe that was not closed, even in appearance, until a year and a half had elapsed. It is worthy of note that Griswold had left his place on "Graham's" about three months before the delivery of the address.

The receipts from lecturing could not have been large, and for one cause or another the editors who were accustomed to publish Poe's work either would not buy it or else delayed to print it. After Griswold's retirement from "Graham's," Poe seems to have contributed freely to the critical department; and there in March, 1844, appeared his only signed article for several months past, a lengthy review of the drama, "Orion," by Richard Hengist Horne, recently published in England. Of this work, which appealed strongly to Poe's delight in pictorial fancy and subdued mystical suggestion, he declared, "It is our deliberate opinion that in all that regards the loftiest and holiest attributes of the true Poetry, 'Orion' has *never* been excelled. Indeed, we feel strongly inclined to say that it has never been *equaled*." After comparing one passage of it with Milton's description of hell, the latter being "*altogether inferior* in graphic effect, in originality, in expression, in the true imagination," he concludes more calmly that "'Orion' will be admitted, by every man of genius, to be one of the noblest, if not the very noblest poetical work of the age." [1]

Poe entered into correspondence with Horne, and endeavored through him to place some of his work in England, as he appears to have done formerly through "Blackwood's" and Dickens; he sent the tale of "The Spectacles," but if anything resulted from the plan, it has escaped identification. Horne replied in two letters: —

LONDON, April 16, 1844.

MY DEAR SIR, — I have received your letter this morning, and shall feel now and at all times happy in forwarding your views here so far as I am able, in these matters of literary engagement. Just at this time, however, and probably for some months to come, I shall not be *likely* to have the power. If you have seen the "New Spirit of the Age," you will readily understand that a great many critics here and some authors are far from pleased with me. The attacks and jeers in magazines and newspapers (though several have treated me very fairly) are nearly all written by friends of the angry parties or

[1] *Works*, vi, 279, 287.

influenced by them. Perhaps I may say a word on this point in the Second Edition now preparing. I mention this to show you *why* I can do so little at present. I need not say to an American that when the storm has blown over, those trees that are not blown down nor injured look all the fresher among the wrecks. I dare say I shall be able to do what you wish before long. I should prefer to do this so that you are fairly remunerated; but if the parties are *not* in a "paying condition," then I will put you in direct communication with them to arrange the matter yourself.

I could most probably obtain the insertion of the article you have sent in "Jerrold's Illuminated Magazine." Jerrold has always spoken and written very handsomely and eloquently about me, and there would be no difficulty. But —I fear this magazine is not doing at all well. I tell you this *in confidence.* They have a large but inadequate circulation. The remuneration would be scarcely worth having — ten guineas a sheet is poor pay for such a page! And now, perhaps, they do not even give that. I will see. My impression, however, is that for the reasons stated previously, I shall not at *present* be able to assist you in the way I could best wish.

Your name is well known to me in the critical literature of America, although I have not seen any American magazine for some months. I have ordered the last two numbers of "Graham's Magazine," but have not received them from my booksellers. I am very grateful for the noble and generous terms in which you speak of my works.

I have written you a business-like, and not a very "spiritual," letter, you will think. Still, as you are kind enough to give me credit for some things of the latter kind, it seemed best at this distance to reply to your wishes practically. I am, dear sir,

Yours truly, R. H. HORNE.[1]

LONDON, April 27, 1844.

MY DEAR SIR, — When I replied to your letter (which I did by the next post of the day on which I received it) I had not seen the number of "Graham's" for March, containing the review of "Orion." Mr. C. Matthews, of New York, had been so good as to inform me there would be a review; and he, at the same time, mentioned that he had sent me a copy of the magazine in question. My friend Miss E. B. Barrett also sent me a note to the same effect. But owing, no

[1] Griswold, MSS.

doubt, to some forgetfulness on the part of the booksellers who were to forward it, the magazine never reached me, nor was it at Wiley & Putnam's when I called the other day. Your MS. of "The Spectacles" is safely lodged in my iron chest with my own MSS. till I find a favorable opportunity for its use.

I have carefully read and considered the review of "Orion" in the magazine. It would be uncandid in me to appear to agree to all the objections; and, amidst such high praise, so independently and courageously awarded, it would be ungrateful in me to offer any self-justificatory remark on any such objections. I shall, therefore, only observe that there are *some* objections from which I can *derive advantage* in the way of revision — which is more than I can say of any of the critiques written on this side of the water. One passage, in particular, I will mention. It is that which occurs at p. 103. "Star-rays that first" — needlessly obscure, as you truly say. For, in fact, I *did* allude to Sleep, as the antecedent — and it should have been printed with a capital letter. What I meant by the passage, if rendered in prose, would be something like this: "The God Sleep, lying in his cave by the old divine sea, feeleth the star-rays upon his eyelids at times; and then his sleep is not perfect, and he dreams, or for a brief interval awakes. Without which awaking he would never have known surprise, nor hope, nor useful action. Because (your poet herein bewitched by a theory he fancies original) we are never *surprised* at anything. however wonderful, in a dream; neither do we *hope;* nor do we perform any action with an idea of its being at all useful." A pretty condition, you see, my imagination had got into while writing this passage. The explanation, if it does not make you angry, will, I think, greatly amuse you.

Are there any of my works which you do not possess, and would like to have? I shall be very happy to request your acceptance of any, if you will let me know how to send them. It strikes me (from some remarks of yours on versification and rhythm) that you do not know my introduction to "Chaucer Modernized." Do you? Would any American bookseller like to reprint "Orion," do you think? If so, I would willingly superintend the sheets, by a slight revision in some half-dozen places, and would write a brief Introduction or Preface addressed to the American Public; and certainly I should at the same time be too happy to express my obligations to the boldness and handsomeness of American criticism. I am, dear sir,

Your obliged, R. H. HORNE.[1]

P. S. In the remark I have made at the close of my letter, as to a reprint of "Orion" by an American bookseller, I forgot to say that I was not particular as to terms; and if they would give me nothing, I was still ready to give them the thing I proposed.

Poe's hand was recognized in "Graham's" by his correspondents, and both Tomlin and Lowell wrote him their compliments:—

JACKSON, TENNESSEE, February 23, 1844.

DEAR SIR,—I have had no letter from you since I sent you the libellous letter of L. A. Wilmer. Did you inflict on him a chastisement equal to the injury he designed, by the publication of such slanders? Previous to the reception of that letter, I had entertained a good opinion of the "Quacks of Helicon" man, and it had been brought about in a great measure by your review of the book. In his former letters, he not only spoke kindly of you, but seemed disposed to become your advocate against the *littérateurs*

[1] Griswold MSS.

of Philadelphia. I hope that you will forgive him, and that he will go and "sin no more." Your review of "Orion" in the February or March number of "Graham's," I have read with much pleasure. The article is one of great ability. I know of no writer whose success in life would give me more sincere pleasure than that of yourself.

Hoping soon to hear from you, I remain ever,

Your friend, JNO. TOMLIN.[1]

ELMWOOD, CAMBRIDGE, March 6, 1844.

MY DEAR FRIEND, — When I received your last letter I was very busily employed upon a *job* article on a subject in which I have no manner of interest. As I had nothing to say, it took me a great while to say it.

I made an expedition to Boston to learn what I could about our lectures there, & found that the lectures for the season are now over. I mean the *Society* lectures. There are different gentlemen employed diligently in lecturing upon "physical sciences" & "the lungs," &c., &c., admission ninepence, children half price, but all the lectures of a more literary class are over. I spoke to the secretary of the Boston Lyceum about the

[1] Griswold MSS.

probability of your success if you came experimentally, & he shook his head. It is not a matter in which I feel myself competent to judge — my bump of hope being quite too large. I asked him about engaging you for next year & he seemed very much pleased with the plan & said that the Society would be glad to do it. This course of lectures has (I think) the highest rank here.

To speak for myself *I* should be delighted both to see & hear you. I like your subject too.

The Boston people want a little independent criticism vastly. I know that we should not *agree* exactly, but we should at least sympathize. You occasionally state a critical proposition from which I *dissent*, but I am always satisfied. I care not a straw *what* a man says, if I see that *he* has *his* grounds for it, & knows thoroughly what he is talking about. You might cut me up as much as you pleased & I should read what you said with respect, & with a great deal more of satisfaction, than most of the praise I get, affords me. It is these halfpenny "critics" — these men who appeal to our democratic sympathies by exhibiting as their only credentials the fact that they are "practical printers" & what not, that are ruining our literature — men who never doubt that they have a full right to pronounce upon the music of Apollo's lute, because they can criticise fitly the filing of a handsaw, & who, making a point of blundering, will commend Hercules (if they commend at all) for his skill at Omphale's distaff.

It will please you to hear that my volume will soon reach a third edition. The editions are of five hundred each, but "run over," as printers say, a little, so that I suppose about eleven hundred have been sold. I shall write to you again soon, giving you a sketch of my life. *Outwardly* it has been simple enough, but inwardly every man's life must be more or less of a curiosity. Goethe made a good distinction when he divided his own autobiography into poetry & fact.

When will Graham give us your portrait? I hope you will have it done well when it is done, & quickly too. Writing to him a short time ago I congratulated him upon having engaged you as editor again. I recognized your hand in some of the editorial matter (critical) & missed it in the rest. But I thought it would do no harm to assume the fact, as it would at least give him a hint. He tells me I am mistaken & I am sorry for it. Why could not you write an article now and then for the "North American Review"?

I know the editor a little, & should like to get you introduced there. I think he would be glad to get an article. On the modern French School of novels for example. How should you like it? The "Review" does not pay a great deal ($2 a page, I believe), but the pages do not eat up copy very fast.

I am sorry I did not know of your plan to lecture in Boston earlier. I might have done something about it. The Lyceum pays some fifty to a hundred dollars, as their purse is full or empty. I will put matters in train for next year, however.

Affectionately your friend,[1]

[Signature cut out.]

P. S. You must not make any autobiographical deductions from my handwriting, as my hand is numb with cold. Winter has come back upon us.

Poe had now formed a new scheme, which is as fine a piece of literary visionariness as was ever elaborated by a penniless author. He unfolds it in the following letter to Lowell, which also contains other matter of contemporary interest.

[1] Griswold MSS.

PHILADELPHIA, March 30, 1844.

MY DEAR FRIEND, — Graham has been speaking to me, lately, about your Biography, and I am anxious to write it at once, always provided you have no objection. Could you forward me the materials within a day or two? I am just now quite disengaged — in fact positively idle.

I presume you have read the Memoir of Willis, in the April number of G. It is written by a Mr. Landor — but I think it full of hyperbole. Willis is *no* genius — a graceful trifler — no more. He wants force and sincerity. He is very frequently far-fetched. In me, at least, he never excites an emotion. Perhaps the best poem he has written is a little piece called "Unseen Spirits," beginning "The Shadows lay — Along Broadway."

You inquire about my own portrait. It has been done for some time — but is better as an engraving, than as a portrait. It scarcely resembles me at all. When it will appear I cannot say. Conrad and Mrs. Stephens will certainly come before me — perhaps Gen. Morris. My Life is not yet written, and I am at a sad loss for a Biographer — for Graham insists upon leaving the matter to myself.

I sincerely rejoice to hear of the success of your volume. To sell eleven hundred copies of a bound book of American poetry, is to do wonders. I hope everything from your future endeavors. Have you read "Orion"? Have you seen the article on "American Poetry" in the "London Foreign Quarterly"? It has been denied that Dickens wrote it — but, to me, the article affords so strong internal evidence of his hand that I would as soon think of doubting my existence. He tells much truth — although he evinces much ignorance and more spleen. Among other points he accuses myself of "metrical imitation" of Tennyson, citing, by way of instance, passages from poems which were written and published by me long before Tennyson was heard of: — but I have at no time made any poetical pretension. I am greatly indebted for the trouble you have taken about the lectures, and shall be very glad to avail myself, next season, of any invitation from the "Boston Lyceum." Thank you, also, for the hint about the "North American Review"; — I will bear it in mind. I mail you, herewith, a "Dollar Newspaper," containing a somewhat extravagant tale of my own. I fear it will prove little to your taste.

How dreadful is the present condition of our Literature! To what are things tending? We want two things, certainly: — an International Copy-Right Law, and a well-founded Monthly Journal, of sufficient ability, circulation, and character, to control, and so give tone to, our Letters. It should be, externally, a specimen of high, but not too refined Taste: — I mean, it should be boldly printed, on excellent paper, in single column, and be illustrated, not merely embellished, by spirited wood designs in the style of Grandville. Its chief aims should be Independence, Truth, Originality. It should be a journal of some 120 pp. and furnished at $5. It should have nothing to do with Agents or Agencies. Such a Magazine might be made to exercise a prodigious influence, and would be a source of vast wealth to its proprietors. There *can* be no reason why 100,000 copies might not, in one or two years, be circulated; but the means of bringing it into circulation should be radically different from those usually employed.

Such a journal might, perhaps, be set on foot by a coalition, and, thus set on foot, with proper understanding, would be irresistible. Suppose, for example, that the élite of our men of letters should combine secretly. Many of them control papers, &c. Let each subscribe, say $200, for the commencement of the undertaking; furnishing other means, as required from time to time, until the work be established. The articles to be supplied by the members solely, and upon a concerted plan of action. A nominal editor to be elected from among the number. How could such a journal fail? I would like very much to hear your opinion upon this matter. Could not the "ball be set in motion"? If we do *not* defend ourselves by some such coalition, we shall be devoured, without mercy, by the Godeys, the Snowdens, *et id genus omne*.

Most truly your friend,

EDGAR A. POE.[1]

The next week after writing this letter Poe put in execution what seems a sudden determination to leave Philadelphia. Whatever was the immediate occasion of his decision, looking back over the five years of his life in that city, with its delusively brilliant openings and sharp reverses of hope, he obeyed the dictates of worldly prudence in deserting a scene where his failures were well known, his character widely distrusted, and his reputation in the city gone. It is plain that there was no time, after the first year of his residence in Philadelphia, when

[1] Lowell MSS.

he had not the reputation, among those who profess to have been his boon-companions, of frequenting drinking places and joining with them in their ways; and his absences from the city, though few, ended in spreeing.[1] He had fought his fight, and lost; and, driven by poverty, he shifted the scene. He seems to have broken up his home at the cottage before this time, and he had not much more than ten dollars in his pocket when he left. Mrs. Clemm remained behind to sell his books and settle up affairs, and with Virginia he went to New York, with no more definite a view than to make a new start in a new community.

[1] Cf. *Harper's New Monthly Magazine*, lxxviii (March, 1889). Mrs. Clemm evidently followed him with anxiety at such times, and as on this occasion (either March or June, 1842), when he was found wandering in the Jersey woods, hunted him up.

CHAPTER IX

THE AUTHOR OF "THE RAVEN"

POE'S account of his departure is given in a letter to Mrs. Clemm, which stands by itself in his correspondence as of a purely domestic kind, illustrative of life within doors. Its confiding and familiar tone explains somewhat, too, how he won the devotion of his mother-in-law to that degree which has secured for her the admiration of all who were intimately acquainted with Poe's home life.

NEW YORK, Sunday Morning,
April 7, just after breakfast.

MY DEAR MUDDY, — We have just this minute done breakfast, and I now sit down to write you about everything. I can't pay for the letter, because the P. O. won't be open to-day. In the first place we arrived safe at Walnut St. wharf. The driver wanted to make me pay a dollar, but I would n't. Then I had to pay a boy a levy to put the trunks in the baggage car. In the meantime I took Sis [Virginia] in the Depôt Hotel. It was only a quarter past six, and we had to wait till seven. We saw the "Ledger" and "Times" — nothing in either — a few words of no account in the "Chronicle." We started in good spirits, but did not get here until nearly three o'clock. We went in the cars to Amboy, about forty miles from N. York, and then took the steamboat the rest of the way. Sissy coughed none at all. When we got to the wharf it was raining hard. I left her on board the boat, after putting the trunks in the Ladies' cabin, and set off to buy an umbrella and look for a boarding-house. I met a man selling umbrellas, and bought one for twenty-five cents. Then I went up Greenwich St. and soon found a boarding-house. It is just before you get to Cedar St., on the west side going up — the left-hand side. It has brown stone steps, with a porch with brown pillars. "Morrison" is the name on the door. I made a bargain in a few minutes and then got a hack and went for Sis. I was not gone more than half an hour, and she was quite astonished to see me back so soon. She did n't expect me for an hour. There were two other ladies waiting on board — so she was n't very lonely. When we got to the house we had to wait about half an hour before the room was ready. The house is old and looks buggy [The letter is cut here for the signature on the other side.] the cheapest board I ever knew, taking into consideration the central situation and the *living*. I wish Kate [Catterina, the cat] could see it — she would faint. Last night, for supper, we had the nicest tea you ever drank, strong and hot, — wheat bread and rye bread — cheese — tea-cakes (elegant), a great dish (two dishes) of elegant ham, and two of cold veal, piled up like a mountain and large slices — three dishes of the cakes and everything in the greatest profusion. No fear of starving here. The landlady seemed as if she could n't press us enough, and we were at home directly. Her husband is living with her — a fat, good-natured old soul. There are eight or ten boarders — two or three of them ladies — two servants. For breakfast we had excellent-flavored coffee, hot and strong — not very clear and no great deal of cream — veal cutlets, elegant ham and eggs and nice bread and butter. I never sat down to a more plentiful or a nicer breakfast. I wish you could have seen the eggs — and the great dishes of meat. I ate the first hearty breakfast I have eaten since I left our little home. Sis is delighted, and we are both in excellent spirits. She has coughed hardly any and had no night sweat. She is now busy mend-ing my pants which I tore against a nail. I went out last night and bought a skein of silk, a skein of thread, two buttons, a pair of slippers, and a tin pan for the stove. The fire kept in all night. We have now got four dollars and a half left. To-morrow I am going to try and borrow three dollars, so that I may have a fortnight to go upon. I feel in excellent spirits, and have n't drank a drop — so that I hope soon to get out of trouble. The very instant I scrape together enough money I will send it on. You can't imagine how much we both do miss you. Sissy had a hearty cry last night, because you and Catterina were n't here. We are resolved to get two rooms the first moment we can. In the meantime it is impossible we could be more comfortable or more at home than we are. It looks as if it were going to clear up now. Be sure and go to the P. O. and have my letters forwarded. As soon as I write Lowell's article, I will send it to you, and get you to get the money from Graham. Give our best love to C.

[Signature cut out.]

Be sure and take home the "Messenger" to Hirst. We hope to send for you *very* soon.[1]

[1] Poe to Mrs. Clemm, MS.

Poe's first business in New York after he got settled was presumably to call on the editor of "The Sun," and offer him the well-known "Balloon Hoax." At least on the following Saturday, April 13, "The Sun" contained a postscript, in double-leaded type, announcing that a balloon had crossed the Atlantic, bringing news, and had arrived at Charleston, South Carolina, and promising that an extra, giving full particulars, should be issued at ten o'clock on that morning. The extra duly appeared, with its narrative, in Poe's usual realistic manner, of a transatlantic voyage by a party of English aeronauts; and at a time when such journalistic fictions were more common and less easily detected than now, it achieved a momentary success.

Lowell now offered to write Poe's life for the series, "Our Contributors," then appearing in "Graham's"; and with this subject Poe's reply was next mainly concerned.

New York, May 28, '44.

My dear Friend, — I received yours last night, forwarded from Philadelphia to this city, where I intend living for the future. Touching the Biography — I would be very proud, indeed, if you would write it, and did, certainly, say to myself, and I believe to Graham — that such was my wish; but as I fancied the job might be disagreeable, I did not venture to suggest it to yourself. Your offer relieves me from great embarrassment, and I thank you sincerely. You will do me justice; and that I could not expect at all hands.

Herewith, I mail you a Life written some time since by Hirst, from materials furnished principally by Thomas and Mr. T. W. White. It is correct, I think, in the main (barring extravagant eulogy), and you can select from it whatever you deem right. The limit is 6 pp. of Graham — as much less as you please. Besides the Tales enumerated in the foot-note, I have written "The Spectacles"; "*The Oblong Box*"; "A Tale of the Ragged Mountains"; "*The Premature Burial*"; "*The Purloined Letter*"; "*The System of Doctors Tar and Fether*"; "The Black Cat"; "The Elk"; "Diddling Considered as one of the Exact Sciences"; "*Mesmeric Revelation*"; "The Gold Bug"; "*Thou art the Man*"; about 60 altogether, including the "Grotesque and Arabesque." Those italicized are as yet unpublished — in the hands of different editors. Of the "Gold Bug" (my most successful tale), more than 300,000 copies have been circulated.

There is an article on "American Poetry" in a late number of the "London Foreign Quarterly," in which some allusion is made to me, as a poet, and as an imitator of Tennyson. I would like you to say (in my defense) what is the fact: that the passages quoted as imitations were written and published, in Boston, before the issue of even Tennyson's first volume. Dickens (*I know*) wrote the article — I have private personal reasons for knowing this. The portrait prepared does not in the least resemble me.

I wrote you a long letter from Philadelphia about seven weeks since — did you get it? You make no allusion to it. In great haste,

Your most sincere friend,

EDGAR A. POE.[1]

The list of the tales still in the hands of editors which Poe gives, brings out strongly one source of the discouragement under which he had to bear up. He had been for ten years a writer of untiring industry, and in that time had produced an amount of work large in quantity and excellent in quality, much of it belonging in the very highest rank of imaginative prose; but his books had never sold, and the income from his

[1] Lowell MSS.

tales and other papers in the magazines when he was not attached to a magazine had never sufficed to keep the wolf from the door. Nothing is plainer, in his life, than that he had difficulty in selling his work and was very poorly paid. He had now prepared a revision of all his tales, and he sent them to Anthon, and solicited his influence with the Harpers to secure their publication by that house in five volumes. He accompanied his request with a review of his career.

June, 1844.

My dear Sir,—Many years have elapsed since my last communication with you, and perhaps you will be surprised at receiving a letter from me now—if not positively vexed at receiving one of so great a length and of such a character. But I trust to your goodness of heart for a patient hearing at the least.

You will have already seen that, as usual, I have a favor to solicit. You have, indeed, been to me in many respects a good genius and a friend, but the request I have to make now is one of vital interest to myself—so much so that upon your granting it, or refusing it, depends, I feel, much if not all of the prosperity, and even comfort, of my future life.

I cannot flatter myself that you have felt sufficient interest in me to have followed in any respect my literary career since the period at which you first did me the honor to address me a note while editor of the "Southern Messenger." A few words of explanation on this point will therefore be necessary here.

As I am well aware that your course of reading lies entirely out of the track of our lighter literature, and as I take it for granted, therefore, that none of the papers in question have met your eye, I have thought it advisable to send you with this letter a single tale as a specimen. This will no doubt put you in mind of the trick of the Skolastikos — but I could not think of troubling you with more than one. I do not think it my best tale, but it is perhaps the best in its particular vein. Variety has been one of my chief aims.

In lieu of the rest, I venture to place in your hands the published opinions of many of my contemporaries [appended to Hirst's Sketch of Poe]. I will not deny that I have been careful to collect and preserve them. They include, as you will see, the warm commendations of a great number of very eminent men, and of these commendations I should be at a loss to understand why I have not a right to be proud.

Before quitting the "Messenger" I saw, or fancied I saw, through a long and dim vista, the brilliant field for ambition which a Magazine of bold and noble aims presented to him who should successfully establish it in America. I perceived that the country, from its very constitution, could not fail of affording in a few years a larger proportionate amount of readers than any upon the earth. I perceived that the whole energetic, busy spirit of the age tended wholly to Magazine literature — to the curt, the terse, the well-timed, and the readily diffused, in preference to the old forms of the verbose and ponderous and the inaccessible. I knew from personal experience that lying *perdu* among the innumerable plantations in our vast Southern and Western countries were a host of well-educated men peculiarly devoid of prejudice, who would gladly lend their influence to a really vigorous journal, provided the right means were taken of bringing it fairly within the very limited scope of their observation.

Now, I knew, it is true, that some scores of journals had failed (for, indeed, I looked upon the best success of the best of them as failure), but then I easily traced the causes of their failure in the impotency of their conductors, who made no scruple of basing their rules of action altogether upon what had been customarily done instead of what was now before them to do, in the greatly changed and constantly changing condition of things.

In short, I could see no real reason why a Magazine, if worthy the name, could not be made to circulate among 20,000 subscribers, embracing the best intellect and education of the land. This was a thought which stimulated my fancy and my ambition. The influence of such a journal would be vast indeed, and I dreamed of honestly employing that influence in the sacred cause of the beautiful, the just, and the true.

Even in a pecuniary view, the object was a magnificent one. The journal I proposed would be a large octavo of 128 pages, printed with bold type, single column, on the finest paper; and disdaining everything of what is termed "embellishment" with the exception of an occasional portrait of a literary man, or some well-engraved wood-design in obvious illustration of the text. Of such a journal I had cautiously estimated the expenses. Could I circulate 20,000 copies at $5, the cost would be about $30,000, estimating all contingencies at the highest rate. There would be a balance of $70,000 per annum.

But not to trust too implicitly to *a priori* reasonings, and at the same time to make myself thoroughly master of all details which might avail me concerning the mere business of publication, I entered a few steps into the field of experiment. I joined the "Messenger," as you know, which was then in its second year with 700 subscribers, and the general outcry was that because a Magazine had never succeeded south of the Potomac, therefore a Magazine never could succeed. Yet, in spite of this, and in despite of the wretched taste of its proprietor, which hampered and controlled me at all points, I increased the circulation in fifteen months to 5500 subscribers paying an annual profit of $10,000 when I left it. This number was never exceeded by the journal, which rapidly went down, and may now be said to be extinct. Of "Graham's Magazine" you have no doubt heard. It had been in existence under the name of the "Casket" for eight years when I became its editor, with a subscription list of about 5000. In about eighteen months afterward, its circulation amounted to no less than 50,000 — astonishing as this may appear. At this period I left it. It is now two years since, and the number of subscribers is now *not more* than 25,000 — but possibly very much less. In three years it will be extinct. The nature of this journal, however, was such that even its 50,000 subscribers could not make it very profitable to its proprietor. Its price was $3, but not only were its expenses immense, owing to the employment of absurd steel plates and other extravagances, which tell not at all, but recourse was had to innumerable agents, who received it at a discount of no less than fifty per cent., and whose frequent dishonesty occasioned enormous loss. But if 50,000 *can* be obtained for a $3 Magazine among a class of readers who really read little, why may not 50,000 be procured for a $5 journal among the true and permanent readers of the land?

Holding steadily in view my ultimate purpose, — to found a Magazine of my own, or in which at least I might have a proprietary right, — it has been my constant endeavour in the mean time, not so much to establish a reputation great in itself as one of that particular character which should best further my special objects, and draw attention to my exertions as Editor of a Magazine. Thus I have written no books, and have been so far essentially a Magazinist [illegible] bearing, not only willingly but cheerfully, sad poverty and the thousand consequent contumelies and other ills which the condition of the mere Magazinist entails upon him in America, where, more than in any other region upon the face of the globe, to be poor is to be despised.

The one great difficulty resulting from this course is unless the journalist collects his various articles he is liable to be grossly misconceived and misjudged by men of whose good opinion he would be proud, but who see, perhaps, only a paper here and there, by accident — often only one of his mere extravaganzas, written to supply a particular demand. He loses, too, whatever merit may be his due on the score of *versatility* — a point which can only be estimated by collection of his various articles in volume form and all together. This is indeed a serious difficulty — to seek a remedy for which is my object in writing you this letter.

Setting aside, for the present, my criticisms, poems, and miscellanies (sufficiently numerous), my tales, a great number of which might be termed fantasy pieces, are in number sixty-six. They would make, perhaps, five of the ordinary novel-volumes. I have them prepared in every respect for the press; but, alas, I have no money, nor that influence which would enable me to get a publisher — although I seek *no* pecuniary remuneration. My sole immediate object is the furtherance of my ultimate one. I believe that if I could get my tales fairly before the public, and thus have an opportunity of eliciting foreign as well as native opinion respecting them, I should by their means be in a far more advantageous position than at present in regard to the establishment of a Magazine. In a word, I believe that the publication of the work would lead forthwith either directly through my own exertion, or indirectly with the aid of a publisher, to the establishment of the journal I hold in view.

It is very true that I have no claims upon your attention, not even that of personal acquaintance. But I have reached a crisis of my life in which I sadly stand in need of aid, and without being able to say why, — unless it is that I so earnestly desire your friendship, — I have always felt a half-hope that, if I appealed to you, you would prove my friend. I know that you have unbounded influence with the Harpers, and I know that if you would exert it in my behalf you could procure me the publication I desire.[1]

Anthon replied five months later, his apparent delay being perhaps due to the summer vacation: —

[1] Griswold MSS.

NEW YORK, November 2, 1844.

DEAR SIR, — I have called upon the Harpers, as you requested, and have cheerfully exerted with them what influence I possess, but without accomplishing anything of importance. They have *complaints* against you, grounded on certain movements of yours, when they acted as your publishers some years ago; and appear very little inclined at present to enter upon the matter which you have so much at heart. However, they have retained, for a second and more careful perusal, the letter which you sent to me, and have promised that, if they should see fit to come to terms with you, they will address a note to you forthwith. Of course, if you should not hear from them, their silence must be construed into a declining of your proposal. My *own advice* to you is to call in person at their store, and talk over the matter with them. I am *very sure* that such a step on your part will remove many of the difficulties which at present obstruct your way.

You do me injustice by supposing that I am a stranger to your productions. I subscribed to the "Messenger" solely because you were connected with it, and I have since that period read and, as a matter of course, admired very many of your other pieces. The Harpers also entertain, as I heard from their own lips, the highest opinion of your talents, but — I remain very sincerely,

Your. friend and well-wisher,

CHARLES ANTHON.[1]

P. S. The MSS. which you were kind enough to send can be obtained by you at any time on calling at my residence. C. A.

A letter from a correspondence otherwise unknown, addressed to Bowen and Gossler, editors of "The Columbia Spy," Columbia, Pennsylvania, throws some light upon Poe's interests and occupations at this obscure period, and differs markedly from his usual correspondence. It may have been intended for insertion in the paper, and if so is a unique example of a kind of composition to which there is some reason to believe that Poe occasionally resorted to make money when he was otherwise unemployed, either anonymously or semi-anonymously as in this signature.

NEW YORK, June 18, [1844].

In point of *natural* beauty, as well as of convenience, the harbor of New York has scarcely its equal in the northern hemisphere; but, as in

[1] Griswold MSS.

the case of Brooklyn, the Gothamites have most greviously disfigured it by displays of landscape and architectural *taste*. More atrocious *pagodas*, or what not,— for it is indeed difficult to find a name for them, — were certainly never imagined than the greater portion of those which affront the eye, in every nook and corner of the bay, and more particularly, in the vicinity of New Brighton. If these monstrosities appertain to taste, then it is to taste in its dying agonies.—— Speaking of harbors; I have been much surprised at observing an attempt, on the part of a Philadelphian paper, to compare Boston, as a port, with New York; and in instituting the comparison, the journal in question is so bold as to assert that the largest class of ships cannot pass the bar of this harbor at low water. I believe this to be quite a mistake; — is it not?—— Foreigners are apt to speak of the great *length* of Broadway. It is no doubt a long street; but we have many much longer in Philadelphia. If I do not greatly err, Front Street offers an unbroken line of houses for *four miles*, and is, unquestionably, the longest street in America, if not in the world. Grant, the gossiping and twaddling author of "Random Recollections of the House of Lords," "The Great Metropolis,"

&c., &c., in mentioning some London thoroughfare of two miles and three quarters, calls it, with an absolute air, "the most extensive in the world." The dogmatic bow-bow of this is the most amusing thing imaginable. I do believe that out of every ten matters which he gives to the public as fact, eight, at least, are downright lies, while the other two may be classed either as "doubtful" or "rigmarole." ——The trial of Polly Bodine will take place at Richmond, on Monday next, and will, no doubt, excite much interest. This woman may, possibly, escape; — for they manage these matters wretchedly in New York. It is difficult to conceive anything more preposterous than the whole conduct, for example, of the Mary Rogers affair. The police seemed blown about, in all directions, by every varying puff of the most unconsidered newspaper opinion. The *truth*, as an end, appeared to be lost sight of altogether. The magistry suffered the murderer to escape, while they amused themselves with playing court, and chopping the technicalities of jurisprudence. Not the least usual error in such investigations, is the limiting of inquiry to the immediate, with total disregard of the collateral, or circumstantial events. It is malpractice to confine evidence and discussion too rigorously within the limits of the seemingly relevant. Experience has shown, and Philosophy will always show, that a vast portion, perhaps the larger portion of truth, arises from the apparently *irre*levant. It is through the spirit of this principle, that modern science has resolved to *calculate upon the unforeseen.* The history of human knowledge has so uniformly shown that to collateral, or incidental, or accidental events, we are indebted for the most numerous and most valuable discoveries, that it has, at length, become necessary, in any prospective view of improvement, to make not only large, but the largest allowances for inventions that shall arise by chance — out of the range of expectation. It is, thus, no longer philosophical to base upon what *has been*, a vision of what *is to be*. Accident is admitted as a portion of the substructure. We make chance a matter of absolute certainty. We subject the unlooked-for and unimagined to the mathematical *formulæ* of the schools. But what I wish now to observe is, that the small magistracies are too prone to ape the airs and echo the rectangular precepts of the courts. And, moreover, *very* much of what is rejected as evidence by a court, is the best of evidence to the intellect. For the court, guiding itself by the general principles of evidence, — the recognized and *booked* principles, — is averse from swerving at particular instances. And this steadfast adherence to principle, with systematic disregard of the conflicting exception, is a sure mode of attaining the *maximum* of attainable truth, in any long sequence of time. The practice, *in mass*, is, therefore, philosophical; but it is none the less certain that it engenders, in many extraordinary instances, a vast amount of individual error. I have good reason to believe that it will do public mischief in the coming trial of Polly Bodine.—— The literary world of Gotham is not particularly busy. Mr. Willis, I see, has issued a very handsome edition of his poems — the only complete edition — with a portrait. Few men have received more abuse, deserving it less, than the author of "Melanie." I never read a paper from his pen, in the "New Mirror," without regretting his abandonment of Glen-Mary, and the tranquillity and leisure he might there have found. In its retirement he might have accomplished much, both for himself and for posterity; but, chained oar of a mere weekly paper, professedly addressing the frivolous and the fashionable, what can he now hope for but a gradual sinking into the slough of the Public Disregard? For *his* sake, I do sincerely wish the "New Mirror" would go the way of all flesh.

Did you see his Biography in "Graham's Magazine"? The style was a little stilted, but the matter was *true*. Mr. W. deserves nearly all, if not quite all, the commendation there bestowed. Some of the newspapers, in the habit of seeing through mill-stones, attributed the article to Longfellow, whose manner it about as much resembled as a virgin of Massaccio does a virgin of Raphael. The real author, Mr. Landor, although a man of high talent, has a certain set of phrases which cannot easily be mistaken, and is as much a uni-stylist as Cardinal Chigi, who boasted that he wrote with the same pen for fifty years. ——

In the "annual" way, little preparation is making for 1845. It is doubtful whether Mr. Keese will publish his "Wintergreen." Mr. Appleton *may* issue something pretty, but cares little about adventure, and would prefer, I dare say, a general decay of the race of gift works, their profit is small. Mr. Ricker is getting up the "Opal," which was first edited by Mr. Griswold, afterwards by Mr. Willis for a *very* brief period, and now by Mrs. Hale, a lady of fine genius and masculine energy and ability. The "Gift," however, will bear away the palm.

By the way, if you have *not* seen Mr. Griswold's "American Series of the Curiosities of Literature," then look at it, for God's sake — or for mine. I wish you to say, upon your word of honor, whether it is, or is not, *per se*, the greatest of *all* the Curiosities of Literature, or whether it is as great a curiosity as the compiler himself.

P——.[1]

After a month's delay, Lowell replied to Poe's communication with regard to the biography.

ELMWOOD, June 27, 1844.

MY DEAR FRIEND, — I have been stealing a kind of vacation from the pen during the last month, & I hope that my lying fallow for a time will increase my future crops, though I cannot bring myself to use the farmer's phrase & wish them to be "*heavier*." Now I ought by this time to have finished the article to accompany your head in Graham, but I have been unable to write anything. I have fits of this kind too often owing to a Constitutional indolence which was not counteracted by proper training in my childhood. You may be sure I am not one of those

[1] Poe to Bowen and Gossler, MS. copy.

who follow a fashion which is hardly yet extinct, & call upon the good, easy world to accept my faults in proof of my genius. I can only mention it to ask forgiveness for my dilatoriness which springs from no want of interest but from sheer indolence — a fault — which your acquaintance with Life & Biography must have convinced you is one of the most incurable. However, I am resolved to set about it now in good earnest — & I have one or two preliminary requests to make. I wish you would (if you can) write me a letter giving me in some sort a spiritual autobiography of yourself. The newspaper ["The Saturday Museum" containing Hirst's sketch of Poe] you sent me will give me enough outward facts — but I want *your own estimate* of your life. Of course you need not write it as if for my use merely in the writing of this article — but as to a friend. I believe that the opinion a man has of himself (if he be accustomed to self-analysis) is of more worth than that of all the rest of the world. If you have a copy of your first volume (of poems) will you send it to me by Harnden, directing it to be kept till called for & writing me a line by mail to warn me of its being on the way. I will return it to you by the same conveyance — as it must be valuable to you & as you have not probably more than one copy. I never saw it, nor can I get it. If you would send at the same time any other of your writings which I could not readily get you will oblige me very much & they shall be safely returned to you.

I agree with you that the article on Griswold's book in the "Foreign Quarterly Review" was fair enough as far as the Conclusions the author came to were concerned — though at the same time I think him as ignorant in political matters as a man can well be — in short, ignorant to the full to be a Reviewer — But you are mistaken as to the authorship of it. It was not (I am quite sure) written by Dickens, but by a friend of his named Forster (or Foster) — the author of a book named "Statesmen of the time of Cromwell." Dickens may have given him hints. . . .

I shall send you my sketch of course before it is printed, so that you can make any suggestions you like or suppress it altogether. I wish it to please you rather than the public.

Affectionately your friend,

J. R. L.[1]

Poe's reply to this request for a "spiritual autobiography" — and especially, what he says

[1] Griswold MSS.

of his own indolence in view of the whole mass of his writings, of which a large portion was perishable — ought to be taken with some allowance for the tendency he had to idealize his own nature. A poet's analysis of his original temperament, if it be sincere, is of the highest value; for a man's conception of his own character, particularly if he be of an introspective turn, counts often as one of the most powerful influences that shape his acts. It should be remembered, too, that in describing himself Poe was not unconscious of the presence of Lowell as his auditor, nor forgetful of the latter's relation to him as his biographer; but, nevertheless, the account falls in with other more disinterested utterances by Poe regarding himself, and in general it has an idiosyncratic character that marks it as genuine.

NEW YORK, July 2, '44.

MY DEAR MR. LOWELL, — I can feel for the "constitutional indolence" of which you complain — for it is one of my own besetting sins. I am excessively slothful and wonderfully industrious — by fits. There are epochs when any kind of mental exercise is torture, and when nothing yields me pleasure but solitary communion with the "mountains and the woods," — the "altars" of Byron. I have thus rambled and dreamed away whole months, and awake, at last, to a sort of mania for composition. Then I scribble all day, and read all night, so long as the disease endures. This is also the temperament of P. P. Cooke, of Virginia, the author of "Florence Vane," "Young Rosalie Lee," and some other sweet poems — and I should not be surprised if it were your own. Cooke writes and thinks as you — and I have been told that you resemble him personally.

I am *not* ambitious — unless negatively. I now and then feel stirred up to excel a fool, merely because I hate to let a fool imagine that he may excel me. Beyond this I feel nothing of ambition. I really perceive that vanity about which most men merely prate, — the vanity of the human or temporal life. I live continually in a reverie of the future. I have no faith in human perfectibility. I think that human exertion will have no appreciable effect upon humanity. Man is now only more active — not more happy — nor more wise, than he was 6000 years ago. The result will never vary — and to suppose that it will, is to suppose that the foregone man has lived in vain — that the foregone time is but the rudiment of the future — that the myriads who have perished have not been upon equal footing with ourselves — nor are we with our posterity. I cannot agree to lose sight of man the individual in man the mass. — I have no belief in spirituality. I think the word a *mere* word. No one has really a conception of spirit. We cannot imagine what is not. We deceive ourselves by the idea of infinitely rarefied matter. Matter escapes the senses by degrees — a stone — a metal — a liquid — the atmosphere — a gas — the luminiferous ether. Beyond this there are other modifications more rare. But to all we attach the notion of a constitution of particles — atomic composition. For this reason only we think spirit different; for spirit, we say, is unparticled, and *therefore* is not matter. But it is clear that if we proceed sufficiently far in our ideas of rarefaction, we shall arrive at a point where the particles coalesce; for, although the particles be infinite, the infinity of littleness in the spaces between them is an absurdity. — The unparticled matter, permeating and impelling all things, is God. Its activity is the thought of God — which creates. Man, and other thinking beings, are individualizations of the unparticled matter. Man exists as a "person," by being clothed with matter (the particled matter) which individualizes him. Thus habited, his life is rudimental. What we call "death" is the painful metamorphosis. The stars are the habitations of rudimental beings. But for the necessity of the rudimental life, there would have been no worlds. At death, the worm is the butterfly — still material, but of a matter unrecognized by our organs — recognized occasionally, perhaps, by the sleep-walker directly — without organs — through the mesmeric medium. Thus a sleep-walker may see ghosts. Divested of the rudimental covering, the being inhabits *space*, — what we suppose to be the immaterial universe, — passing everywhere, and acting all things, by mere volition, cognizant of all secrets but that of the nature of God's volition, — the motion, or activity, of the unparticled matter.

You speak of "an estimate of my life," — and, from what I have already said, you will see that I have none to give. I have been too deeply conscious of the mutability and evanescence of temporal things to give any continuous effort to anything — to be consistent in anything. My life has been *whim* — impulse — passion — a longing for solitude — a scorn of all things present, in an earnest desire for the future.

I am profoundly excited by music, and by

some poems, — those of Tennyson especially — whom, with Keats, Shelley, Coleridge (occasionally), and a few others of like thought and expression, I regard as the *sole* poets. Music is the perfection of the soul, or idea, of Poetry. The *vagueness* of exaltation aroused by a sweet air (which should be strictly indefinite and never too strongly suggestive) is precisely what we should aim at in poetry. Affectation, within bounds, is thus no blemish.

I still adhere to Dickens as either author, or dictator, of the review. My reasons would convince you, could I give them to you, but I have left myself no space. I had two long interviews with Mr. D. when here. Nearly everything in the critique, I heard from him, or suggested to him, personally. The poem of Emerson I read to him.

I have been so negligent as not to preserve copies of any of my volumes of poems — nor was either worthy of preservation. The best passages were culled in Hirst's article. I think my best poems "The Sleeper," "The Conqueror Worm," "The Haunted Palace," "Lenore," "Dreamland," and the "Coliseum," — but all have been hurried and unconsidered. My best tales are "Ligeia," the "Gold-Bug," the "Murders in the

Rue Morgue," "The Fall of the House of Usher," the "Telltale Heart," the "Black Cat," "William Wilson," and "The Descent into the Maelström." "The Purloined Letter," forthcoming in the "Gift," is perhaps the best of my tales of ratiocination. I have lately written for Godey "The Oblong Box" and "Thou art the Man," — as yet unpublished. With this I mail you the "Gold-Bug," which is the only one of my tales I have on hand.

Graham has had, for nine months, a review of mine on Longfellow's "Spanish Student," which I have "used up," and in which I have exposed some of the grossest plagiarisms ever perpetrated. I can't tell why he does not publish it. — I believe G. intends my Life for the September number, which will be made up by the 10th August. Your article should be on hand as soon as convenient.

Believe me your true friend,

E. A. Poe.[1]

The philosophic lucubrations in the foregoing were taken from his metaphysical tale, "Mesmeric Revelation," about to be published in the "Columbian Magazine" for August, and were

[1] Lowell MSS.

afterwards more fully developed. Poe returned to the same metaphysical subject in a letter [1] to Chivers, July 10, written in reply to a communication dated May 15, from Oaky Grove, Georgia; but he was more concerned with his correspondent's inquiry whether the "Penn Magazine," in which Poe had asked him to join financially two years before, was abandoned, and with the offer which accompanied the question. "I expect," said Chivers, "to receive my part of my father's estate in July next, and should like to unite with you, provided it would be to my interest to do so." Poe answered that the "Stylus" (the change of name was apparently unknown to Chivers) was only postponed, and encouraged him to come on to New York for a consultation. Six weeks later he sent the "Mesmeric Revelation" to Lowell, and gave the noticeable information that he was engaged on his "Critical History of American Literature," a book at which he kept working until death.

New York, August 18, 1844.

My dear Friend, — With this letter I take the liberty to mail you a number of the "Colum-

[1] Poe to Chivers. The Poe-Chivers Papers, *Century Magazine*, January–February, 1903.

bian Magazine," in which you will find a paper on "Mesmeric Revelation." In it I have endeavored to amplify some ideas which I suggested in my last letter.

You will observe many corrections and alterations. In fact the article was wofully misprinted; and my principal object in boring you with it now, is to beg of you the favor to get it copied (with corrections) in the Brother Jonathan — I mean the Boston Notion — or any other paper where you have interest. If you can do this without trouble, I would be very deeply indebted to you. I am living so entirely out of the world, just now, that I can do nothing of the kind myself.

In what are you occupied? — or is it still the far niente? For myself I am very industrious — collecting and arranging materials for a "Critical History of American Literature." Do you ever see Mr. Hawthorne? He is a man of rare genius. A day or two since I met with a sketch by him called "Drowne's Wooden Image" — delicious. The leading idea, however, is suggested by Michäel Angelo's couplet: —

> Non ha l' ottimo artista alcun concetto
> Chè un marmo solo in se non circonscriva.

To be sure Angelo half stole the thought from Socrates.

How fares it with the Biography? I fear we shall be late.

Most truly your friend,

EDGAR A. POE.[1]

Poe's correspondence with Thomas had languished, but was now pleasantly resumed, in the old strain, and contains further evidence of the effort Poe made, in the first year of his residence, to establish himself.

NEW YORK, September 8, 1844.

MY DEAR THOMAS, — I received yours with sincere pleasure, and nearly as sincere surprise; for while you were wondering that I did not write to *you*, I was making up my mind that you had forgotten *me* altogether.

I have left Philadelphia, and am living, at present, about five miles out of New York. For the last seven or eight months I have been playing hermit in earnest, nor have I seen a living soul out of my family — who are well and desire to be kindly remembered. When I say "well," I only mean (as regards Virginia) as well as usual. Her health remains excessively precarious.

Touching the "Beechen Tree" [a poem by

[1] Lowell MSS.

Thomas], I remember it well and pleasantly. I have not yet seen a published copy, but will get one forthwith and notice it as it deserves — and it deserves much of high praise — at the very first opportunity I get. At present I am so much out of the world that I may not be able to do anything *immediately*.

Thank God! Richard (whom you know) is himself again. Tell Dow so: but he won't believe it. I am working at a variety of things (all of which you shall behold in the end) — and with an ardor of which I did not believe myself capable.

You said to me hurriedly, when we last met on the wharf in Philadelphia, that you believed Robert Tyler really wished to give me the post in the Custom House. This I also really think; and I am confirmed in the opinion that he could not, at all times, do as he wished in such matters, by seeing ——— ——— at the head of the "Aurora" — a bullet-headed and malicious villain who has brought more odium upon the Administration than any fellow (of equal littleness) in its ranks, and who has been more indefatigably busy in both open and secret vilification of Robert Tyler than any individual, little or big, in America.

Let me hear from you again very soon, my dear Thomas, and believe me *ever*

Your friend, POE.[1]

At the end of the month he received the biography by Lowell: —

ELMWOOD, September 27, 1844.

MY DEAR FRIEND, — I kept back the biography a short time in order to send it on by a private hand. It is not half so good as it ought to be, but it was written under many disadvantages, not the least of which was depression of spirits which unfits a man for anything. I wish you to make any suggestions about it that may occur to you, and to reject it entirely if you do not like it.

I have mentioned Chatterton in it rather too slightingly; will you be good enough to modify what I say of him a little? His "Minstrel's Song in Ella" is better than the rest of his writings.

You will find the package at No. 1 Nassau Street, *up stairs*. It was addressed to the care of *C. F. Briggs*. If his name is not upon the door, you will probably see the name of "Dougherty" or "Jones." As ever, your friend,

J. R. LOWELL.[2]

[1] Griswold MSS. [2] Stoddard, civ, cv.

It was at this time that, according to Willis, Mrs. Clemm called upon him and solicited employment for Poe, who was then, she said, ill. Willis, who was just converting his weekly paper, the "New Mirror," into the "Evening Mirror," a daily, with a weekly issue in addition, was in need of a subordinate, and in consequence of Mrs. Clemm's visit Poe was engaged as an assistant — a "mechanical paragraphist," to use Willis's phrase — in the "Mirror" office. There, during the fall, at a desk in a corner, he sat from nine in the morning until the paper went to press, ready for whatever work might befall. He discharged the duties of the daily routine punctually, listened good-humoredly to the request that he would dull the edge of a criticism or soften a misanthropic sentiment, and conformed with entire fidelity to the suggestions made. Such is Willis's sketch of his subordinate, and he adds in general terms that through a considerable period he saw only "one presentment of the man, — a quiet, patient, industrious, and most gentlemanly person, commanding the utmost respect and good feeling by his unvarying deportment and ability."[1] It needs no keen eye to read between the lines of this de-

[1] *The Home Journal*, October 13, 1849.

scription the real facts, — that the pay was small, the labor perfunctory and uninteresting, and the spirit of the poet himself, compelled to subdue his saturnine temper to the geniality of his chief, was chafing within. It was a striking instance of Pegasus in harness.

The first number of "The Evening Mirror" appeared October 7, 1844, and the next day the literary columns contained this passage upon Elizabeth Barrett Browning: —

"Miss Barrett is worth a dozen of Tennyson and six of Motherwell — equal perhaps in original genius to Keats and Shelley."

Two months later this was followed up by another unmistakable sentence on the same poetess: —

"We do not believe there is a poetical soul embodied in this world that — as a centre of thought — sees further out toward the periphery permitted to angels, than Miss Barrett." [1]

These critical dicta could have been no one's but Poe's; and as his hand is readily discerned in the literary paragraphing at many other points, it is most likely that he was employed on the daily from its start. It is as certain, on the other hand, as internal evidence can make it, that he

[1] *Evening Mirror*, December 7, 1844.

NATHANIEL P. WILLIS

never before this time made, as has been stated,[1] one of Willis's staff of writers.

A month after the receipt of the biography from Lowell, Poe acknowledged it, and again reverted to his scheme for the association of authors in a Magazine Company.

NEW YORK, October 28, '44.

MY DEAR FRIEND, — A host of small troubles growing from the *one* trouble of poverty, but which I will not trouble you with in detail, have hitherto prevented me from thanking you for the Biography and all the well-intended flatteries which it contains. But, upon the principle of better late than never, let me thank you now, again and again. I sent it to Graham on the day I received it — taking with it only one liberty in the

[1] Ingram, i, 248. The statement that Poe contributed translations from the French to the *New Mirror* from April, 1843, to its discontinuance (which is wrongly said to have taken place before Poe left Philadelphia), and signed them with his initials, rests on a negligent examination of the files. The translations referred to begin January 3, 1843 (i, 9), and are signed E. P.; they continue to the end, but afterwards they are also signed at the beginning of the articles "By a Lady." For example, i, 307, 355, etc. The complete list is published in *The Virginia Poe*, xvi, 368–371. They are, perhaps, from the pen of Emily Percival.

way of modification. This I hope you will pardon. It was merely the substitution of another brief poem for the last you have done me the honor to quote.

I have not seen your marriage announced, but I presume from what you said in your penultimate letter, that I may congratulate you now. Is it so? At all events I can wish you no better wish than that you may derive from your marriage as substantial happiness as I have derived from mine.

A long time ago I wrote you a long letter to which you have never replied. It concerned a scheme for protecting ourselves from the imposition of publishers by a coalition. I will state it again in brief. Suppose a dozen of the most active or influential men of letters in this country should unite for the purpose of publishing a magazine of high character. Their names to be kept secret, that their mutual support might be the more effectual. Each member to take a share of the stock at $100 a share. Each, if required, to furnish one article each month — the work to be sustained altogether by the contributions of the members, or by unpaid contributions from others. As many of the members as possible to be taken from those connected otherwise with the press: — a black-ball to exclude any one suggested as a member by those already conjoined — this to secure unanimity. These, of course, are mere hints in the rough. But suppose that (the scheme originating with yourself and me) we write to any others or, seeing them personally, engage them in the enterprise. The desired number being made up, a meeting might be held, and a constitution framed. A point in this latter might be that an editor should be elected periodically from among the stockholders.

The advantages of such a coalition seem to me very great. The Magazine could be started with a positive certainty of success. There would be no expense for contributions, while we would have the best. Plates, of course, would be disdained. The aim would be to elevate without stupefying our literature — to further justice — to resist foreign dictation — and to afford (in the circulation and profit of the journal) a remuneration to ourselves for whatever we should write.

The work should be printed in the very best manner, and should address the aristocracy of talent. We might safely give, for $5, a pamphlet of 128 pages, and, with the support of the variety of our personal influence, we might easily extend the circulation to 20,000, — giving $100,000. The expenses would not exceed $40,000, — if indeed they reached $20,000 when the work should be fairly established. Thus there would be $60,000 to be divided among twelve, — $5000 per annum apiece.

I have thought of this matter long and cautiously, and am persuaded that there would be little difficulty in doing even far *more* than I have ventured to suggest.

Do you hear anything more about the Lectures? Truly yours,

E. A. Poe.[1]

Lowell did not answer until the middle of December, when he wrote to pave the way for Briggs, who was about to start the "Broadway Journal" in New York and desired an introduction.

Elmwood, December 12, 1844.

My dear Friend, — You will forgive me for not writing sooner & for writing so little now, when I tell you that I have been for some time keeping a printing office agoing at the rate of from eight to twenty pages a day. I am printing

[1] Lowell MSS.

a volume of prose (in conversation form) about poets and everything else, ["Conversations on Some of the Old Poets"] & not having prepared my copy, am obliged to write & print at once. You will like some parts of the book and dislike others.

My object in writing this is to introduce you to my friend Charles F. Briggs who is about to start a literary weekly paper in New York & desires your aid. He was here a month or two since, & I took the liberty of reading to him what I had written about you & to-day I received a letter from him announcing his plan & asking your address. Not knowing it, & not having time to write him I thought that the shortest way would be to introduce you to him. He will pay & I thought from something you said in your last letter that pay would be useful to you. I also took the liberty of praising you to a Mr. Colton, who has written "Tecumseh" . . . & whom I suspect, from some wry faces he made on first hearing your name, you have cut up. He is publishing a magazine & I think I convinced him that it would be for his interest to engage you permanently. But I know nothing whatever of his ability to pay.

I am not to be married till I have been delivered of my book; which will probably be before Christmas, & I shall spend the winter in Philadelphia. I shall only stop one night in New York on my way on. Returning I shall make a longer stay & shall of course see you. You will like Briggs & he will edit an excellent paper. Opposite, I write a note to him.

Yr. affectionate friend,

J. R. Lowell.[1]

P. S. You must excuse me if I have blundered in recommending you to Colton. I know nothing of your circumstances save what I gleaned from your last letter, &, of course, said nothing to him which I might not say as an entire stranger to you. It is never safe to let an editor (as editors go) know that an author *wants* his pay.

I was in hopes that I should have been able to revise my sketch of you before it appeared. It was written under adverse circumstances & was incomplete. If you do not like this method of getting acquainted, send Briggs your address. *His* is No. 1 Nassau St. I never wrote an introductory letter before & do not own a complete letter writer — so you must excuse any greenness about it.

[1] Griswold MSS.

Nothing of Poe's in the "Mirror" during the first three months requires notice. Since his arrival in New York, however, in the preceding April, some of his pieces in editors' hands had got published: "A Tale of the Ragged Mountains," a picturesque story of metempsychosis ascribed to the influence of Hoffmann, in "Godey's" for June, and the two inferior grotesques, "The Oblong Box" and "Thou art the Man," also in "Godey's" for September and October; "Dreamland," a new poem, in "Graham's" for June; "The Angel of the Odd," a title which appears for the first time, in the "Columbian" for October; "The Literary Life of Thingum Bob," a satirical extravaganza, said to be aimed at Graham, on the ways of editors and the means of popularity, which had at last found its indulgent victim in the "Southern Literary Messenger" for December, where it appeared anonymously; "The Purloined Letter," in the "Gift" for 1845, closing the series of the ratiocinative tales. In the "Democratic Review," too, for November and December, the first installments of the miscellaneous notes called "Marginalia" were issued; and as one reads them and the later collections, which continued to be published until Poe died, one cannot but admire the audacity of their author, who could thus resell clippings from his old book reviews since the beginning of his career, by merely giving them a new title. It was a dexterous filching back from Time of the alms for oblivion already given and stored away in that capacious wallet. Doubtless Poe looked on editors as fair game, — if they would not buy his new tales, let them purchase his old criticisms. But an event was soon to occur that made any manuscripts by Poe treasure-trove. Probably the editors, who had almost emptied their pigeon-holes of his accumulated contributions, were sorry they had not delayed longer.

In the "Evening Mirror," January 29, 1845, "The Raven" was published, with a highly commendatory card from Willis; and a few days later "The American Whig Review" for February, from the advance sheets of which this poem had been copied, was the centre of literary interest and the prey of editorial scissors throughout the length and breadth of the country. In the magazine the author was masked under the pseudonym "Quarles," but in this journal he had been named as E. A. Poe. The popular response was instantaneous and decisive. No brief poem ever established itself so immediately, so widely, and so imperishably in men's minds. "The Raven" became, in some sort, a national bird, and the author the most notorious American of the hour. It happened — and for this Godey and Graham must have blessed their stars, that in their respective magazines of this same month the former published "The 1002 Tale," the voyage of Sinbad among the wonders made known by modern science, and the latter Lowell's sketch of Poe.

The history of the composition of the "Raven" has been variously told, but it is possible to reconcile the different accounts. Mrs. Weiss relates, on Poe's authority, that the bird was originally an owl, and that the poem "had lain for more than ten years in his desk unfinished, while he would at long intervals work on it."[1] Whatever may have been the history of this earlier conception, the true germ is contained in Poe's review of "Barnaby Rudge," published in "Graham's," February, 1842: —

"The raven, too, intensely amusing as it is, might have been made, more than we now see it, a portion of the conception of the fantastic Barnaby. Its croakings might have been prophetically heard in the course of the drama. Its

[1] Mrs. Weiss, p. 185.

character might have performed, in regard to that of the idiot, much the same part as does, in music, the accompaniment in respect to the air. Each might have been distinct. Each might have differed remarkably from the other. Yet between them there might have been wrought an analogical resemblance, and although each might have existed apart, they might have formed together a whole which would have been imperfect in the absence of either." This is precisely the relation which exists in the poem between the raven and the lover.

It is related [1] that Poe was, at some time the following summer, at the Barhyte trout-ponds, Saratoga Springs, New York, and mentioned the poem "to be called 'The Raven'" to Mrs. Barhyte, who was a contributor to the "New York Mirror." The next summer, 1843, according to this same tradition, agreeing with the tale told at Philadelphia of such a visit, he was again at the same resort; and a conversation between him and a lad about the bird in the poem is reported, and it is added that Mrs. Barhyte was shown the written composition. This lady died in April, 1844, and these statements seem

[1] *Home Journal* (by Dr. William Elliot Griffis), November 5, 1884.

to be derived from Mr. Barhyte's recollection of what his wife said. It must have been this draft of the poem which Rosenbach saw in Philadelphia as early as the winter of 1843-44. "I read 'The Raven' long before it was published," says this writer, "and was in Mr. George R. Graham's office when the poem was offered to him. Poe said that his wife and Mrs. Clemm were starving, and that he was in very pressing need of the money. I carried him fifteen dollars contributed by Mr. Graham, Mr. Godey, Mr. McMichael, and others, who condemned the poem, but gave the money as a charity."[1] He had this poem, which may be correctly described as a draft, at least, when, in 1844, he went to New York and boarded at Mrs. Brennan's, on the Bloomingdale road, near what is now the eastern corner of Eighty-fourth Street and Broadway, where he is also said[2] to have stayed, accompanied by his family, in the previous summer. There he read the poem to his

[1] The *American*, February 26, 1887.

[2] *Poe and the Raven* (by General James R. O'Beirne), the New York *Mail and Express*, quoted in the Augusta *Chronicle*, April 30, 1900; the earliest account of Poe's residence in the house and the reminiscences of Mrs. Brennan is given by Gill, 1877. Cf. *Frank Leslie's Illustrated Weekly*, September, 1833 (by Tyrrell).

landlady before its publication in the "Mirror"; and as he removed, late in the fall of 1844, to 15 Amity Street, it is clear that whatever revision he gave it was done there.[1] He offered the poem to the "Whig Review" anonymously, through John Augustus Shea, an old West Point schoolmate then pursuing literature in the city, to whom he sent the last correction in a note.[2] It will be remembered, however, that Colton, the editor of the "Whig," had been spoken to by Lowell in Poe's favor, and it is unlikely that he was ignorant of the authorship. Willis may have taken the text from an advance copy of the magazine or from a proof. Such seems to have been the composition of "The Raven."

Poe now withdrew from the "Mirror," much to the regret of his employer. His contributions

[1] It is also related by his tavern companions of Sandy Welsh's cellar in Ann Street that the poem was a sort of joint-product of all their wits, being "produced stanza by stanza at small intervals, and submitted by Poe piecemeal to the criticism and emendation of his intimates," until it was "voted complete." Specific instances of such emendation are reported from Colonel Du Solle. *Scribner's* (by F. G. Fairfield), October, 1875. Mrs. Weiss (p. 99), also on Du Solle's authority, tells the same anecdote with variations.

[2] *The Virginia Poe*, i, 217–220. Judge George Shea, son of J. A. Shea, told the author the entire story some time about 1893 at "The Players," New York.

HOUSE WHERE "THE RAVEN" WAS WRITTEN

Near 84th Street, New York

had been of the slightest interest, and contained nothing novel, except his attack on Longfellow's collection of fugitive poems, called "The Waif," — the beginning of the "Longfellow war." His connection with the paper had turned to his own benefit by the frequent puffs of himself, both direct and indirect, which it published, and by the literary introductions which his position afforded him. He was, however, always dissatisfied with his situation, which certainly was a humble one. In the issue of January 20, 1845, in which Lowell's critical estimate of him was reprinted, he was editorially praised, his capacities as a magazine editor pointed out, and himself described as "ready for propositions." [1] No proposition of the kind was made, but an arrangement was entered into by which he became associated with Charles F. Briggs, then known as "Harry Franco," in the management of "The Broadway Journal," a weekly which had issued its first number on the 4th of January previous.

Briggs was a writer of light literature, from Nantucket, and ambitious of editing a paper. A month before this time he wrote to his friend Lowell, "I have made arrangements for pub-

[1] *Evening Mirror*, January 20, 1845.

lishing the first number of my long-talked-of paper in January. It will be published by John Bisco, a shrewd Yankee from Worcester, who has been a school-teacher in New Jersey, and was once the publisher of the 'Knickerbocker.'" Further on he adds, "If you know Poe's address, send it on to me when you write." In consequence of Lowell's introduction Poe contributed to the first two numbers of the "Journal" a review of Miss Barrett (Mrs. Browning), and from that time was a regular writer at the rate of one dollar a column. He sent the review, and also a copy of "The Raven" to Horne, January 25, 1845, but the reply was delayed till late in the spring, when Horne wrote: —

LONDON, May 17, 1845.

MY DEAR SIR, — After so long a delay of my last letter to you, I am at all events glad to hear that it reached you — or rather that you, in diving among the shoals at the Post-Office, had contrived to fish it up. But matters do not seem to mend in this respect; for your present letter of the date of January 25, 1845, only reached my house at the latter end of April. In short, we might as well correspond from Calcutta, as far as time is concerned. However, I am glad that the letters reach their destination at all, and so that none are lost we must be patient.

I have only just returned from a nine months' absence in Germany. I principally resided, during this time, in the Rhine Provinces. I take the earliest opportunity of thanking you for all attentions.

As I thought your letter to me contained more of the bright side of criticism than the "Broadway Journal," I sent it to my friend Miss Barrett. She returned it with a note—half of which I tear off, and send you (*confidentially*) that you may see in what a good and noble spirit she receives the critique — in which, as you say, the shadows do certainly predominate. Well, for my own part, I think a work should be judged of its merits *chiefly* — since faults and imperfections are certain to be found in all works, but the highest merits only in a few. Therefore the highest merits seem to me to be naturally the first and main points to be considered. Miss Barrett has read the "Raven," and says she thinks there is a fine lyrical melody in it. When I tell you that this lady "says" you will be so good as to understand that I mean "writes" — for although I have corresponded with Miss Barrett these five or six years, I have never seen her to this day.

Nor have I been *nearer* to doing so than talking with her father and sisters.

I am of the same opinion as Miss Barrett about the "Raven"; and it also seems to me that the poet intends to represent a very painful condition [of] mind, as of an imagination that was liable to topple over into some delirium, or an abyss of melancholy, from the continuity of one unvaried emotion.

Tennyson I have not seen nor heard from yet, since my return. It is curious that you should ask me for the opinions of the only two poets with whom I am especially intimate. Most of the others I am acquainted with, but am not upon such terms of intellectual sympathy and friendship, as with Miss Barrett and Tennyson. But I do not at this moment know where Tennyson is.

You mention that an American publisher would probably like to reprint "Orion," and I therefore send a copy for that purpose, or probability. I also send a copy in which I have written your name, together with a copy of "Gregory VII," and two copies of "Introductory Comments" (to the second edition of the "New Spirit of the Age") of which I beg your acceptance. Of "Chaucer Modernized" I do not possess any other copy than the one in my own library, and I believe it is out of print; but if you would like to have a copy of Schlegel's lectures on "Dramatic Literature" (to which I wrote an introduction to the second edition), I shall be happy to forward you the volume, and any others of my own you would like to have — that is, if I have copies of them. "Cosmo de' Medici," for instance, I could send you. I have made no revision of "Orion" for the proposed new edition. The fact is, I have not time, and *moreover* am hardly disposed to do much to it, after so many editions. I had rather write (almost) another long poem. I shall be happy to send you a short poem or two for your magazine, directly it is established, or for the first number, if there be time for you to let me know. I am, dear sir,

Yours truly, R. H. HORNE.[1]

The inclosure, from Mrs. Browning to Horne, was as follows: —

58 WIMPOLE ST., May 12, 1845.

You will certainly think me mad, dear Mr. Horne, for treading upon my own heels (room for the [illegible], in another letter. But I am uncomfortable about my message to Mr. Poe, lest it should not be grateful enough in the sound of

[1] Griswold MSS.

it. Will you tell him what is quite the truth, that in my own opinion he has dealt with me most generously, and that I thank him for his candour as for a part of his kindness. Will you tell him also that he has given my father pleasure, which is giving it to *me* more than twice. Also the review is very ably written — and the reviewer has so obviously and thoroughly *read* my poems, as to be a wonder among critics. Will you tell Mr. Poe this, or to this effect, dear Mr. Horne, all but part of the last sentence, which peradventure may be somewhat superfluous. I heard from dear Miss Mitford this morning, and she talks delightfully of taking lodgings in London soon; of coming not for a day only, nor for a week only [end of sheet [1]].

Poe's association with Briggs continued in an undefined way. "The Raven" was reprinted in the "Journal," slightly revised, February 8, and the office-boy of the day, writing fifty-seven years afterwards, gives a scene of the editorial den.

"It was one cold day in winter, when everybody in the 'Literary Journal' office from myself on up was busily at work, that Poe came

[1] Griswold MSS.

into the office, accompanied by the great actor named Murdock. They went to Poe's desk, and Mr. Poe summoned the entire force, including myself, about him. There were less than a dozen of us, and I was the only boy.

"When we were all together, Poe drew the manuscript of 'The Raven' from his pocket and handed it to Murdock. He had called us to hear the great elocutionist read his newly-written poem. Murdock read, and what with the combined art of two masters, I was entranced. It is the most cherished memory of my life that I heard the immortal poem read by one whose voice was like a chime of silver bells. . . . In the next issue of the 'Literary Journal' 'The Raven' appeared in the place of honor." [1]

The first trial Poe made of the value of his popularity was to lecture in the library of the New York Historical Society, on February 28, when between two and three hundred persons gathered to hear him. His subject was, as before, American Poetry, and in substance the address was the old monologue, sharp, bitter, and grim, on the sins of editors and the stupidity of versifiers, relieved by the elocutionary effect of a

[1] *Sunday World-Herald,* Omaha (by Alexander T. Crane), July 13, 1902.

few fine poems and too generous praise where he thought praise was due. He dealt with Mrs. Sigourney, Mrs. Welby, Mrs. Osgood, Seba Smith, the Davidsons, Bryant, Halleck, Longfellow, Sprague, and Dana. The inference is that the lecture was made up by piecing together his old book reviews, and was probably textually the same with that delivered at Philadelphia, except that he now omitted reference to Griswold, with whom he was endeavoring to renew his acquaintance, plainly from selfish motives. He was still playing the part of the fearless critic, and he found some listeners to follow Lowell's lead and commend him for his audacity, while they acknowledged the usefulness of his ungracious service; but there were many more in whose minds his words rankled. He was a good speaker, having natural gifts of elocution and an effective manner. Willis, in noticing the lecture, sketches him with the elegant facility that now, to our changed taste, reads so much like nonsense: —

"He becomes a desk, — his beautiful head showing like a statuary embodiment of Discrimination; his accent drops like a knife through water, and his style is so much purer and clearer than the pulpit commonly gets or requires that the effect of what he says, besides other things, pampers the ear." [1]

The impression Poe first made on Briggs is told in the following passages of the latter's correspondence with Lowell: —

"I like Poe exceedingly well; Mr. Griswold has told me shocking bad stories about him, which his whole demeanor contradicts." [2]

"Poe tells me that Graham refused to print his tale of the 'Gold Bug,' and kept it in his possession nine months. I never read it before last week, and it strikes me as among the most ingenious pieces of fiction that I have ever seen. If you have not read it, it will repay you for the trouble when you do. He told me furthermore that the poem which you have quoted from the 'House of Usher,' —

> "'In a valley, fair and shady [*sic*]
> By good angels tenanted,' etc.,

he sent to O'Sullivan for the 'Democratic,' and it was returned to him. You see by these what the judgments of Magazine editors amount to. . . . I have always strangely misunderstood Poe, from thinking him one of the Graham and Godey species, but I find him as different as possible. I

[1] *Evening Mirror*, March 12, 1845.

[2] Briggs to Lowell, January 6, 1845. MS.

think that you will like him well when you come to know him personally."[1]

Briggs, under this impression, now associated Poe with himself in "The Broadway Journal"; and, under the impetus of the popularity of "The Raven," Wiley & Putnam undertook to bring out in the summer a selection from his tales, and later an edition of his poems.

[1] Briggs to Lowell, January 27, 1845. MS.

CHAPTER X

THE BROADWAY JOURNAL

At the beginning of March Poe was announced as co-editor, with Henry S. Watson and Briggs, of "The Broadway Journal." The correspondence of Briggs with Lowell shows plainly the relations between him and his new chief. The "Journal" was at the time becoming notorious by the "Longfellow war," which, as Briggs remarked, was "all on one side." It had been begun by Poe, in the "Mirror," and had followed with him into the new office. He had long had this bee in his bonnet, and was only repeating a charge that he had made from his first Philadelphia days. He was now endeavoring mightily to sustain the accusation of plagiarism against the poet, and incidentally he glanced at Lowell as guilty of the same offense, whether knowingly or not. On March 8, 1845, Briggs wrote: —

"Poe is only an assistant to me, and will in no manner interfere with my own way of doing things. It was requisite that I should have his or some other person's assistance, on account of my liability to be taken off from the business of the paper, and as his name is of some authority I thought it advisable to announce him as an editor. Mr. Watson's name will command the support of a good portion of the musical interest in this city and in Boston, and by putting forth his name as musical editor I can gain his time for a *pro rata* dividend on the amount of patronage which he may obtain. He is the only musical critic in the country and a thorough good fellow. Poe has left the 'Mirror.' Willis was too Willisy for him. Unfortunately for him (Poe), he has mounted a very ticklish hobby just now, Plagiarism, which he is bent on riding to death, and I think the better way is to let him run down as soon as possible by giving him no check. Wiley & Putnam are going to publish a new edition of his tales and sketches. Everybody has been raven-mad about his last poem, and his lecture, which W. Story went with me to hear, has gained him a dozen or two of waspish foes who will do him more good than harm." [1]

A week later, March 16, he returns to the same subject: —

"Poe is a monomaniac on the subject of pla-

[1] Briggs to Lowell. MS.

giarism, and I thought it best to allow him to ride his hobby to death in the outset and be done with it. It all commenced with myself. When he was in the 'Mirror' office he made what I thought a very unjustifiable charge against my friend Aldrich [James Aldrich], who is one of the best fellows in the world, and I replied to it as you saw. Somebody in Boston, 'Outis,' whose name I forget, replied to P. on behalf of Longfellow and Aldrich, and so the war began. It will end as it began, in smoke. But it will do us some good by calling public attention to our paper. Poe is a much better fellow than you have an idea of. . . . The 'Journal' gains strength every day, and I am very sanguine of success."[1]

Three days later he writes again more fully:

"I thought it best to gain Poe's services as a critic because he already has a reputation for reviewing, and I could gain them by allowing him a certain portion of the profits of the paper. He thought it would gain the 'Journal' a certain number of subscribers immediately if his name were published in connection with it. I did not much like the plan, but he had had more experience than myself in the matter, so I consented.

[1] Briggs to Lowell. MS.

. . . I retain precisely the same authority I did in the beginning. . . . Poe's fol-de-rol about plagiarism I do not like, but the replies which it provokes serve us as advertisements, and help us along. As he dealt more severely by me and my friend Aldrich than anybody else I do not think that anybody has any right to complain of his thumps. I think that you are too sensitive in regard to Longfellow; I really do not see that he has said anything offensive about him. . . . Poe has indeed a very high admiration for Longfellow, and so he will say before he is done. For my own part I did not use to think well of Poe, but my love for you and implicit confidence in your judgment led me to abandon all my prejudices against him when I read your account of him. The Rev. Mr. Griswold, of Philadelphia, told me some abominable lies about him, but a personal acquaintance with him has induced me to think highly of him. Perhaps some Philadelphian has been whispering foul things in your ear about him. Doubtless his sharp manner has made him many enemies. But you will think better of him when you meet him." [1]

While Briggs was thus explaining his own position and defending Poe from the strictures of

[1] Briggs to Lowell. MS.

Lowell, who had now ceased to correspond with him, the "Broadway Journal" was pressing the attack. The attitude of Poe toward Longfellow has become sufficiently clear in the course of the preceding narrative; he was a jealous admirer. The present, and most notorious, imbroglio was occasioned by the publication of "The Waif," a collection of fugitive pieces by minor authors, edited by Longfellow. In the "Mirror" Poe had said, —

"We conclude our notes on the 'Waif' with the observation that, although full of beauties, it is infected with a *moral taint* — or is this a mere freak of our own fancy? We shall be pleased if it be so; — but there *does* appear, in this little volume, a very careful avoidance of all American poets who may be supposed especially to interfere with the claims of Mr. Longfellow. These men Mr. Longfellow can continuously *imitate* (*is* that the word?) and yet never incidentally commend." [1]

The discussion thus begun was followed up in succeeding issues with the protests of Longfellow's friends and the editorial comment in reply, extenuating on Willis's part, vindicatory on Poe's, until Willis withdrew from the discussion

[1] *Evening Mirror*, January 14, 1845.

in a card in which he stated his entire dissent from "all the disparagement of Longfellow" that had been published in the "Mirror"; and soon he admitted to its columns a lengthy defense of him by one "Outis," just after Poe left the office to join Briggs.

On March 1 the new editor of the "Broadway Journal" began his reply to "Outis," which was continued in weekly installments through five numbers. So far as it related to Longfellow it repeated textually the charge made in "Burton's" in regard to the "Midnight Mass for the Dying Year"; discredited a letter in which Longfellow had personally explained the error in consequence of which he had translated a song of Motherwell's back into English from the German of Wolff, under the impression that it was original with the latter; and finally charged new plagiarisms, particularly in the case of "The Spanish Student," some scenes of which Poe traced to his own "Politian" in a violent passage in which probably the old review is incorporated.

To sum up Poe's strictures as urged here and in earlier and later writings, Longfellow was a plagiarist, a didactic poet, and a writer of hexameters. In this there is so much truth as is involved in the milder statement that he belonged to the poets of cultivation rather than of irresistible original genius, that he frequently wrote to illustrate or enforce morality, and that his ear was not offended by the English hexameter. That Poe was sincere in his opinions, though he enforced them rudely and with the malicious pleasure of an envious rival, there can be little question; that Longfellow never pilfered from Poe, and that in the unconscious adaptations natural to a poet of culture he never imitated him, there can be no doubt at all. In the elusive search for motives in the case, it is best to remain content with Longfellow's charitable opinion: "The harshness of his criticisms I have never attributed to anything but the irritation of a sensitive nature, chafed by some indefinite sense of wrong."[1]

Poe's other contributions to the "Journal" during the time that he had "a third interest" (as he described to Griswold his salary of a third of the profits) were plentiful, but not fresh.[2] The

[1] *Southern Literary Messenger*, November, 1849. Cf. *Monats-Hefte*, liii, pp. 119, 538, 677, *Edgar Poe gegen Henry Longfellow*, von Fr. Spielhagen.

[2] He reprinted, sometimes with slightly changed names and other revision, representing the Anthon copy, *Lionizing*, *Berenice*, *Bon-Bon*, *The Oval Portrait*, *The Philosophy of Furni-*

very early grotesque, "Peter Snook," and the long-rejected tale, "The Premature Burial," of which no earlier publication is found, were the freshest stories. But it should be remembered that his tales were salable, and therefore reserved for the magazines. He also utilized passages from old book reviews by incorporating them in new notices. His new papers were for the most part hack-work articles on anastatic printing, street-paving, magazine literature, etc., etc.; the only noteworthy pieces being a critical baiting of W. W. Lord, who had committed the unpardonable sin of plagiarizing from the author of "The Raven," and the exhaustive review of some volumes of Mrs. Browning's, already mentioned. In this last, although nearly all the space is taken up with unfavorable comment in detail, Miss Barrett is at the conclusion lifted to the highest pinnacle but one: "She has surpassed all her poetical contemporaries of either sex (with a single exception)," that exception being Tennyson.

The state of Poe's mind at this time is best seen in a characteristic letter to Thomas: —

ture, Three Sundays in a Week, The Pit and the Pendulum, Eleonora, Shadow, The Assignation, and *Morella;* and of his poems, *To F——, The Sleeper, To One in Paradise,* and *The Conqueror Worm.*

May 4, 1845

My dear Thomas, — In the hope that you have not yet *quite* given me up as gone to Texas, or elsewhere, I sit down to write you a few words. I have been intending to do the same thing ever since I received your letter before the last — but for my life and soul I could not find, or make, an opportunity. The fact is, that being seized of late with a fit of industry, I put so many irons in the fire all at once that I have been quite unable to get them out. For the last three or four months I have been working fourteen or fifteen hours a day, — hard at it all the time, — and so, whenever I took pen in hand to write, I found that I was neglecting something that *would be* attended to. I never knew what it was to be a slave before.

And yet, Thomas, I have made no money. I am as poor now as ever I was in my life — except in hope, which is by no means bankable. I have taken a third pecuniary interest in the "Broadway Journal," and for everything I have written for it have been, of course, so much out of pocket. In the end, however, it will pay me well — at least the prospects are good. Say to Dow for me that there never has been a chance for my repaying him, without putting myself to greater inconvenience than he himself would have wished to subject me to, had he known the state of the case. Nor am I able to pay him now. The Devil himself was never so poor. Say to Dow, also, that I am sorry he has taken to dunning in his old age — it is a diabolical practice, altogether unworthy "a gentleman and a scholar" — to say nothing of the Editor of the "Madisonian." I wonder how he would like me to write him a series of letters, — say one a week, — giving him the literary gossip of New York, or something of more general character. I would furnish him such a series for whatever he could afford to give me. If he agrees to this arrangement, ask him to state the length and character of the letters — how often — and how much he can give me. Remember me kindly to him, and tell him I believe that dunning is his one sin — although at the same time, I do think it is the unpardonable sin against the Holy Ghost spoken of in the Scriptures. I am going to mail him the "Broadway Journal" regularly, and hope he will honor me with an exchange.

My dear Thomas, I hope you will never imagine, from any seeming neglect of mine, that I have forgotten our old friendship. There is no one in the world I would rather see at this moment than yourself; and many are the long talks we have about you and yours. Virginia and Mrs. Clemm beg to be remembered to you in the kindest terms. Do write me fully when you get this, and let me know particularly what you are about.

I send you an early number of the "B. Journal" containing my "Raven." It was copied by Briggs, my associate, before I joined the paper. The "Raven" has had a great "run," Thomas — but I wrote it for the express purpose of running — just as I did the "Gold Bug," you know. The bird beat the bug, though, all hollow.

Do not forget to write immediately, and believe me,

Most sincerely your friend, POE.[1]

During the year 1844, from his arrival in New York, Poe was abstemious. Mrs. Barhyte, Willis, and others, who saw him daily, bear testimony to this. It was a time when he, for the most part, kept apart from general association with men by his residence and work in the country. He had returned to the city, 15 Amity Street, in November, 1844, and had since led a more social life, but without excesses; after the publica-

[1] Griswold MSS.

tion of "The Raven" he began to fall into old habits. The first information of this sort comes from the reminiscent office-boy of the "Journal," who idolized him. He relates that Poe was invited to repeat the lecture of February 28, and gives the only account of what happened on that evening late in March: —

"The night set for the second lecture was a very bad one. It stormed incessantly, with mingled rain and hail and sleet. In consequence there were scarcely a dozen persons present when Poe came upon the platform and announced that, under the circumstances, the lecture could not be given, and those in the audience would receive their money back at the door. I was one of those present, as Poe had given me a complimentary ticket to the lecture, and badly as I was disappointed, I could see upon his face that my master was much more so. It was a little thing, it is true, but he was a man easily upset by little things. The next morning he came to the office, leaning on the arm of a friend, intoxicated with wine."[1] The same authority states that this was the only occasion on which he saw anything of the sort.

[1] *Sunday World-Herald,* Omaha (by Alexander T. Crane), July 13, 1902.

Toward the last of May Lowell passed through the city on his way from Philadelphia, where he had for a few months been on the staff of the "Pennsylvania Freeman," and called on Poe. Neither of them was much pleased. Lowell thus describes the meeting: —

"I saw Poe only once. . . . I suppose there are many descriptions of him. He was small; his complexion of what I should call a clammy-white; fine, dark eyes, and fine head, very broad at the temples, but receding sharply from the brows backwards. His manner was rather formal, even pompous, but I have the impression he was a little soggy with drink — not tipsy — but as if he had been holding his head under a pump to cool it."[1]

Mrs. Clemm herself described the interview in a letter to Lowell, after Poe's death: —

LOWELL, 9th March, 1850.

DEAR SIR, — . . . How much I wish I could see you! how quickly I could remove your wrong impression of my darling Eddie! The day you saw him in New York *he was not himself*. [Italics in letter.] Do you not remember that I never left the room? Oh, if you only knew his

[1] Lowell to the author, March 12, 1884.

bitter sorrow when I told him how unlike himself he was while you were there, you would have pitied him! he always felt particularly anxious to possess your approbation. If he spoke unkindly of you (as you say he did), rely on it, it was when he did not know of what he was talking. . . .

Most respectfully,

MARIA CLEMM.[1]

Poe, on his part, said to Chivers: "He [Lowell] called to see me the other day, but I was very much disappointed in his appearance as an intellectual man. He was not half the noble-looking person that I expected to see." [2]

Chivers had come to New York on the occasion of the publication of his volume, "The Lost Pleiad, and Other Poems," and also with a desire to confer with Poe as to his association with him in the "Stylus," with a view to fur-

[1] Mrs. Clemm to Lowell. Lowell MSS. The author would not have printed these passages had not his account of the interview been called in question by Professor Harrison. *The Virginia Poe*, i, 203, 204.

[2] The Poe-Chivers Papers, the *Century Magazine* (by the author), August–September, 1903. The author is not at liberty to quote from the Chivers papers themselves. The habits of Poe during these months are abundantly shown by this and other testimony, and the brief statement in the former biography sufficiently substantiated.

nishing the capital for that enterprise. He arrived either in June or July, and met Poe[1] on Nassau Street in an intoxicated condition. Chivers went home with him — he was then living at 195 Broadway — and narrates the incidents of the walk, chief of which was an encounter with Lewis Gaylord Clark, editor of the "Knickerbocker," whom Poe threatened to attack; but Clark, seeing how matters stood, bowed himself out of the way. Chivers gives a detailed account of Poe's reception by Mrs. Clemm. The next day when Chivers called, Poe was not to be found. On the next he was in bed, feigning illness, as Chivers thought, in order to excuse himself for not delivering a poem he engaged to give before a meeting of the societies of New York University. Chivers continued to see him, during his stay, and Poe noticed his new book of poems, August 2, in the "Journal."

A pleasant anecdote of Poe, and the lasting impression he made on a working-boy during the year, are given in Mr. Crane's reminiscences, already quoted: —

"Poe was a quiet man about the office, and was uniformly kind and courteous to every one, and, with congenial company, he would grow

[1] *Ibid.*

cheerful and even playful. I saw him every day, for, as you may imagine, our office rooms did not consist of a great many compartments, and office-boy and editor were pretty close together. He came to the office every day about nine o'clock and worked until three or four in the afternoon, and he worked steadily and methodically too.

"Not a great while after I had gone to work on the paper, on a hot August afternoon, while wrapping and addressing Journals, I was overcome with the heat and fainted dead away. Poe was writing at his desk. When I recovered consciousness I was stretched out on the long table at which I had been at work and Poe was bending over me bathing my wrists and temples in cold water. He ministered to me until I was able to stand up, and then he sent me home in a carriage.

"This act of kindness, coupled with his uniform gentle greetings when he entered the office of a morning, together with frequent personal inquiries and words of encouragement, made me love and trust my editor." [1]

The history of the "Broadway Journal" in the mean time was interesting. When the first vol-

[1] *Sunday World-Herald*, Omaha, July 13, 1902.

ume was approaching its end, Briggs wrote to Lowell, June 29, 1845, reviewing his plans: —

"I have arrangements on foot with a new publisher for the 'Journal' who will enable me to give it a fresh start, and I trust very soon to be able to give you an earnest of its profits. I shall haul down Poe's name; he has latterly got into his old habits and I fear will injure himself irretrievably. I was taken at first with a certain appearance of independence and learning in his criticisms, but they are so verbal, and so purely selfish that I can no longer have any sympathy with him."[1]

Lowell's own interview, however, in the previous month had prepared him for the following passage in Briggs's next letter, in explanation of what seemed a sudden demise of the "Journal":

"The non-appearance of the 'Broadway Journal' has probably surprised you. I had made arrangements with a new publisher, — a very good business man, — and had agreed upon terms with Bisco to buy his interest; but when I came to close with him he exacted more than I had stipulated for, and finding that he was determined to give me trouble I refused to do anything with the 'Journal.' I had the first number

[1] Briggs to Lowell. MS.

of the new volume all ready to be issued, with a handsomely engraved title, etc.; but, as I could not put the new publisher's name upon it without Bisco's consent, I let it go a week, meaning to issue a double number — not doubting that I could agree with him upon some terms; but he had fallen into the hands of evil advisers, and became more extortionate than ever. Poe in the mean time got into a drunken spree, and conceived an idea that I had not treated him well, for which he had no other grounds than my having loaned him money and persuaded Bisco to carry on the 'Journal' himself. As his doing so would give me a legal claim upon him, and enable me to recover something from him, I allowed him to issue one number, but it is doubtful whether he issues another. Mr. Homans, the publisher, with whom I had agreed to undertake the publication of the 'Journal,' is an educated man and a thorough good fellow, with a very extensive book-selling connection. He is still desirous of taking hold of the 'Journal,' and has made me a very liberal offer to go on with him if he can purchase Bisco's share. But I do not yet know how the affair will terminate.

"Poe's mother-in-law told me that he was quite tipsy the day that you called upon him, and that he acted very strangely; but I perceived nothing of it when I saw him in the morning. He was to have delivered a poem before the societies of the New York University a few weeks since, but drunkenness prevented him. I believe he had not drunk anything for more than eighteen months until within the past three months, but in this time he has been very frequently carried home in a wretched condition. I am sorry for him. He has some good points, but, taken altogether, he is badly made up. I was deceived by his superficial talents when I first met him, and relied too much upon the high opinion which you had expressed of him. His learning is very much like that of the famous Mr. Jenkinson in the 'Vicar of Wakefield.' He talks about dactyls and spondees with surprising glibness; and the names of metres being caviare to nine men out of ten, he has gained a reputation for erudition at a very cheap rate. He makes quotations from the German, but he can't read a word of the language." [1]

Some further explanation of the matter was given August 1: —

"I did not give you sufficient particulars to enable you to understand my difficulties with

[1] Briggs to Lowell, July 16, 1845. MS.

Bisco and Poe. Neither has done anything without my full consent, and I have nothing to complain of but their meanness, which they could n't help. I had told P. a month before that I should drop his name from the 'Journal.' He said I might keep it there if I wanted to, although he intended to go into the country and devote his time to getting up books, and would not therefore be able to assist me. I had also told Bisco that I would have nothing more to do with him after the close of the first volume, and that I would not carry it on unless I could find a publisher to my mind. I did find such a publisher, and Bisco, thinking that I was very anxious to go on with it, was more exacting in his demands for his share of the 'Journal' than I thought just, so I told him I would not take it; and he, thinking to spite me, and Poe, thinking to glorify himself in having overmastered me, agreed to go on with it. I laughed at their folly, and told them to go ahead; but I still hold the same right that I ever did, and could displace them both if I wished to do so. But seeing so much poltroonery and littleness in the business gave me a disgust to it, and I let them alone, hoping to get back from Bisco some money which I had advanced him." [1]

[1] Briggs to Lowell. MS.

Three weeks later he wrote a characterization of Poe more in detail: —

"You have formed a correct estimate of Poe's characterless character. I have never met a person so utterly deficient of high motive. He cannot conceive of anybody's doing anything, except for his own personal advantage; and he says, with perfect sincerity, and entire unconsciousness of the exposition which it makes of his own mind and heart, that he looks upon all reformers as madmen; and it is for this reason that he is so great an egoist. He cannot conceive why the world should not feel an interest in whatever interests him, because he feels no interest himself in what does not personally concern him. Therefore, he attributes all the favor which Longfellow, yourself, or anybody else receives from the world as an evidence of the ignorance of the world, and the lack of that favor in himself he attributes to the world's malignity. It is too absurd for belief, but he really thinks that Longfellow owes his fame mainly to the ideas which he has borrowed from his (Poe's) writings in the 'Southern Literary Messenger.' His presumption is beyond the liveliest imagination. He has no reverence for Homer, Shakespeare, or Milton, but thinks that 'Orion' is the greatest poem in the language. He has too much prudence to put his opinions into print, — or, rather, he can find nobody impudent enough to print them, — but he shows himself in his private converse. The Bible, he says, is all rigmarole. As to his Greek, — you might see very well if it were put in your eye. He does not read Wordsworth, and knows nothing about him." [1]

As has been incidentally mentioned above, the "Journal" was suspended for one week; and when the first number of the second volume appeared, a week later, it bore Poe's name as sole editor. Since he describes himself as "one third proprietor," in his old terms, it seems probable that he agreed to go on with Bisco for one third of the profits, just as before, but having entire charge. Bisco himself declared that he meant to get rid of Briggs, and, in order to do so, took up with Poe. There was from the first some financial tangle between the parties, which, fortunately, there is no need to unravel. The result of the difference was to install Poe in full control. One of his acts was to have a fling at Briggs, in connection with which a last extract from the latter's correspondence has its interest:

"You take Poe's *niaiseries* too seriously. I

[1] Briggs to Lowell, August 21, 1845. MS.

only cared for his unhandsome allusion to me in the B. J. because it proved him a baser man than I thought him before. . . . The truth is that I have not given him the shadow of a cause for ill-feeling; on the contrary he owes me now for money that I lent him to pay his board and keep him from being turned into the street. But he knows that I am possessed of the secret of his real character and he no doubt hates me for it. Until it was absolutely necessary for me to expose some of his practices to save myself from contempt, I never breathed a syllable of his ill habits, but I tried in vain to hide them from observation out of pure compassion, for I had not known him long before I lost all respect for him and felt a loathing disgust for his habits. I did not much blame him for the matter of his remarks about Jones, although the manner of them was exceeding improper and unjust; the real cause of his ire was Jones' neglecting to enumerate him among the humorous writers of the country, for he has an inconceivably extravagant idea of his capacities as a humorist. The last conversation I had with Poe he used all his power of eloquence in persuading me to join him in the joint editorship of the 'Stylus.'"[1]

[1] Briggs to Lowell, October 13, 1845. MS.

Poe remained simply editor, with his third interest for pay, until October. In the first number of his editing was a review of his own "Tales,"[1] just published by Wiley & Putnam as No. 2 in their "Library of American Books," and selected by Duyckinck from the seventy previously sent to Anthon and declined by the Harpers in the previous November. Duyckinck certainly had chosen from Poe's numerous and uneven stories those on which his fame has proved itself to be founded. Poe, however, declared in private, "Those selected are *not* my best, nor do they fairly represent me in any respect."[2] He meant that they were too much of one kind, whereas he had aimed at diversity in his writings; in other words, the grotesque tales were slighted, and hence the universality of his genius and the versatility of his talents were not illustrated. During the first months of his sole editorship he reprinted, as before, his

[1] *Tales.* By Edgar A. Poe. New York: Wiley & Putnam, 1845, pp. 228. The contents are, in order: *The Gold Bug, The Black Cat, Mesmeric Revelation, Lionizing, The Fall of the House of Usher, The Descent into the Maelström, The Colloquy of Monos and Una, The Conversation of Eiros and Charmion, The Murders of the Rue Morgue, The Mystery of Marie Roget, The Purloined Letter, The Man in the Crowd.*

[2] Poe to Eveleth, Ingram, ii, 24.

THE BLACK CAT

old tales and poems,[1] as now revised for book publication and one paper whose previous issue, before June, 1844, is unknown, "Diddling Considered as one of the Fine Arts;" of criticism there was nothing noteworthy except a flattering review of Hirst and a satirical one of Hoyt, both poetasters.

In October occurred one of the best known incidents of Poe's life. In the summer he had visited Boston, and now was invited to give a poem before the Boston Lyceum (it will be remembered that Lowell had at Poe's request formerly interested himself to obtain an engagement for him to lecture before the same organization), and he accepted. On the evening appointed, October 16, a lecture, which was the

[1] *How to write a Blackwood Article, The Masque of the Red Death, The Literary Life of Thingum-Bob, The Business Man, The Man who was Used Up, Never Bet the Devil your Head, The Tell-Tale Heart, William Wilson, Why the Little Frenchman wears his Hand in a Sling, The Landscape Garden, The Tale of Jerusalem, The Island of the Fay, MS. Found in a Bottle, The Duc de L'Omelette, King Pest,* and *The Power of Words.* Of his poetry he used *The Coliseum, Zante, Israfel, Silence, Science, Bridal Ballad, Eulalie, Lenore, A Dream, Catholic Hymn, Romance, City in the Sea, To the River ——, The Valley of Unrest, To F——, To ——* ("The bowers whereat"), *Song* ("I saw thee"), and *Fairyland.* He had also reprinted, in the *Whig, The Doomed City* and *The Valley Nis.*

second of the course, having been given by Caleb Cushing, Poe came forward on the platform of the Odeon, and, after some prefatory remarks about the foolishness of didacticism, read "Al Aaraaf." The audience, the hour being late, began to disperse, but enough persons remained to enjoy his recitation of "The Raven," with which the entertainment closed. The audience was disappointed, and afterwards some Boston papers commented somewhat severely on the performance, especially when the truth came out that the poem given was a juvenile production, written years before. Poe, when he returned to New York, declared that he had acted of malice prepense.

"It would scarcely be supposed that we would put ourselves to the trouble of composing for the Bostonians anything in the shape of an *original* poem. We did not. We had a poem (of about five hundred lines) lying by us — one quite as good as new — one, at all events, that we considered would answer sufficiently well for an audience of transcendentalists. *That* we gave them — it was the best that we had — for the price — and it *did* answer remarkably well. Its name was *not* 'The Messenger Star' — who but Miss Walter would ever think of so delicious a little bit of invention as that? We had no name for it at all. The poem is what is occasionally called a 'juvenile poem' — but the fact is, it is anything but juvenile now, for we wrote it, printed it, and published it, in book form, before we had fairly completed our tenth year. We read it *verbatim*, from a copy now in our possession, and which we shall be happy to show at any moment to any of our inquisitive friends." [1] He goes on to say, "Over a bottle of champagne that night, we confessed to Messrs. Cushing, Whipple, Hudson, Fields, and a few other natives who swear not altogether by the frog-pond — we confessed, we say, the soft impeachment of the hoax."

This was Poe's explanation. The fact was, that he had undertaken an engagement, and being unable to write a poem for the occasion he resorted to his old compositions, and selected "Al Aaraaf" as the most available. He then attempted to extricate himself from the situation by turning the incident into burlesque.

Poe became sole proprietor of the "Journal" October 24. Mr. Bisco says that he made over his rights to Poe for the consideration of a promissory note for $50, signed by Poe, and indorsed by Horace Greeley, who had at one time

[1] The *Broadway Journal*, November 1, 1845.

written on political topics for the paper; and when it came due Bisco collected it, as was to be anticipated, from the indorser. It is plain, however, that there were also other notes given in this transaction or afterwards. Greeley himself refers to the incident, with sharp pleasantry: —

"A gushing youth once wrote me to this effect: —

"'DEAR SIR, — Among your literary treasures, you have doubtless preserved several autographs of our country's late lamented poet, Edgar A. Poe. If so, and you can spare one, please inclose it to me, and receive the thanks of yours truly.'

"I promptly responded as follows: —

"'DEAR SIR, — Among my literary treasures, there happens to be exactly *one* autograph of our country's late lamented poet, Edgar A. Poe. It is his note of hand for fifty dollars, with my indorsement across the back. It cost me exactly $50.75 (including protest), and you may have it for half that amount. Yours, respectfully.'

"That autograph, I regret to say, remains on my hands, and is still for sale at first cost, despite the lapse of time and the depreciation of our currency." [1]

[1] *Recollections of a Busy Life.* By Horace Greeley, pp. 196, 197.

Thus Poe at last owned and edited the "Journal," but he needed capital to run it. In August he had written to Neilson Poe,[1] with whom he had reëstablished connections, that he should start a magazine in January; but this was probably only a reference to the "Stylus," which he may have hoped to float with the financial aid of Chivers, who had set that date as the time when he would be ready to undertake it. He wrote to Chivers, August 11, "my prospects about Maga are glorious"[2] and that there was "a fortune" in the "Broadway Journal," for whose immediate needs he asked a loan of fifty dollars for two months; and again, August 29, reminding him of this request; and to Kennedy, October 26, in the same strain:—

NEW YORK, Octo. 26, '45.

MY DEAR MR. KENNEDY, — When you were in New York I made frequent endeavours to meet you — but in vain — as I was forced to go to Boston.

I stand much in need of your aid, and beg you to afford it me, if possible — for the sake of the position which you already have enabled me to obtain. By a series of manœuvres, almost

[1] Poe to Neilson Poe, August 8, 1845. MS.

[2] Poe to Chivers. The New York *Observer*, April 26, 1900.

incomprehensible to myself, I have succeeded in getting rid, one by one, of all my associates in "The Broadway Journal," and (as you will see by last week's paper) have now become sole editor and owner. It will be a fortune to me if I can hold it — and if I can hold it for one month I am quite safe — as you shall see. I have exhausted all my immediate resources in the purchase — and I now write to ask you for a small loan — say $50. I will punctually return it in 3 months.

Most truly yours,

EDGAR A. POE.[1]

HON. J. P. KENNEDY.

Chivers continued to put him off, but Kennedy declined, and this letter from his old friend is interesting, as probably the last and also as showing the writer's temper toward his protégé: —

DEAR POE, — I was in Virginia when your letter came to Baltimore and did not return until very recently, which will account for my delay in acknowledging it. I take great pleasure in hearing of your success in your career, and am an attentive reader of what comes from your pen.

[1] Kennedy MSS.

You have acquired a very honorable reputation in letters, but nothing less than I predicted at the time of our first acquaintance. When in New York, a month ago, I called at your "Broadway Journal" establishment in the hope of meeting you, but was told you were just setting out for Providence, and as I received your card the same day I took it for granted you had left it only in the moment of your departure and I therefore made no further effort to see you. I trust you turn the "Journal" to a good account. It would have given me pleasure to assist you in this enterprise in the manner your letter suggested, but that I could not do. Good wishes are pretty nearly all the capital I have for such speculations. I hear of you very often, and although I perceive you have some enemies, it may gratify you to know that you have also a good array of friends. When it falls in your way to visit Baltimore both Mrs. Kennedy and myself would be much pleased to receive you on our old terms of familiar acquaintance and regard.

Very truly yours,

J. P. KENNEDY.[1]

EDGAR A. POE, Esqr.

BALT. December 1, 1845.

[1] Griswold MSS.

Poe also appealed to his publishers, Wiley & Putnam. He had placed in their hands, apparently in September, the material for a volume of poems for immediate issue, and was also preparing for them a volume, the "American Parnassus," probably a variant title of that work on his contemporaries which occupied his attention continuously. In consequence of these engagements, as well as of their issue of his "Tales" in the summer, he had financial dealings with them, and their representative, Duyckinck, was now his chief adviser in literary ways. He seems to have already drawn the fifty dollars mentioned in the following letter, previous to his visit to Boston in October.

Thursday Morning.

My dear Mr. Duyckinck, — I am still dreadfully unwell, and fear that I shall be very seriously ill. Some matters of domestic affliction have also happened which deprive me of what little energy I have left — and I have resolved to give up the B. Journal and retire to the country for six months, or perhaps a year, as the sole means of recruiting my health and spirits. Is it not possible that yourself or Mr. Matthews might give me a trifle for my interest in the

EVERT A. DUYCKINCK

papers. Or, if this cannot be effected, might I venture to ask you for an advance of $50 on the faith of the "American Parnassus"?— which I will finish as soon as possible. If you could oblige me in this manner I would feel myself under the deepest obligation. Will you be so kind as to reply by the bearer?

Truly yours, EDGAR A. POE.[1]

Poe now wrote again: —

Thursday Morning — 13th [November, 1845].
85 Amity St.

MY DEAR DR. DUYCKINCK, — For the first time during two months I find myself entirely myself — dreadfully sick and depressed, but still myself. I seem to have just awakened from some horrible dream, in which all was confusion and suffering — relieved only by the constant sense of your kindness, and that of one or two other considerate friends. I really believe that I have been mad — but indeed I have had abundant reason to be so. I have made up my mind to a step which will preserve me, for the future,

[1] Poe to Duyckinck. Bulletin of the New York Public Library, VI, i (January, 1902). The letter is undated, but, read in connection with the next letter and the context, may be safely referred to the late summer of 1845.

from at least the greater portion of the troubles which have beset me. In the mean time, I have need of the most active exertion to extricate myself from the embarrassments into which I have already fallen — and my object in writing you this note is (once again), to beg your aid. Of course I need not say to you that my most urgent trouble is the want of ready money. I find that what I said to you about the prospects of the B. J. is strictly correct. The most trifling immediate relief would put it on an excellent footing. All that I want is time in which to look about me; and I think that it is your power to afford me this.

I have already drawn from Mr. Wiley, first $30 — then 10 (from yourself) — then 50 (on account of the "Parnassus") — then 20 (when I went to Boston) — and finally 25 — in all 135. Mr. Wiley owes me, for the "Poems," 75, and admitting that 1500 of the "Tales" have been sold, and that I am to receive 8 cts a copy — the amount which you named, if I remember — admitting this, he will owe me $120. on them: — in all 195. Deducting what I have received there is a balance of 60 in my favor. If I understood you, a few days ago, Mr. W. was to settle with me in February. Now, you will already have anticipated my request. It is that you would ask Mr. W. to give me, to-day, in lieu of all farther claim, a certain sum whatever he may think advisable. So dreadfully am I pressed, that I would willingly take even the $60 actually due (in lieu of all farther demand) than wait until February:— but I am sure that you will do the best for me that you can.

Please send your answer to 85 Amity St. and believe me — with the most sincere friendship and ardent gratitude

Yours, EDGAR A. POE.[1]

On November 15 Poe again appealed to Chivers and said that he had paid entirely the price of the "Journal" except one hundred and forty dollars, which would fall due January 1, 1846.

The lack of capital continuing to be a pressing trouble, he wrote to his cousin, George Poe, touching the matter:—

NEW YORK, November 30, '45.

DEAR SIR, — Since the period when (no doubt for good reasons) you declined aiding me with the loan of $50, I have perseveringly struggled against a thousand difficulties, and have suc-

[1] Poe to Duyckinck, *loc. cit.*

ceeded, although not in making money, still in attaining a position in the world of letters, of which, under the circumstances, I have no reason to be ashamed.

For these reasons — because I feel that I have exerted myself to the utmost — and because I believe that you will appreciate my efforts to elevate the family name — I now appeal to you once more for aid.

With this letter I send you a number of "The Broadway Journal," of which, hitherto, I have been merely editor, and one third proprietor. I have lately purchased the whole paper, and, if I can retain it, it will be a fortune to me in a short time; — but I have exhausted all my resources in the purchase. In this emergency I have thought that you might not be indisposed to assist me.

I refrain from saying any more — for I feel that if your heart is kindly disposed toward me, I have already [1]

[Rest, with signature, cut off.]

On the next day, December 1, he wrote [2] to Halleck, who seems to have assisted him at

[1] Poe to George Poe. MS.

[2] Poe to Halleck. The New York *Observer*, April 26, 1900.

other times in a spirit of generous friendship, and asked a loan of one hundred dollars for three months. Halleck sent the money, and, as in Greeley's case, the note was preserved as an autograph.

While these embarrassments were annoying him, Poe used his paper for the reproduction of his works [1] as formerly, the only tale not elsewhere known being "The Spectacles," which he had formerly sent to Horne. Of his original work, since he left the "Mirror," he had published in the "Democratic,"—"The Power of Words," a metaphysical tale: in the "Whig,"—"Some Words with a Mummy," a grotesque on the old theme that "there is nothing new under the sun," with some unusual satire on politics; "The Facts in the Case of M. Valdemar," that tale which for mere physical disgust and foul horror has no rival in literature; a new poem, "Eulalie," and a review of "The American Drama," in which he dealt mainly with Willis's "Tortesa," and once more with Longfellow's "Spanish Student" at great length: in "Graham's,"—"The Imp of the Perverse," the last

[1] *Some Words with a Mummy, The Devil in the Belfry, A Tale of the Ragged Mountains, Four Beasts in One, The Oblong Box, Mystification, Loss of Breath.*

of the tales of conscience, and the absurd madhouse grotesque, "Dr. Tarr and Prof. Fether"; and, in "Godey's," two installments of the clippings from old magazines, called "Marginalia." These publications include all his new writings during the year, outside of the "Journal."

The "Journal" showed vigorous management; its advertisements had been largely increased, and its circulation is said to have lessened. The last numbers of December are full of promises regarding the future; but George Poe not responding, the Greeley note becoming due, and other friends than Halleck being obdurate, the demise of the paper suddenly took place. Its last expenses appear to have been paid by T. H. Lane, who through a long life remembered with pleasure this brief association with Poe and always spoke in his behalf. On December 26 was published the following: —

VALEDICTORY

Unexpected engagements demanding my whole attention, and the objects being fulfilled so far as regards myself personally, for which "The Broadway Journal" was established, I now, as its editor, bid farewell — as cordially to foes as to friends. EDGAR A. POE.

What other objects Poe achieved, except the republication of much that he had previously written in prose and verse, it is hard to see. One more number was issued, January 3, with the assistance of Thomas Dunn English, with which the "Journal" expired.

Just at the close of the year, apparently on December 31, Poe's collected poems had been issued by Wiley & Putnam, under the title "The Raven, and Other Poems."[1] He dedicated the volume to Mrs. Browning, then Miss Barrett, and sent her a copy, which drew forth this reply:

5 WIMPOLE ST., April, 1846.

DEAR SIR,—Receiving a book from you seems to authorize or at least encourage me to

[1] *The Raven, and Other Poems.* By Edgar A. Poe. New York: Wiley & Putnam, 1845. The contents were, in order, *The Raven, Valley of Unrest, Bridal Ballad, The Sleeper, The Coliseum, Lenore, Catholic Hymn, Israfel, Dream-land, Sonnet — To Zante, City in the Sea, To One in Paradise, Eulalie — A Song, To F——s S. O——d, To F——, Sonnet — Silence, The Conqueror Worm, The Haunted Palace, Scenes from Politian.* Then followed, with the foot-note still published, *Poems in Youth: Sonnet — To Science, Al Aaraaf, Tamerlane, A Dream, Romance, Fairy-land, To ——, To the River ——, The Lake — To ——, Song, To Helen.* It is scarcely necessary to add that the youthful poems are not printed exactly "*verbatim,* without alteration from the original edition," but the changes, nevertheless, are not important.

try to express what I have felt long before — my sense of the high honor you have done me in [illegible] your country and of mine, of the dedication of your poems. It is too great a distinction, conferred by a hand of too liberal a generosity. I wish for my own sake I were worthy of it. But I may endeavour, by future work, to justify a little what I cannot deserve anywise, now. For it, meanwhile, I may be grateful — because gratitude is the virtue of the humblest.

After which imperfect acknowledgment of my personal obligation may I thank you as another reader would thank you for this vivid writing, this power which is felt! Your "Raven" has produced a sensation, a "fit horror," here in England. Some of my friends are taken by the fear of it and some by the music. I hear of persons haunted by the "Nevermore," and one acquaintance of mine who has the misfortune of possessing a "bust of Pallas" never can bear to look at it in the twilight. I think you will like to be told that our great poet, Mr. Browning, the author of "Paracelsus" and the "Bells and Pomegranates," was struck much by the rhythm of that poem.

Then there is a tale of yours ["The Case of M. Valdemar"] which I do not find in this volume, but which is going the round of the newspapers, about mesmerism, throwing us all into "most admired disorder," and dreadful doubts as to whether "it can be true," as the children say of ghost stories. The certain thing in the tale in question is the power of the writer, and the faculty he has of making horrible improbabilities seem near and familiar.

And now will you permit me, dear Mr. Poe, as one who though a stranger is grateful to you, and has the right of esteeming you though unseen by your eyes — will you permit me to remain

Very truly yours always,

ELIZABETH BARRETT BARRETT.[1]

The volume contained nearly all the poetry he had ever written, and the versions are those now established in the text. In the preface he speaks in dispraise of his work, saying that he thinks nothing in this volume of much value to the public, or very creditable to himself. "Events not to be controlled," he continues, in the well-known words, "have prevented me from making at any time any serious effort in what, under happier circumstances, would have been the field of my choice. With me poetry has been not

[1] Griswold MSS.

a purpose, but a passion; and the passions should be held in reverence; they must not — they cannot at will be excited, with an eye to the paltry compensations, or the more paltry commendations, of mankind."[1]

The poems which this proud apology prefaced comprise the poetic labors of their author up to the close of this year, and although a few were to be added before his death, they illustrate fully his poetic powers. In attempting an estimate of their worth, it is useful to recur once more to the theory which Poe had now completely developed regarding the aims and scope of poetry; for it is his own comment on his own text. To put it in the fewest words, Poe believed that of the pleasures that spring from Truth, which satisfies the intellect, or from Passion, which excites the heart, or from Beauty, which elevates the soul, the latter is the most pure, keen, and absorbing; and this because it appeals to that sense of harmony and feeds that yearning for its manifestation which belongs to the immortal part of man. In the moods aroused through the sentiment of beauty man is most clearly conscious of his eternal nature, and in the lifting up of his spirit under such influences penetrates (so

[1] *Works*, x, 4.

THE RAVEN

Poe thought) to the divine. This subtle power is possessed by all beauty in its sensible forms as built by God in nature; but the suggestions of something fairer beyond and above nature, which arise in its presence, stimulate man to attempt to reach this unknown loveliness by recombining the elements he perceives, and thus in imagination (which repeats the creative act of God) to fashion by art, under the guidance of his own instinct, an ideal beauty which shall be a new and purer source of spiritual emotion. This creation of beauty is the end of all the fine arts, but in music and in poetry it is most directly accomplished. It would, however, be an error to suppose that Poe, in thus adopting the doctrines of Coleridge and rejecting passion and truth and morality as poetic themes, meant to sever poetry by distinct boundaries from those regions of life; on the contrary, he expressly states that "the incitements of Passion, the precepts of Duty, and even the lessons of Truth" may be advantageously introduced into a poem, if they are only subordinated and blended in by the skill of the artist who understands how to use them for the heightening of the effect of mere beauty; and furthermore, it should be observed that to beauty itself Poe assigns both a moral value, as lending attraction to virtue, and an intellectual value, as leading out to the mystical province of that truth which, withdrawn from the probing of the reason, is fathomed by the imagination alone. Such a speculation may be regarded as a baseless reverie or as profound philosophy; but it is essential to keep in mind the fact, not only that Poe made beauty the theme of poetry, but also that he found its value in intimations of the divine; or, in other words, that he was devoted to a mystical æstheticism. Of the minor articles of his creed it is necessary to recall only those which assert that a poem should be brief; should aim at a single artistic effect, but not to the exclusion of a secondary suggested meaning; and should be touched, if possible, by a certain quaintness, grotesqueness, or peculiarity of rhythm or metre, to give it tone.

One who reflects upon the character of mind implied by the holding of this theory, the elements of which assimilated and united only very slowly in Poe's case, cannot be surprised at the objections ordinarily urged against Poe's verses. They are said to be vague, destitute of ideas, insubstantial, unreal, full of artifice, and trenching on the domain of music. That these phrases accurately describe the impression made by the poems on many minds by no means strangers to the poetic sentiment may be granted without hesitation; and if any one maintains that from certain points of view such words are justly applied, it would be futile to dissent. The diversity of criticism upon Poe's verse is largely due to the assumption that it can be measured intelligibly by any other than his own standard. The poet strives, Poe thought, to bring about in others the state felt in himself; and in his own case that was one of brooding reverie, a sort of emotional possession, full of presentiment, expectancy, and invisible suggestion, the mood that is the habitat of superstition; vagueness was the very hue in which he painted. Again, if in his prose tales he declares repeatedly that he meant not to tell a story, but to produce an effect, much more is it to be thought that in poetry he aimed not to convey an idea, but to make an impression. He was a dreamer. When he came to poetic expression which must needs be the genuine manifestation of the soul's secret, he had no wisdom and no romance to disclose, of any earthly reality, and he was forced to bring out his meagre store of visionary facts, to which his random and morbid feelings alone gave credibility. To say of such works that they are destitute of ideas and insubstantial is not criticism,—it is mere description. Even for that slight framework of the things of sense which Poe had to shape in order to allegorize his moods at all, he seems but little indebted to nature. The purely imaginary character of his landscape has been touched on, again and again, hitherto; it is indicative of the obvious fact that he never regarded nature as anything but the crucible of his fancies. To qualify his conceptions as unreal is merely to gather into a colorless word the quivering eastern valley, the flaming city isled in darkness, the angel-thronged, star-lighted theatre of the Worm's conquest, the wind-blown kingdom by the sea, the Titanic cypress alley, the night's Plutonian shore, or any other of those dim tracts,

"Out of space, out of time,"

where his spirit wandered. So, too, if any one presses the charge of artifice home, it must be allowed just, though it attaches only to the later poems and is the excess of art. No poet was ever less spontaneous in excellence than Poe. When one reads, at successive stages of his career, the same old stanzas in new versions, and notices how they grew out of rudeness of many different descriptions into such perfection as they reached, he perceives before him an extraordinary example of growth in the knowledge and exercise of the poetic art, — the pulse of the machine laid bare. The changes are minute and almost innumerable, the approaches to perfection are exceedingly gradual, the last draft is sometimes only slightly related to the earliest; but — and this is the point that proves Poe primarily a careful artist rather than an inspired poet — in every instance the alteration is judicious, the step is a step forward. One who achieves success mainly by self-training in art comes to rely on art overmuch; and so he degenerates into artifice, or visible art, puts his faith in mechanism, and trusts his fame to cogs and levers of words and involutions of sounds; or it may happen, as was perhaps finally the case with Poe, that a weakened hand keeps facility with the tools when the work slips from his grasp. At least, so much truth lies in this last objection of the artificiality of Poe's work as to justify the more expressive statement that he was, in verse as in prose, essentially a skillful literary artist. And furthermore, music was an essential element of his art. It is true that his ear for verbal melody was at first very defective, and was never perfect, but in much of his best work the rhythmic movement is faultless in its flow and its simplicity. This is not, however, all that is meant by saying that he borrowed effects from music. In his verses sonorousness counts independently of its relation to the meaning of the words, and the poem seems at intervals to become merely a volume of sound, in which there is no appeal to the mind at all, but only a stimulation of the feelings as by the tones of an instrument. In the management of the theme, too, particularly in his later verse, the handling of the refrain, the recurrence to the same vocal sounds and the same order of syllabic structure, the movement of the whole poem by mere new presentations of the one idea, as in "The Raven," or of the same group of imagery, as in "Ulalume," partakes of the method of musical composition. In these ways Poe did appropriate the effects of music, and they blended with the other characteristics of his art as sound and color in nature, to make that vague impression on the mind of which he sought the secret. It belongs to his originality that he could thus exercise his mastery in the borderland between poetry and music, where none before him had power.

After all, to meet the last circumscription of his praise, he did not write a dozen poems of the best rank. Those of his youth, already sufficiently characterized, were works of promise in a boy, but they would not have made a bubble as they sank in the waters of oblivion. Of those composed in manhood (and as such should be reckoned the present versions of "The Sleeper," "The Valley of Unrest," "The City in the Sea," "To One in Paradise," and possibly "Israfel") the first fine one was "The Haunted Palace," nor was that to be free from later improvements; and from its appearance until his death Poe's poems of the same level can be counted on the fingers. To the world, indeed, he is the genius of one poem only, "The Raven"; unless, to support his name, the fame of "The Bells" and of "Ulalume" be added. There is no occasion to examine either these three or any others of the dozen that are justly immortal; they all belong to the class of poems that make their way at once or not at all. Yet it may serve to define and possibly to elucidate Poe's genius if it be incidentally noticed that, except in his single lyric "Israfel," the theme of his imagination is ruin; and that in the larger number of these few best poems it is the special case of ruin which he declared the most poetic of all, — the death of a beautiful woman. It is of no concern that the treatment was radically different, so that in each instance a poem absolutely unique was created; the noteworthy fact is, at present, that Poe's genius was developed in its strength by brooding over a fixed idea, as the insane do; and when, under great excitement, some other mode of expression was imperative, it was found only in such objective work as the marvelous allegory of "The Conqueror Worm," or in such spirit-broken confession as that other allegory of "The Haunted Palace," which in intense, imaginative self-portraiture is scarcely excelled in literature. The secret life, the moments of strongest emotion, the hours of longest reach, implied by such motives as these, make that impenetrable background of shadow against which in these poems the poet stands relieved forever,— the object of deep gloom, whether his sufferings were imaginary or real, inevitable or self-imposed, the work of unregarding fate or the strict retribution of justice.

But when the utmost has been said adversely, the power of these dozen poems is undiminished even over those who admit their vagueness, their lack of ideas, their insubstantial and unreal quality, their sometimes obvious artifice, their likeness to musical compositions, and their scant number. Poe would himself have considered such censures as praises in disguise, and scoffed at their authors as dull-mettled rascals, like Partridge at the play. The power, after all, remains; first and foremost a power of long-practiced art, but also of the spell itself, of the forms evoked independently of the magic that compels them, — a fascination that makes the mind pause. If one is not subdued by this, at least at moments, there are some regions of mortality unknown to him; he will never disembark on No Man's Land. If one is not sensible of the exquisite construction here shown, the poetic art is as much a mystery to him as was Prospero's to Caliban. But if one with the eye to see and the heart to understand remains fascinated by these poems, he forgets Poe's own gospel of the ends of art, and does not perceive the meaning of the irony that made the worshiper of beauty the poet of the outcast soul.[1] If it be the office of poetry to intimate the divine, it must be confessed these works of Poe intimate the infernal; they

[1] "L'adorateur de la beauté devint le poète de l'âme damnée. C'est vrai: mais si Poe n'atteignit guère cette beauté extatique à laquelle il aspirait, n'atteignit-il pas en son inspiration mélancholique à une perfection artistique qui est aussi de la beauté?" *Edgar Poe, sa vie et son Œuvre* par Émile Lauvrière, Paris, 1904, p. 434.

are variations struck on the chord of evil that vibrates in all life, throbs of the heart of pain, echoes of ruin that float up from the deep within the deep, the legend and pæan and ritual of hopeless death; they belong to the confusions of a superstitious mind, the feebleness of an unmanned spirit, the misery of an impotent will. Profound in knowledge of the obscure sources of feeling; almost magical in the subtlety of their lure; bold, clear, and novel in imagination; ideal, startlingly original, married to strange and revealing music, these poems fulfill all conditions of Poe's standard save one, and that the supreme one.

A fresh phase of Poe's fascination for women emerged in the period of which the other incidents have now been detailed, — his relations with the poetesses of the New York coterie and their circle. After the publication of "The Raven" he had attended, from time to time, most often alone, but sometimes in company with his invalid wife, the receptions at which the *littêrateurs* of the metropolis, particularly the ladies, used to meet. These gatherings took place commonly at Dr. Orville Dewey's, the eloquent preacher; or at James Lawson's, distinguished in Poe's mind as a man interested in our literature although a Scotchman, and as an enthusiast in all matters of taste although himself devoid of it; or at Miss Anne Charlotte Lynch's, a poetess of the Willis group, whose weekly receptions in Waverley Place were thronged by literary men, artists, poetesses, and others of like pursuits. At such resorts, in the midst of a variously constituted company, Poe would sit, dressed in plain black, but with the head, the broad, retreating white brow, the large, luminous, piercing eyes, the impassive lips, that gave the visible character of genius to his features; and if the loud, bluff pleasantry of the humorist physician, Dr. Francis, or the high-keyed declamation of Margaret Fuller in her detested transcendentalist Boston dialect, would permit, he would himself, in his ordinary subdued, musical tones exercise his charm on women of lesser note, among whom — to mention only a few that come within the scope of this narrative — were Mrs. Elizabeth Oakes-Smith, once known as the author of "The Sinless Child" (which Poe thought the most original long American poem excepting Maria del Occidente's "Bride of Seven"); Mrs. Elizabeth Frieze Ellet, whose hand Poe took in an evil hour; and Mrs. Mary Gove, afterwards

Mrs. Nichols, "a Mesmerist, a Swedenborgian, a phrenologist, a homœopathist, and a disciple of Priessnitz," and, adds Poe, "what more I am not prepared to say."[1] Notwithstanding his natural reserve his manners were pleasing, and his conversation, although said to be best when but one or two were present, was engaging and impressive even in the constraint and inconsequence of general talk. Upon women his voice and look had a magical power, partly the social charm peculiar to the Virginia society in which he was bred, but also flowing from his own personality, idealized now through his authorship of "The Raven," and often pathetic by the pallor of illness and poverty. He fascinated women from his youth, and his relation to them had always been romantic, so far as it existed at all; he now appealed to sentimental women by his figure, history, and actions, and to kind-hearted women by his sufferings. Early in 1845 he had formed such an attachment with Mrs. Francis Sargent Osgood, a poetess of thirty and the wife of an American artist, who on publishing her first volume, seven years before, in London, had been taken up as a protégée by Mrs. Norton. Poe had noticed her verses with great favor, and

[1] *Works*, viii, 62.

FRANCES SARGENT OSGOOD

in his New York lecture, in February, especially, eulogized her in warm terms. Shortly after this latter incident Willis one day handed her "The Raven," with the author's request for her judgment on it, and for an introduction to herself. She assented, and a few days later Poe called at the Astor House to see her.

"I shall never forget," she wrote, "the morning when I was summoned to the drawing-room by Mr. Willis to receive him. With his proud and beautiful head erect, his dark eyes flashing with the electric light of feeling and of thought, a peculiar, an inimitable blending of sweetness and hauteur in his expression and manner, he greeted me, calmly, gravely, almost coldly, yet with so marked an earnestness that I could not help being deeply impressed by it. From that moment until his death we were friends; although we met only during the first year of our acquaintance." [1]

Some verses addressed to Poe, in the character of Israfel, by Mrs. Osgood, were published in the "Broadway Journal" April 5; and to these Poe replied April 26, with a version of his stanzas, originally written for the "Messenger," and here entitled "To F——" and signed

[1] Griswold, liii.

"E."; and he later addressed her again in the "Journal," September 13, with four lines of the eight originally written for Miss Eliza White at Richmond. The course of this friendship, however, by her own statement, had not run smooth from the start. He sought her with the characteristic vehemence of his nature. "I never thought of him till he sent me his 'Raven' and asked Willis to introduce him to me, and immediately after I went to Albany, and afterwards to Boston and Providence to avoid him, and he followed me to each of those places and wrote to me, imploring me to love him, many a letter which I did not reply to, until his *wife* added her entreaties to his and said that I might save him from infamy, and her from death, by showing an affectionate interest in him."[1] The young poetess thus became intimate with the Poes now at 85 Amity Street, and to her pen is due the only description of the family, at this time, that has been preserved: —

"It was in his own simple yet poetical home that to me the character of Edgar Poe appeared in its most beautiful light. Playful, affectionate,

[1] Mrs. Osgood to Griswold. Griswold MSS. A version of Poe's pursuit of Mrs. Osgood, quite different in tone, is given by her brother-in-law. *The Critic*, October 3, 1885.

witty, alternately docile and wayward as a petted child, for his young, gentle, and idolized wife, and for all who came, he had, even in the midst of his most harassing literary duties, a kind word, a pleasant smile, a graceful and courteous attention. At his desk beneath the romantic picture of his loved and lost Lenore, he would sit, hour after hour, patient, assiduous, and uncomplaining, tracing, in an exquisitely clear chirography and with almost superhuman swiftness, the lightning thoughts — the 'rare and radiant fancies' — as they flashed through his wonderful and ever-wakeful brain. I recollect, one morning, toward the close of his residence in this city, when he seemed unusually gay and light-hearted. Virginia, his sweet wife, had written me a pressing invitation to come to them; and I, who never could resist her affectionate summons, and who enjoyed his society far more in his own home than elsewhere, hastened to Amity Street. I found him just completing his series of papers entitled 'The Literati of New York.' 'See,' said he, displaying in laughing triumph several little rolls of narrow paper (he always wrote thus for the press), 'I am going to show you by the difference of length in these the different degrees of estimation in which I hold all you literary people. In each of these one of you is rolled up and fully discussed. Come, Virginia, help me!' And one by one they unfolded them. At last they came to one which seemed interminable. Virginia laughingly ran to one corner of the room with one end, and her husband to the opposite with the other. 'And whose lengthened sweetness long drawn out is that?' said I. 'Hear her!' he cried. 'Just as if her little vain heart did n't tell her it's herself!'"[1]

Mrs. Osgood was a kind friend, and while her indulgence in sentimentality is sufficiently evident in these reminiscences, and plainly affected her more than she was conscious of, she was pleased to think, with Virginia, that her influence over Poe was for his good. If on his part there were in this Platonic friendship, as she declares, "many little poetical episodes, in which the impassioned romance of his temperament impelled him to indulge," they were not new to the family circle that encouraged them; and on her own part, his devoted admirer obtained from him a solemn promise not to use stimulants, and, she naïvely states, he so far observed his word as never to appear before her when affected by them.

[1] Griswold, lii, liii.

Facsimile of original MS.
By courtesy of Mrs. W. M. Griswold

A Valentine.

By Edgar A. Poe.

To ——— ——— ———

For her this rhyme is penned, whose luminous eyes,
  Brightly expressive as the twins of Lœda,
Shall find her own sweet name that, nestling, lies
  Upon the page, enwrapped from every reader.
Search narrowly these lines! — they hold a treasure
  Divine — a talisman — an amulet
That must be worn *at heart*. Search well the measure —
  The words — the syllables! Do not forget

[illegible] point, or you may lose your labor;

And yet there is in this no Gordian knot

Which one might not undo without a sabre

If one could merely comprehend the plot.

Enwritten upon the leaf where now are peering

Eyes scintillating soul, there lie *perdus*

Three eloquent words oft uttered in the hearing

Of poets, by poets — as the name is a poet's, too.

Its letters, although naturally lying

(Like the knight Pinto — Mendez Ferdinando —)

Still form a synonym for Truth. —— Cease trying!

You will not read the riddle though you do the best you *can* do.

Valentine's Eve, 1848.

The correspondence between the two was fraught with evil consequences; for, one day, after the Poes had removed to the village of Fordham, whither they went when the cherry trees blossomed in 1846, Mrs. Ellet, who was calling on them, saw an open letter from Mrs. Osgood to Poe, couched in language which in her judgment required friendly interference. This lady consulted with her friends, and the scandalized bevy of interlopers prevailed on Mrs. Osgood to commission some of them to demand the return of her portion of the too-sugared correspondence. It seems strange that Mrs. Osgood did not herself make the request quietly, if she thought she had committed herself improperly; instead of doing so, however, she sent Margaret Fuller and a companion, who astonished the poet with their credentials. In a moment of exasperation he is said to have remarked that Mrs. Ellet had better come and look after her own letters, — a chance word that seems to have canceled all his considerate flattery of that versifier in the past ten years. The ladies returned to New York with their bundle; and Poe says that he gave Mrs. Ellet her own packet without awaiting her application, and hence was surprised when her brother demanded of him, a few days later, what he had no longer in his possession. Mrs. Osgood did not meet Poe after the first year of their acquaintance, but precisely when she ceased to do so is obscure.[1]

While this romance was verging to its catastrophe, immediately after the issue of his poems, Poe offered to Wiley & Putnam on January 6, 1846, another selection from his tales, asking fifty dollars for the copyright: he had made the selection himself, and describes it as "a far better one than the first — containing for instance 'Ligeia,' which is undoubtedly the best story I have written"; but this offer was fruitless.[2] Duyckinck was his trusted adviser, and he submitted to him correspondence before sending it, and requested his services in placing notices of him in the papers; as, for instance, on April 28, 1846, when he solicited a notice of his

[1] Mrs. Weiss (p. 127 *et seq.*) connects with the final scenes the tale told by Rosalie Poe, who visited her brother toward the end of June. On her arrival he was absent from the cottage, "on a business trip," said Mrs. Clemm, and in such difficulties that money had to be scraped together to send him for his return. He was "scolded" at first, but nursed through a night of illness and partial delirium during which "he begged for morphine," and it was some days before he recovered. The evidence which connects this incident with Mrs. Osgood seems inconclusive.

[2] Poe to Duyckinck, *loc. cit.* p. 8.

declining an invitation of the literary societies of the University of Vermont to read a poem in the following August.[1] He still occasionally contributed to "Graham's," which in March published an installment of "Marginalia" and in April "The Philosophy of Composition" with its notorious analysis of the genesis of "The Raven"; but "Godey's" had become the mainstay of his support, where he had written criticisms in each number since the previous November, noticing Mathews, Mrs. Smith, Simms, Mrs. Hewitt, Mrs. Osgood, and Bryant, and now published "The Literati."

[1] Poe to Duyckinck, *loc. cit.* p. 8.

CHAPTER XI

THE LITERATI

"THE LITERATI" was a series of papers, not called forth by current books, but a sort of "Autography" expanded, and probably, with the preceding critical papers, made up all Poe had yet written of his projected work on current American literature. It began to appear in May and continued through six numbers; it dealt with thirty-eight authors resident in New York, and Poe professed to give in the main not merely his own opinion of them, but that of literary society as expressed in private. The sketches themselves are distinctly the work of a magazinist, both in conception and execution; in fact, they are simply somewhat hurriedly recorded impressions of literary people and their works, interspersed, according to Poe's inveterate habit, with extracts from, or paraphrases of, his old book reviews since the time of the "Messenger." Being written with taking frankness, and in that spirit of oblivious indifference to what the world would say which had won a hearing for Poe's criticism, the series was the literary hit of the season. Few of these characterizations (they include personal as well as literary qualities) are in any way humiliating to their subjects. None, it is true, not even that of Mrs. Osgood, is unreservedly laudatory; but if limitations of capacity are marked out sharply and freely, praise is, as a rule, generously given within the bounds. Against Lewis Gaylord Clark of "The Knickerbocker" Poe had an old grudge, and just at this time Briggs had succeeded to Fay and Griswold as the peculiar object of his spleen; but with these exceptions, although some of the nobodies might have been nettled at the cavalier manner in which their merits were circumscribed or themselves patronized, there were very few with any just cause for complaint, since Poe was not so much the prince of critics as to anticipate exactly the judgment of posterity by ignoring them. In respect to the more important ones, Willis, Halleck, and Margaret Fuller, his decisions were final and have been sustained. There was a good deal of discussion, however, among the disturbed mediocrities; Godey was implored by the honey-tongued and browbeaten by the loud-mouthed, but he refused to be intimidated by either method, as he assured the public in a card; and, in particular, Thomas Dunn English was roused to open combat.

English, whom Poe facetiously called "Thomas Dunn Brown," was a doctor, lawyer, novelist, editor, and poet of twenty-seven years of age, and lived to be a representative to Congress in old age; Poe, despite his foolish disclaimer of personal acquaintance, had known him well in Philadelphia, and had associated with him in New York, now that both had come to that city. English had aided the last number of the "Journal," when Poe left it. No mortal ever held a pen who would not resent such an article as was Poe's in this instance, — a sort of grotesque in criticism. English secured forthwith the columns of the "Daily Telegraph," from a friend, and poured out on Poe, at once, a flood of words. He reviewed his association with Poe from his Philadelphia days, and especially during the week already sufficiently described above by Chivers, the period of the Boston poem, and that of the imbroglio over the Osgood-Ellet letters, and described the personal encounter in which Poe's last visit to him, relating to the last episode, ended on his refusal, as he later declared, to represent Poe in dealing with Lummis, Mrs. Ellet's brother-in-law. He added, and this was the gravamen of the matter,. a specific accusation of obtaining money from himself under false pretenses and a tale of forgery, — namely, that a respectable merchant of the city had circulated a story of that nature with regard to Poe, and that Poe, after demanding an explanation and receiving little, had abandoned the legal proceedings which English, who had been his intermediary with both the merchant and the lawyers, had suggested. Poe wrote a reply dated some days later, in which he exercised his powers of recrimination at a length and with an effect that makes one think of the lion and the jackal. He does not deny anything in respect to his own failings, and the passage in which he acknowledges them is the clearest statement he ever made publicly with regard to them: —

"The errors and frailties which I deplore, it cannot at least be asserted that I have been the coward to deny. Never, even, have I made attempt at *extenuating* a weakness which is (or, by the blessing of God, *was*) a calamity, although those who did not know me intimately had little reason to regard it otherwise than as a crime. For, indeed, had my pride, or that of my family permitted, there was much — very much — there was everything — to be offered in extenuation. Perhaps, even, there was an epoch at which it might not have been wrong in me to hint — what by the testimony of Dr. Francis and other medical men I might have demonstrated, had the public, indeed, cared for the demonstration — that the irregularities so profoundly lamented were the *effect* of a terrible evil rather than its cause. — And now let me thank God that in redemption from the physical ill I have forever got rid of the moral."

He was in a sense precluded from any detailed denial of incidents or words that occurred when he was intoxicated, as in severe attacks he had no memory of them. On the occasion when he visited English in his office and the personal encounter took place, in which both claimed the victory, he was apparently suffering from such an attack, accompanied, as on other occasions, by fear; he was in an irresponsible state, and the brother of Mrs. Ellet was then an object of apprehension to him. This is the natural explanation of what is now known of the entire affair. On recovering himself he "did not remember," as his friends were accustomed to say of his excesses, and the incident with English was recent and notorious. He could not deny; and he confined his defense to an explanation of the tale of forgery, and printed a letter, dated July 5, 1845, in which the merchant withdrew the charge as having been due to some misunderstanding of the words of his informant, who denied having uttered it or having any knowledge about it. In consequence of this retraction Poe had given up his idea of a suit-at-law. Had he not himself indulged in intemperate personal abuse of English, there would have been nothing to mar his rejoinder. He submitted the reply to Duyckinck and asked him to show it also to the latter's partner, Cornelius Mathews, in a letter, June 29,[1] and sent it to Godey, who published it in the "Philadelphia Spirit of the Times," July 10, at a cost of ten dollars. Poe wrote to Godey with regard to it a few days later: —

NEW YORK, July 16, 1846.

MY DEAR SIR, — I regret that you published my "Reply" in "The Times." I should have found no difficulty in getting it printed here in a *respectable* paper and gratis. However, as I have the game in my own hands, I shall not stop to complain about trifles.

[1] Poe to Duyckinck, *loc. cit.* p. 9.

I am rather ashamed that, knowing me to be as poor as I am, you should have thought it advisable to make the demand *on me* of the $10. I confess that I thought better of you — but let it go — it is the way of the world.

The man or men who told you that there was anything wrong in *the tone* of my "Reply" were either my enemies, or your enemies, or asses. When you see them, tell them so from me. I have never written an article upon which I more confidently depend for *literary* reputation than that "Reply." Its merit lay in being *precisely* adapted to its purpose. In this city I have had upon it the favorable judgments of the best men. All the error about it was yours. You should have done as I requested — published it in the "Book." It is of no use to conceive a plan if you have to depend upon another for its execution.

Please distribute twenty or thirty copies of the "Reply" in Philadelphia, and send me the balance through Harnden.

What paper, or papers, have copied E.'s attack?

I have put this matter in the hands of a competent attorney, and you shall see the result. Your charge, $10, will of course be brought before the court as an item when I speak of damages.

In perfect good feeling, yours truly,

POE.[1]

It *would* be as well to address your letters to West Farms. Please put "Miss Lynch" in the next number. I enclose the "Reveillé" article. I presume that, ere this, you have seen the highly flattering notices of the "Picayune," and the "Charleston Courier."

Poe also brought suit against the "Mirror," which copied the libel; no witnesses appearing, he was adjudged damages, February 17, 1847, in the sum of $225, with costs to the defendant.

Notwithstanding wrath, Poe's "Literati" was not a prose Dunciad; and the impression that his criticism in general was an anathema on American mediocrity is an entirely false one. Not infrequently, indeed, he exposed some fool's folly with the raillery and zest of a boy's untroubled enjoyment in the low comedy of the situation; now and then, in a more bitter mood, he could with deliberate leisure pull some insect of the hour to pieces, or impale a Bavius or two upon the highway. He looked on himself as a

[1] Griswold MSS.

public executioner, and was proud of the office. On the whole, however, his commendation equaled, if it did not exceed, his condemnation, and more than one of those whom he extolled to the skies has long since sunk back to the dust. The peculiarity of his position was, not that he was an unjust judge, but that he was the only judge; not that his censures were undeserved, but that he seemed to pronounce a sentence without fear or favor. He thus drew about himself a swarm of enemies; and as his life offered only too fair an opportunity they used their advantage to take revenge in scandal, as did English, but in secret. In these critical decisions of Poe's, speaking generally, he was not habitually actuated by any unworthy motive, any personal consideration of friendliness or enmity, or any hope of gain or fear of loss. Now and then, as in the case of Griswold, he was stung into telling truth when he might otherwise have held his peace; or he apologized, as to Mathews, for the violence of some earlier critique, or lowered the key of his laudation when friendship ceased, as with Lowell. Worldly motives swayed his mind, now more, now less; personal feelings entered into his verdicts; but his claim to impartiality, sincerity, and integrity seems to be generally sustained, or to be invalidated by the praise he gave to his feminine friends rather than by the contempt he poured out on his masculine foes.

It is thought in some quarters that Poe's criticism, in general, and particularly its destructive portions, was very valuable. It is even said that he raised the level of our current literature. The race of chameleon poets, however, is not yet extinct, and they feed on the green trees of Tennyson, Browning, and Swinburne as once on those of Moore, Mrs. Hemans, and Keats. Reputations are still made by the coteries of a publisher's anteroom and sustained by mendacious advertising. The motives that influence the editorial judgments of the press have changed but little in two generations. If, as is true, mediocrities of our time are more clever in their imitation and more painstaking in their drudgery, this is rather to be ascribed to the general rise of the standard of literary excellence, due to the intellectual movement of the age, than to the influence of a single free lance like Poe. The good that criticism can do to the producers of literature is trifling; its work is to improve the popular taste, and to make the best that is written widely known and easily apprehensible; to authors it is, for many reasons, well-nigh useless.

Destructive criticism of imaginative work, especially, is ordinarily futile, and in Poe's case no exception need be made. The good he did was infinitesimal; it would have been far better to leave such work to the scythe of Time.

Of the excellence of Poe's criticism in itself, however, there can be no question. He was the disciple of Coleridge; and, being gifted with something of Coleridge's analytic powers, he applied the principles he thus derived with skill and effect. No one, too, could subject himself to so long a self-training, and become so perfect in his own subtle art, without developing a refined taste of the highest value in criticism. The test of his ability as a critic, the severest test to which a man can be put, is the quickness and certainty of his recognition of unknown genius. In this Poe succeeded; the rank he gave to the American poets, young and old (and in the case of the best of them he had only their earliest work to judge by), is the rank sustained by the issue, and his success in dealing with the English reputations of the future was not less marked. To Tennyson, Dickens, and Longfellow he brought early applause; Mrs. Browning, Lowell, and Hawthorne were foreknown by him when their names were still in doubt. It is no diminution of his just praise that he so far shared in human weakness as to obey an obscure jealousy, notably in Longfellow's case; or to be misled by a prejudice, as with Emerson or any other transcendentalist; or to hail many a poetaster, particularly in petticoats, as of Apollo's band. He was as extreme in eulogy as in denunciation; and, especially in the case of Southern writers, he sometimes indulged in so laudatory a strain as to be guilty of absurdity. His decisions in more than one instance, like those on Moore, and in a less degree on Dickens, were merely contemporary; and in other cases, like that of Horne's "Orion," were esoteric and whimsical. His silence, too, regarding the great men of the past, such as Shakespeare, and the unanimous report of his violent depreciation of them in conversation, must count in settling his own virtues as a critic. He was, it is easy to see now, prejudiced here and partial there; foolish, or interested, or wrong-headed; carping, or flattering, or contemptuous. Yet he was the first of his time to mark the limitations of the pioneer writers, such as Irving, Bryant, and Cooper, and to foresee the future of the younger men who have been mentioned; he was, too, though he originated no criterion, the first to take criticism from mere advertising, puffery, and friendship, and submit it to the laws of literary art. This was much to do, and in his lifetime, whatever were his deficiencies, was regarded as his great distinction; it was the more honorable because of the offense that was now and then bound to be given, even if Poe had been the wisest and kindest of men instead of the reckless, erratic, and unscholarly judge he was. For, to come to the rationale of the matter, it was by no means learning, in which he was a charlatan, nor inborn sense, nor intellectual honesty, nor moral insight, nor power of imaginative sympathy, that gave his criticism value, — in all these he was deficient; but it was merely the knowledge of the qualities and methods of artistic effect, which came to him in the development of his own genius under the controlling influence of Coleridge's reason and imagination. His criticism is thus largely a series of illustrations of literary art as he himself practiced it.

These particular articles upon his contemporaries in the same city, however, did him no service and were ill-advised. They were vulnerable on both sides, both in friendship and in enmity. The censorious spirit had grown upon him, and his reluctance to admit excellencies in any but the mediocre, with a few exceptions, was marked. The papers showed in many places an unamiable character, and fell in only too readily with his depreciation of Longfellow and others to make for him a reputation for ill-nature. In fact, personal feeling entered into his critical writing, in the later time, to a degree that makes it a part of the autobiography of the man. The inexpediency of these articles, however, was pointed out to him, and other advice given, by William Gilmore Simms, in a letter, July 30, 1846, which again illustrates the attitude of the literary men of his country toward him: —

New York, July 30, 1846.

Dear Sir, — I received your note a week ago, and proceeded at once to answer it, but being in daily expectation of a newspaper from the South, to which, in a letter, I had communicated a paragraph concerning the matter which you had suggested in a previous letter, I determined to wait until I could enclose it to you. It has been delayed somewhat longer than I had anticipated, and has in part caused my delay to answer you. I now send it you, and trust that it will answer the desired purpose; though I must frankly say that I scarcely see the necessity of noticing the sort of scandal to which you refer. I note with regret the very desponding character of your last letter. I surely need not tell you how deeply and sincerely I deplore the misfortunes which attend you — the more so as I see no process for your relief and extrication, but such as must result from your own decision and resolve. No friend can well help you in the struggle which is before you. Money, no doubt, can be procured; but this is not altogether what you require. Sympathy may soothe the hurts of self-esteem, and make a man temporarily forgetful of his assailants; but in what degree will this avail, and for how long, in the protracted warfare of twenty or thirty years? You are still a very young man, and one too largely and too variously endowed not to entertain the conviction as your friends entertain it — of a long and manful struggle with, and a final victory over, fortune. But this warfare the world requires you to carry on with your own unassisted powers. It is only in your manly resolution to use these powers after a legitimate fashion, that it will countenance your claims to its regards and sympathy; and I need n't tell you how rigid and exacting it has ever been in the case of the poetical genius, or, indeed, the genius of any order. Suffer me to tell

WILLIAM GILMORE SIMMS

you frankly, taking the privileges of a true friend, that you are now perhaps in the most perilous period of your career — just in that position — just at that time of life — when a false step becomes a capital error — when a single leading mistake is fatal in its consequence. You are no longer a boy. "At thirty wise or never." You must subdue your impulses; and in particular, let me exhort you to discard all associations with men, whatever their talents, whom you cannot esteem as men. Pardon me for presuming thus to counsel one whose great natural and acquired resources should make him rather the teacher of others. But I obey a law of my own nature, and it is because of my sympathies that I speak. Do not suppose yourself abandoned by the worthy and honorable among your friends. They will be glad to give you welcome *if you will suffer them.* They will rejoice — I know their feelings and hear their language — to countenance your return to that community — that moral province in society — of which, let me say to you respectfully and regretfully, you have been, according to all reports, but too heedlessly, and perhaps too scornfully, indifferent. Remain in obscurity for a while. You have a young wife, — I am told a suffering and an interesting one, — let me entreat you to cherish her, and to cast away those pleasures which are not worthy of your mind, and to trample those temptations under foot which degrade your person, and make it familiar to the mouth of vulgar jest. You may [do] all this by a little circumspection. It is still within your power. Your resources from literature are probably much greater than mine. I am sure they are quite as great. You can increase them so that they shall be ample for all your legitimate desires; but you must learn the worldling's lesson of prudence — a lesson, let me add, which the literary world has but too frequently and unwisely disparaged. It may seem to you very impertinent — in most cases it is impertinent — that he who gives nothing else should presume to give counsel. But one gives that which he can most spare, and you must not esteem me indifferent to a condition which I can in no other way assist. I have never been regardless of your genius, even when I knew nothing of your person. It is some years since I counseled Mr. Godey to obtain the contributions of your pen. He will tell you this. I hear that you reproach him. But how can you expect a Magazine proprietor to encourage contributions which embroil him with all his neighbors? These broils do you no good — vex your temper, destroy your peace of mind, and hurt your reputation. You have abundant resources upon which to draw, even were there no Grub Street in Gotham. Change your tactics, and begin a new series of papers with your publisher. The printed matter which I send you might be quoted by Godey, and might be ascribed to me. But, surely, I need not say to you that, to a Southern man, the annoyance of being mixed up in a squabble with persons whom he does not know, and does not care to know, — and from whom no Alexandrine process of cutting loose would be permitted by society, — would be an intolerable grievance. I submit to frequent injuries and misrepresentations, content — though annoyed by the [illegible] — that the viper should amuse himself upon the file, at the expense of his own teeth. As a man, as a writer, I shall always be solicitous of your reputation and success. You have but to resolve on taking and asserting your position, equally in the social and the literary world, and your way is clear, your path is easy, and you will find true friends enough to sympathize in your triumphs. Very sincerely though sorrowfully,

Your friend and ser'vt,

W. Gilmore Simms.[1]

[1] Griswold MSS.

P. S. If I could I should have been to see you. But I have been, and am still, drudging in the hands of the printers, kept busily employed night and day. Besides, my arrangements are to hurry back to the South where I have a sick family. A very few days will turn my feet in that direction.

Poe had also written to Cooke earlier in the spring, on April 16, and requested that he would continue the biography written by Lowell and bring it up to date. He received an answer almost at the same time as the letter from Simms: —

August 4, 1846.

My dear Sir, — . . . You propose that I shall take up your memoir where Lowell drops it, and carry it on to the present date of your publications. I will do so, if my long delay has not thrown the work into the hands of some other friend, with entire pleasure. I, however, have not "Graham's Magazine" for February, 1845, and if you still wish me to continue the memoir you must send that number to me. I some months ago procured your Tales and Poems, and have read them collectively with great pleasure. That is a wonderful poem ending —

> "Hell rising from a thousand thrones
> Shall do it reverence."

"Lenore," too, is a great poem. The closing stanza of "To One in Paradise" (I remember it as published in "The Visionary") is the perfection of melody. "The Raven" is your *best* poem.

John Kennedy, talking with me about your stories, old and recent, said, "The man's imagination is as truth-like and minutely accurate as De Foe's" — and went on to talk of your "Descent into the Maelström," "MS. Found in a Bottle," "Gold Bug," etc. I think this last the most ingenious thing I ever read. Those stories of criminal detection, "Murders of the Rue Morgue," etc., a prosecuting attorney in the neighborhood here declares are miraculous. I think your French friend, for the most part, fine in his deductions from overlaid and unnoticed small facts, but sometimes too minute and hair-splitting. The stories are certainly as interesting as any ever written. The "Valdemar Case" I read in a number of your "Broadway Journal" last winter — as I lay in a turkey-blind, muffled to the eyes in overcoats, etc., and pronounce it without hesitation the most damnable, *vraisemblable*, horrible, hair-lifting, shocking, ingenious chapter of fiction that any brain ever conceived, or hand traced. That gelatinous, viscous sound of the man's voice! There never was such an idea before. That story scared me in broad day, armed with a double-barrel Tyron turkey-gun. What would it have done at midnight in some old ghostly country-house?

I have always found some one remarkable thing in your stories to haunt me long after reading them. The teeth in "Berenice"; the changing eyes of Morella; that red and glaring crack in the "House of Usher"; the pores of the deck in the "MS. Found in a Bottle"; the visible drops falling into the goblet in "Ligeia," etc., etc., — there is always something of this sort to stick by the mind — by mine at least.

My wife is about to enter the carriage, and as I wish to send this to the P. O. by her I must wind up rapidly. I am *now* after an interval of months again at work in the preparation of my poems for publication. I am *dragging*, but perhaps the mood will presently come. I bespeak a review of my Book at your hands when I get it out. I have not time now to copy "Rosalie Lee." It is in Griswold's last edition. I am grateful to you for the literary prop you afford me; and trust to do something to justify your commendations. I talked recently with a little lady who had heard a lecture of yours in which you praised my poetry—in New York. She had taken up the notion that I was a great poetic roaring "Lion."

Do with my MS. as you choose. What do you design as to the "Stylus"? Write to me without delay, if you can rob yourself of so much time.[1]

Poe at once replied:—

NEW YORK, August 9, 1846.

MY DEAR SIR,—Never think of excusing yourself (to me) for dilatoriness in answering letters—I know too well the unconquerable procrastination which besets the poet. I will place it all to the accounts of the turkeys. Were I to be seized by a rambling fit, one of my customary *passions* (nothing less) for vagabondizing through the woods for a week or a month together, I would not—in fact I *could* not—be put out my mood, were it even to answer a letter from the Grand Mogul informing me that I had fallen heir to his possessions.

Thank you for the compliments. Were I in a serious humor just now, I would tell you frankly how your words of appreciation make my nerves

[1] Griswold MSS.

thrill — not because you praise me (for others have praised me more lavishly), but because I feel that you comprehend and discriminate. You are right about the hair-splitting of my French friend — that is all done for effect. These tales of ratiocination owe most of their popularity to being something in a new key — I do not mean to say that they are not ingenious — but people think them more ingenious than they are — on account of their method, and *air* of method. In the "Murders in the Rue Morgue," for instance, where is the ingenuity of unravelling a web which you yourself (the author) have woven for the express purpose of unravelling? The reader is made to confound the ingenuity of the suppositious Dupin with that of the writer of the story.

Not for the world would I have had any one else to continue Lowell's memoir until I had heard from you. I wish *you* to do it (if you will be so kind) and nobody else. By the time the book appears you will be famous (or all my prophecy goes for nothing), and I shall have the *éclat* of your name to aid my sales. But, seriously, I do not think that any one so well enters into the poetical portion of my mind as yourself — and I deduce this idea from my intense appreciation of those points of your own poetry which seem lost upon others.

Should you undertake the work for me, there is one topic — there is one particular in which I have had wrong done me, and it may not be indecorous in me to call your attention to it. The last selection of my Tales was made from about seventy, by Wiley & Putnam's reader, Duyckinck. He has what he thinks a taste for ratiocination, and has accordingly made up the book mostly of analytic stories. But this is not *representing* my mind in its various phases — it is not giving me fair play. In writing these Tales one by one, at long intervals, I have kept the book-unity, always in mind — that is, each has been composed with reference to its effect as part of *a whole*. In this view, one of my chief aims has been the widest diversity of subject, thought, and especially *tone* and manner of handling. Were all my Tales now before me in a large volume, and as the composition of another, the merit which would principally arrest my attention would be the wide *diversity and variety*. You will be surprised to hear me say that (omitting one or two of my first efforts) I do not consider any one of my stories *better* than another. There is a vast variety of kinds, and, in degree of value, these kinds vary — but each tale is equally good *of its kind.* The loftiest kind is that of the highest imagination — and for this reason only "Ligeia" may be called my *best* tale. I have much improved this last since you saw it, and I mail you a copy, as well as a copy of my best specimen of analysis — "The Philosophy of Composition."

Do you ever see the British papers? Martin F. Tupper, author of "Proverbial Philosophy," has been paying me some high compliments — and indeed I have been treated more than well. There is one "British opinion," however, which I value highly — Miss Barrett's. She says [the letter has been printed above] . . . Would it be in bad taste to quote these words of Miss B. in your notice? Forgive these egotisms (which are rendered in some measure necessary by the topic), and believe me that I will let slip *no* opportunity of reciprocating your kindness.

Griswold's new edition I have not yet seen (is it out?), but I will manage to find "Rosalie Lee." Do not forget to send me a few personal details of yourself — such as I give in "The New York Literati." When your book appears I propose to review it fully in Colton's "American Review." If you ever write to him, please suggest to him that I wish to do so. I hope to get your volume before mine goes to press — so that I may speak more fully.

• I will forward the papers to which I refer *in a day or two* — not by to-day's mail.

Touching "The Stylus": this is [the] one great purpose of my literary life. Undoubtedly (unless I die) I will accomplish it — but I can afford to lose nothing by precipitancy. I cannot say yet when or how I shall get to work — but when the time comes, I will write to you. I wish to establish a journal in which the men of genius may fight their battles upon some terms of equality with those dunces, the men of talent. But, apart from this, I have *magnificent* objects in view. May I but live to accomplish them!

Most cordially your friend,

EDGAR A. POE.[1]

A single letter from Hawthorne also belongs to this period.

SALEM, June 17, 1846.

MY DEAR SIR, — I presume the publishers will have sent you a copy of "Mosses from an Old Manse" — the latest (and probably the last) collection of my tales and sketches. I have read your occasional notices of my productions with

[1] Griswold MSS.

great interest — not so much because your judgment was, upon the whole, favorable, as because it seemed to be given in earnest. I care for nothing but the truth; and shall always much more readily accept a harsh truth, in regard to my writings, than a sugared falsehood.

I confess, however, that I admire you rather as a writer of tales than as a critic upon them. I might often — and often do — dissent from your opinions in the latter capacity, but could never fail to recognize your force and originality in the former. Yours very truly,

NATH. HAWTHORNE.[1]

While this episode of "The Literati" was going on, the private fortunes of Poe, as has been seen, had fallen to a low ebb; he was struggling with poverty, and was disabled by ill-health; his wife grew no better in the cottage at Fordham, and penury starved their home.

[1] Griswold MSS.

CHAPTER XII

THE COTTAGE AT FORDHAM

THE cottage to which Poe had retired in the spring of 1846, although at the best a mean dwelling, was the pleasantest retreat he had known. It was a one story and a half house, then standing on King's Bridge Road, at the top of Fordham Hill. Within, on the ground-floor, were two small apartments, a kitchen and sitting-room; and above, up a narrow stairway, two others, one — Poe's room — a low, cramped chamber, lighted by little square windows like port-holes, the other a diminutive closet of a bedroom, hardly large enough to lie down in. Mrs. Gove, on whose recollections all later biographers have relied for their knowledge, paints the interior: —

"On this occasion I was introduced to the young wife of the poet, and to the mother, then more than sixty years of age. She was a tall, dignified old lady, with a most lady-like manner, and her black dress, though old and much worn, looked really elegant on her. She wore a widow's cap, of the genuine pattern, and it suited exquisitely with her snow-white hair. Her features were large, and corresponded with her stature, and it seemed strange how such a stalwart and queenly woman could be the mother of her *petite* daughter. Mrs. Poe looked very young; she had large black eyes, and a pearly whiteness of complexion which was a perfect pallor. Her pale face, her brilliant eyes, and her raven hair gave her an unearthly look. One felt that she was almost a disrobed spirit, and when she coughed it was made certain that she was rapidly passing away.

"The mother seemed hale and strong, and appeared to be a sort of universal Providence to her strange children.

"The cottage had an air of taste and gentility that must have been lent to it by the presence of its inmates. So neat, so poor, so unfurnished, and yet so charming a dwelling I never saw. The floor of the kitchen was white as wheaten flour. A table, a chair, and a little stove that it contained seemed to furnish it completely. The sitting-room floor was laid with check matting; four chairs, a light stand, and a hanging bookshelf completed its furniture. There were pretty presentation copies of books on the little shelves,

POE'S COTTAGE, FORDHAM

and the Brownings had posts of honor on the stand. With quiet exultation Poe drew from his side-pocket a letter he had recently received from Elizabeth Barrett Browning. He read it to us." [1]

Outside, however, the broad views, in contrast with the dwarfed interior, had a fine spaciousness. Old cherry trees were rooted in the grassy turf, out of which cropped here and there the granite of the underlying rock; and a stone's throw to the east of the veranda, overgrown with vines, rose the ledge itself, overhung by sighing pines, and looking off far across the meadows, woods, and villages, to the glimmer of ocean on the dim horizon. Of this little home in the pleasant country there are many reminiscences, curiously intermingling the beauty of nature with the poor life of the three occupants. Mrs. Clemm made upon all who saw her an impression of dignity, refinement, and especially of deep motherly devotion to her children; Virginia, at the age of twenty-five, retained her attractiveness, but the large black eyes and raven hair contrasted sadly with the white pallor of her face; Poe himself, gnawed by poverty and pride, anticipating grief, and nursing the bitterness that springs from helplessness in the sight of suffering borne by

[1] *Six Penny Magazine*, February, 1863.

those dear to us, was restless and variable, the creature of contradictory impulses, alternating between the eagerness of renewed hope and the dull maze of the ever-recurring disappointment. Friends called on him, and found him anxious over his poverty, or inspirited by the letter from Mrs. Browning, or finding distraction with his pets, — a bobolink he had caught and caged, or a parrot some one had given him, or his favorite cat. The family seem always to have had a bird, or a cat, or growing flowers. He says he had fallen "dreadfully ill," and from the end of February was unable to write a line for the magazines for more than five months, or to go out of the house or help himself in any way; at the end of July he was still apologizing for his handwriting as something done with great difficulty, but he was then getting better, though slowly.[1] Except his letter to English and a review or two, he seems to have done no mental work. He had but just recovered from the business trip of which his sister Rosalie, who was visiting the cottage, told the unhappy issue, and he himself the beginning in a letter to Virginia, which is unique in his correspondence: —

[1] Poe to Chivers, July 22, 1846. *The Century Magazine*, February, 1903.

June 12, 1846.

MY DEAR HEART — MY DEAR VIRGINIA, — Our mother will explain to you why I stay away from you this night. I trust the interview I am promised will result in some *substantial good* for me — for your dear sake and hers — keep up your heart in all hopefulness, and trust yet a little longer. On my last great disappointment I should have lost my courage *but for you* — my little darling wife. You are my *greatest* and *only* stimulus now, to battle with this uncongenial, unsatisfactory, and ungrateful life.

I shall be with you to-morrow [illegible] P. M., and be assured until I see you I will keep in *loving remembrance* your *last words* and your fervent prayer!

Sleep well, and may God grant you a peaceful summer with your devoted

EDGAR.[1]

Poe's ill-health continued, and as the summer went on he grew no better, and daily Virginia failed and faded. Mrs. Clemm wrote to Rosalie despairing letters, and foretold the poor-house. Autumn came, the snow and the cold and the seclusion, and affairs grew desperate; the wolf

[1] Ingram, ii, 88, 89.

was already at the door when by happy chance Mrs. Gove again called on the Poes, and found the dying wife in the summer sitting-room, which had been taken for her use. The scene requires her own description: —

"I saw her in her bed-chamber. Everything here was so neat, so purely clean, so scant and poverty-stricken, that I saw the poor sufferer with such a heartache as the poor feel for the poor.

"There was no clothing on the bed, which was only straw, but a snow-white counterpane and sheets. The weather was cold, and the sick lady had the dreadful chills that accompany the hectic fever of consumption. She lay on the straw bed, wrapped in her husband's great-coat, with a large tortoise-shell cat in her bosom. The wonderful cat seemed conscious of her great usefulness. The coat and the cat were the sufferer's only means of warmth, except as her husband held her hands, and her mother her feet. Mrs. Clemm was passionately fond of her daughter, and her distress on account of her illness and poverty and misery was dreadful to see.

"As soon as I was made aware of these painful facts, I came to New York and enlisted the sympathies and services of a lady, whose heart and hand were ever open to the poor and miserable.

A feather bed and abundance of bed-clothing and other comforts were the first-fruits of my labor of love. The lady headed a private subscription, and carried them $60 the next week. From the day this kind lady saw the suffering family of the poet, she watched over them as a mother watches over her babe. She saw them often, and ministered to the comfort of the dying and the living." The lady was Mrs. Shew.

The work of relief was taken up by Mrs. Hewitt, who wrote to Mrs. Osgood, December 20, 1846: —

The Poes are in the same state of physical and pecuniary suffering — indeed worse than they were last summer, for now the cold weather is added to their accumulation of ills. I went to enquire of Mr. Post about them. He confirmed all that I had previously heard of their condition. Although he says Mrs. Clemm has never told him that they were in want, yet she borrows a shilling often, *to get a letter from the office* — but Mrs. Gove had been to see the Poes and found them living in the greatest wretchedness. I am endeavoring to get up a contribution for them among the editors, and the matter has got into print — very much to my regret, as I fear it will hurt Poe's pride to have his affairs made so public.

MARY.[1]

The necessitous condition of the family, much to Poe's mortification, was made public by a paragraph in "The Express," which appears to have been kindly meant, since it merely appealed to his friends in his behalf: —

"We regret to learn that Edgar A. Poe and his wife are both dangerously ill with the consumption, and that the hand of misfortune lies heavy upon their temporal affairs. We are sorry to mention the fact that they are so far reduced as to be barely able to obtain the necessaries of life. This is indeed a hard lot, and we hope that the friends and admirers of Mr. Poe will come promptly to his assistance in his bitterest hour of need." [2]

Willis, who saw this notice, gave greater currency to the facts by an article in his own paper, the "Home Journal," in which he made his friend's destitution the text of a plea for an authors' house of refuge, and said what it was well to say, under the circumstances, in regard to Poe's character: —

[1] Griswold MSS. [2] Griswold, xi.

"In connection with this public mention of Mr. Poe's personal matters, perhaps it will not be thought inopportune if we put on its proper footing a public impression which does him injustice. We have not seen nor corresponded with Mr. Poe for two years, and we hazard this delicate service without his leave, of course, and simply because we have seen him suffer from the lack of such vindication, when his name has been brought injuriously before the public, and have then wished for some such occasion to speak for him. We refer to conduct and language charged against him, which, were he at the time in sane mind, were an undeniable forfeiture of character and good feeling. To blame, in some degree, still, perhaps he is. But let charity for the failings of human nature judge of the degree. Mr. Poe was engaged with us in the editorship of a daily paper, we think, for about six months. A more considerate, quiet, talented, and gentlemanlike associate than he was for the whole of that time, we could not have wished. Not liking the unstudent-like necessity of coming every day into the city, however, he left us, by his own wish alone, and it was one day soon after that we first saw him in the state to which we refer. He came into our office with his usual gait and manner, and, with no symptoms of ordinary intoxication, he talked like a man insane. Perfectly self-possessed in all other respects, his brain and tongue were evidently beyond his control. We learned afterwards that the least stimulus — a single glass of wine — would produce this effect upon Mr. Poe, and that rarely as these instances of easy aberration of caution and mind occurred, he was liable to them, and while under their influence, voluble and personally self-possessed, but neither sane nor responsible. Now Mr. Poe very possibly may not be willing to consent to even this admission of any infirmity. He has little or no memory of them afterwards, we understand. But public opinion unqualifiedly holds him blamable for what he has said and done under such excitements, and while a call is made in a public paper for aid, it looks like doing him a timely service to, at least, partially exonerate him." [1]

Poe, who felt humiliated by these disclosures, of which Willis sent him a copy with a friendly note, wrote an open letter in reply, December 30, 1846, in which he tried hard to deny the actual misery of his condition, but only succeeded in forcing his pen to the guarded assertion that he

[1] *Home Journal*, December 19, 1846.

had indeed been in want of money in consequence of his long illness, but that it was not altogether true that he had materially suffered from privation beyond the extent of his capacity for suffering. This labored statement, however, which is given in nearly his exact words, was soon afterwards acknowledged, in a letter to Mrs. Locke, of Lowell, Mrs. Osgood's sister-in-law, who sent him some verses, and followed them with more solid expressions of interest, to be only an indulgence of his natural pride, which impelled him, he wrote, "to shrink from public charity, even at the cost of truth in denying those necessities which were but too real."[1]

Within a month, however, all his new hopes and old troubles were lost sight of in view of the rapidly approaching death of his wife. On January 29, 1847, he wrote to Mrs. Shew, whose attention had been unremitting during all these winter weeks, the following note: —

KINDEST — DEAREST FRIEND, — My poor Virginia still lives, although failing fast and now suffering much pain. May God grant her life until she sees you and thanks you once again! Her bosom is full to overflowing — like my own

[1] Griswold MSS.

— with a boundless — inexpressible gratitude to you. Lest she may never see you more — she bids me say that she sends you her sweetest kiss of love and will die blessing you. But come — oh come to-morrow! Yes, I *will* be calm — everything you so nobly wish to see me. My mother sends you, also, her "warmest love and thanks." She begs me to ask you, if possible, to make arrangements at home so that you may stay with us To-morrow night. I enclose the order to the Postmaster. Heaven bless you and farewell!

EDGAR A. POE.[1]

FORDHAM, January 29, '47.

In response, Mrs. Shew called to take a last leave of the invalid, who asked her to read some letters from the second Mrs. Allan,[2] exculpating Poe from causing any difficulty at his old home, and gave her Poe's picture and his mother's jewel-case as keepsakes. Curiously enough Poe's old Baltimore flame, Virginia's girlhood friend, who had also visited them in Amity Street, was

[1] Ingram, ii, 107.

[2] It is incredible that the second Mrs. Allan ever wrote to the Poes, but Poe may have preserved letters from the first Mrs. Allan during his early absence from home. The letters have never been found.

there on the same day, and she, Virginia, and Poe being together, Virginia united their hands and said: "Mary, be a friend to Eddie, and don't forsake him; he always loved you, — did n't you, Eddie?"[1] On the next day, Saturday, January 30, Virginia died. Her husband, wrapped in the military cloak that had once served to cover her, followed the body to the tomb,[2] to which it was consigned in the presence of a few friends, Mrs. Ann S. Stephens, Mrs. Shew, "Mary," Willis, and Morris being among them.

Poe is represented as very ill after this event; and although in the middle of March he partially recovered under the nursing of Mrs. Shew and his mother-in-law, he was again ill, and his life was believed to be endangered. It was necessary to raise fresh funds for his relief, and by the interest of various friends one hundred dollars were collected at once, and afterwards other sums were contributed. Mrs. Shew, who, as has been said, had received a medical educa-

[1] *Harper's Magazine*, (March, 1889), *loc. cit.*

[2] The tomb belonged to a Valentine family, unconnected with the Richmond Valentines; at some time after its demolition the remains of Virginia were re-interred beside Poe's grave at Baltimore. Cf. a curious article, *The Bones of Annabel Lee.*

tion, decided that Poe "in his best health had lesion of one side of the brain"; and she adds in her diary, "As he could not bear stimulants or tonics, without producing insanity, I did not feel much hope that he could be raised up from brain fever, brought on by extreme suffering of mind and body, — actual want and hunger and cold having been borne by this heroic husband in order to supply food, medicine, and comforts to his dying wife, until exhaustion and lifelessness were so near at every reaction of the fever that even sedatives had to be administered with extreme caution."[1] It was at this time that he dictated, in half-delirious states of mind, the romantic and unfounded story, which he obliged Mrs. Shew to write down, of his voyage to France, his duel, and his French novel.

Through all this period Mrs. Clemm was his household protector, and the portrait of her drawn by Willis shows the scene in yet another aspect: —

"Winter after winter, for years, the most touching sight to us, in this whole city, has been that tireless minister to genius, thinly and insufficiently clad, going from office to office with a poem, or an article on some literary subject, to

[1] Ingram, ii, 115.

MARIA CLEMM

sell — sometimes simply pleading in a broken voice that he was ill, and begging for him — mentioning nothing but that 'he was ill,' whatever might be the reason for his writing nothing; and never, amid all her tears and recitals of distress, suffering one syllable to escape her lips that could convey a doubt of him, or a complaint, or a lessening of pride in his genius and good intentions. Her daughter died, a year and a half since, but she did not desert him. She continued his ministering angel, — living with him, caring for him, guarding him against exposure, and, when he was carried away by temptation, amid grief and the loneliness of feelings unreplied to, and awoke from his self-abandonment prostrated in destitution and suffering, *begging* for him still. If woman's devotion, born with a first love, and fed with human passion, hallow its object, as it is allowed to do, what does not a devotion like this — pure, disinterested, and holy as the watch of an invisible spirit — say for him who inspired it?"[1]

On recovering from illness and depression sufficiently to resume work in some degree, Poe confined himself to his home. He rose early, ate moderately, drank only water, and took abun-

[1] *Home Journal*, October 13, 1849.

dance of exercise in the open air. From time to time he visited Mrs. Shew in the city, and she in turn called upon him, and would frequently advise him to contract marriage, with the warning that he could be saved from sudden death only by a prudent, calm life with a woman who had sufficient strength and affection to manage his affairs for him. On his part, he restrained his reply to remarks, which she termed ironical, regarding her ignorance of the world's evil. The circumstances of the family may have been temporarily improved by the payment of the sum for damages in the libel suit; it is said that the sum was eaten up by lawyers' fees, but that Poe gave a tea-party on the occasion, and was especially attentive to one fair guest. His life was, indeed, by no means so gloomy and solitary as has been thought. In this summer and autumn he entertained more than one old friend, like Eliza White of his early Richmond days, or new acquaintances, like the English ladies, who carried away bright recollections of his home. He had still the caged birds to pet, and now in addition he amused his leisure with cultivating a flower garden, in which were beds of mignonette, heliotrope, and dahlias. Frequently he would walk some miles to the westward, along uneven country roads lined with orchards, to the High Bridge, on whose lofty granite arches, a hundred and forty-five feet above high-water, the great aqueduct crosses Harlem River; and there on the elevated grassy causeway, used only by foot-passengers, he would pace by day or night, or would lean on the low parapet, alone. The ledge, too, back of his house, with its pines and the wide prospect, was one of his haunts, and thither he would retreat to escape literary callers, or to dream out the metaphysical rhapsody over which he was brooding; for it was in such solitary places that he planned "Eureka." He had always been a rambler in all weathers, a sentimentalist with women, and a dreamer, and his personal life went on much in the beaten path of his temperament, after as before Virginia's death.

This period was one of comparative inactivity, yet Poe's name did not pass out of the public notice. Just before the death of his wife, at the moment when the public appeal was made for him, he had been cheered by echoes of his first reputation in Europe: —

December 30, '46.

DEAR DUYCKINCK, — Mrs. Clemm mentioned to me, this morning, that some of the

Parisian papers had been speaking about my "Murders in the Rue Morgue." She could not give me the details — merely saying that you had told her. The "Murders in the R. M." was spoken of in the Paris "Charivari," soon after the first issue of the tale in Graham's Mag: — April, 1841. By the enclosed letter from Stonehaven, Scotland, you will see that the "Valdemar Case" still makes a talk, and that a pamphlet edition of it has been published by Short & Co. of London under the title of "Mesmerism in Articulo Mortis." It has fairly gone the rounds of the London Press, commencing with "The Morning Post." "The Monthly Record of Science" &c. gives it with the title "The Last Days of M. Valdemar. By the author of the Last Conversation of a Somnambule" — (Mesmeric Revelation).

My object in enclosing the Scotch letter and the one from Miss Barrett, is to ask you to do me a favor which (*just at this moment*) may be of great importance. It is, to make a paragraph or two for some one of the city papers, stating the facts here given, in connexion with what you know about the "Murders in the Rue Morgue." If this will not give you too much trouble, I will be deeply obliged. If you think it advisable, there is no objection to your copying any portion of Miss B.'s letter. Willis or Morris will put in anything you may be kind enough to write; but as the "Home Journal" has already said a good deal about me, some other paper would be preferable.

Truly yours, POE.[1]

"The Literati" had been immediately succeeded, in November, 1846, in "Godey's," by a tale of Italian vengeance, "The Cask of Amontillado," and in the December "Graham's" was an installment of "Marginalia."

In the earlier part of 1847 there had been nothing published but a few lines of verse, and as the year wore on only one review. Willis remained his literary friend, took pains to copy his poems, advertise his plans, and commend his genius whenever opportunity offered; and

[1] Poe to Duyckinck, *loc. cit.* p. 10. The passage referred to is doubtless that given by Griswold, p. xxxv, as from *L'Entre Acte*, October 20, 1846. Poe had unwittingly been the cause of a suit between two Paris papers, each of which had translated *The Murders in the Rue Morgue* without acknowledgment. *The Revue des Deux Mondes*, October 15, 1846, contained a critical notice by Forgues, and Isabelle Meunier translated some of his tales in the *Démocratie Pacifique* and other papers, apparently the same collected in *Les Contes d'Edgar Poe*, Paris, 1846.

Poe on his part kept him informed in regard to his doings. In the "Home Journal," March 13, appeared the lines mentioned, "To M. L. S——," Mrs. Shew, of inferior poetic merit, and characterized by the peculiar and sometimes dissonant cadences of the later unrhymed poems. A week later the same paper announced as soon to be published, "The Authors of America, in Prose and Verse, by Edgar A. Poe," but the work did not appear. The review of Hawthorne in the November "Godey's," in which Poe decides that Hawthorne is not original, after all, but only peculiar, was perhaps written long before, when Poe received the book from the author. "Ulalume" marked the close of this period in the poet's career. It is the first poem characteristic of his genius since "The Raven." "Many times," says his friend Burr, "after the death of his beloved wife, was he found at the dead hour of a winter night, sitting beside her tomb almost frozen in the snow, where he had wandered from his bed, weeping and wailing." This is the figure that goes with the poem, like an illustration, interpreting it to the sense. It is autobiography translated into imagination, and speaking a new language, — a cast shadow of despair, with tarn and sepulchre for attribute and symbol, — a vision of the soul that sees its own wraith in all that is. It is a difficult poem, and was caviare to the general then, as perhaps such personal allegorizing art must always be.

In December the poem was published in the "Whig," and reprinted by Willis in accordance with the following request from Poe, which may serve as an example of several such letters: —

FORDHAM, December 8.

MY DEAR MR. WILLIS, — Many thanks for the kind expressions in your note of three or four weeks ago.

I send you an "American Review" — the number just issued — in which is a ballad by myself, but published anonymously. It is called "Ulalume" — the page is turned down. I do not care to be known as its author just now; but I would take it as a great favor if you would copy it in the H. J., with a word of *inquiry* as to who wrote it: — provided always that you think the poem worth the room it would occupy in your paper — a matter about which I am by no means sure. Always yours gratefully,

EDGAR A. POE.[1]

[1] Poe to Willis. MS.

Willis prefaced his reprint with the desired inquiry as to the authorship of "Ulalume," and described it, in words that may not have seemed to Poe indicative of sympathetic insight, as an "exquisitely piquant and skillful exercise of rarity and niceness of language," and "a curiosity in philologic flavor." Since this extraordinarily inane characterization, the best opinion has differed widely in regard to this ballad, and still most men of poetic sensibility would say no more in its favor than did Willis. It is built out of the refrain, the most difficult mode of construction, and consequently it requires in the reader not only a willingness to accept monotony as a means of expression, but a content with it; the thought moves so slowly, with such slight advances from its initial stage, with such difficult increments of meaning and indistinguishable deepening of tone, that, like the workings of an expiring mind, it only just keeps wearily in action; its allegorizing, moreover, is further from nature than is usual even with Poe, and implies by its very simplicity that long familiarity with its imagery that Poe possessed. For these and other reasons, the sympathetic mood, without which no such poem is comprehended, must be of rare occurrence in this case; but if

ULALUME

ever that mood comes, — that physical exhaustion and mental gloom and dreaming upon the dark, in which the modes of expression in this poem are identical with those of nature, — then, in spite of jarring discords, cockney rhymes, and coarse types of mystery and horror, this poem may well seem the language of a spirit sunk in blank and moaning despair, and at every move beaten back helplessly upon itself. It was written at the period of Poe's lowest physical exhaustion. The criticism that finds in the ballad he thus wrote merely a whimsical experiment in words has little to go on; it is more likely that, taking into consideration, too, the lack of finish in conjunction with the justness of touch in its essential structure, we have, in this poem, the most spontaneous, the most unmistakably genuine utterance of Poe, the most clearly self-portraying work of his hand. That, to most readers, it is unintelligible, and is suggestive of humor rather than of pathos, only marks how far Poe was now removed, through one and another influence, from normal humanity. As the winter advanced he applied himself wholly to thinking out what he then believed would prove his best title to the remembrance of posterity, "Eureka."

A glimpse of him at this work is afforded by an affectionate reminiscence of Mrs. Clemm's, which was reported by Mr. R. E. Shapley, of Philadelphia, in a newspaper, and has by chance been preserved: —

"He never liked to be alone, and I used to sit up with him, often until four o'clock in the morning, he at his desk, writing, and I dozing in my chair. When he was composing 'Eureka,' we used to walk up and down the garden, his arm around me, mine around him, until I was so tired I could not walk. He would stop every few minutes and explain his ideas to me, and ask if I understood him. I always sat up with him when he was writing, and gave him a cup of hot coffee every hour or two. At home he was simple and affectionate as a child, and during all the years he lived with me I do not remember a single night that he failed to come and kiss his 'mother,' as he called me, before going to bed."

In the main parts this account seems to apply to the whole period of his widowerhood, and portrays the family interior, the intimate domestic scene, as it was in the latter years, when Poe came back to the shelter of his mother-in-law and to work from his various ventures and visits in the outer world.

CHAPTER XIII

EUREKA

Poe began to appear in the world at the opening of the new year, 1848; and concurrently the continuation of Lowell's sketch of him by Cooke appeared, in January, in the friendly "Messenger." He brought forward again the great ambition of his life and announced the resurrection of the "Stylus." He communicated the plan to several correspondents, as the means by which he meant to reëstablish himself in the literary world.

He sent out the old prospectus, with its well-worn announcements that the management was to bear the mark of individuality, the contributions to be selected solely on the ground of merit, the criticism to be independent, sincere, and fearless, and with the promise of "Literary America," by the editor, being "a faithful account of the literary productions, literary people, and literary affairs of the United States," to be begun in the first number. Poe's plan was to make a personal canvass through the country, as had been so successfully done by his friend Mr. Freeman Hunt in launching his "Merchants' Magazine" a few years previous. With the view of raising the money for this journey he advertised a lecture in the Society Library, on the "Cosmogony of the Universe," and at his request Willis besought public favor for it in his paper, the "Home Journal," and added a good word for the projected "Stylus," the founding of which was said to be the ultimate object of the lecture. On February 3, in response to these notices, about sixty persons assembled, the night unfortunately being stormy, and, it is said, were held entranced for two hours and a half by an abstract of "Eureka," although the charm must have been exercised by the personality of the poet rather than the substance of what he uttered; and indeed Poe seems to have been an eloquent and impressive speaker, as he had good right to be both by inheritance and by the natural endowments of his voice and person.

The lecture was imperfectly reported by a few of the city papers, but made no impression. Financially it had failed of its purpose, and therefore Poe, seeing no better means of obtaining funds, determined to publish the entire work, and at once offered it to Mr. Putnam, who many years afterward wrote an account[1] of the interview which shows very clearly both Poe's physical and mental state. He says that Poe was in a tremor of excitement and declared with intense earnestness and solemnity that the issue of the book was of momentous interest, that the truths disclosed in it were of more consequence than the discovery of gravitation, and that an edition of fifty thousand copies would be but a beginning. Mr. Putnam confesses that he was impressed, and two days later accepted the manuscript. An edition of five hundred copies was printed without delay and published early in the summer, in good form, under the title "Eureka; A Prose Poem," [2] and introduced by the well-known preface: —

"To the few who love me and whom I love — to those who feel rather than to those who think — to the dreamers and those who put faith in dreams as in the only realities — I offer this Book of Truths, not in its character of Truth-Teller, but for the Beauty that abounds in its Truth; constituting it true. To them I present the composition as an Art-Product alone: —

[1] *Putnam's Magazine*, iv, 471. N. S. (October, 1869.)

[2] *Eureka: A Prose Poem.* By Edgar A. Poe. New York: George P. Putnam, 1848, pp. 143.

let us say as a Romance; or, if I be not urging too lofty a claim, as a Poem.

"*What I here propound is true:* — therefore it cannot die: — or if by any means it be now trodden down so that it die, it will 'rise again to the Life Everlasting.' Nevertheless it is as a Poem only that I wish this work to be judged after I am dead."

It is obviously impossible to grant Poe's request. He has written a physical explanation of the universe and based it on metaphysical principles; he has declared it a true account, and he must stand by his words. Moreover, the speculative activity of Poe's mind grew out of its analytical activity; the metaphysical essays virtually begin when the ratiocinative tales end, in 1845, and thus in the history of Poe's mental development, "Eureka," the principal work of his last years, necessarily occupies a crowning point. The earliest indication that such topics occupied his mind occurs in the review of Macaulay's "Essays" in June, 1841: "That we know no more to-day of the nature of Deity — of its purposes — and thus of man himself — than we did even a dozen years ago — is a proposition disgracefully absurd; and of this any astronomer could assure Mr. Macaulay. Indeed, to our own mind, the *only* irrefutable argument in support of the soul's immortality — or, rather, the only conclusive proof of man's alternate dissolution and rejuvenescence *ad infinitum* — is to be found in analogies deduced from the modern established theory of the nebular cosmogony." [1] After this utterance the metaphysical tales followed, but the speculations of Poe were not fully developed until the publication of "Eureka." In the following criticism, which necessarily partakes somewhat of the abstract nature of its subject, only what is peculiar to Poe will be dwelt on; and it may as well be premised that the end in view is not the determination of abstract truth, but simply the illustration alike of Poe's genius and character by the light of his speculations.

Poe's hypothesis is as follows: The mind knows intuitively — by inductive or deductive processes which escape consciousness, elude reason, or defy expression — that the creative act of Deity must have been the simplest possible; or, to expand and define this statement, it must have consisted in willing into being a primordial particle, the germ of all things, existing without relations to aught, or, in the technical phrase, unconditioned. This particle, by virtue of the

[1] *Works*, vii, 126.

divine volition, radiated into space uniformly in all directions a shower of atoms of diverse form, irregularly arranged among themselves, but all, generally speaking, equally distant from their source; this operation was repeated at intervals, but with decreased energy in each new instance, so that the atoms were impelled less far. On the exhaustion of the radiating force, the universe was thus made up of a series of concentric hollow spheres, like a nest of boxes, the crusts of the several spheres being constituted of the atoms of the several discharges. The radiating force at each of its manifestations is measured by the number of atoms then thrown off; or, since the number of atoms in any particular case must have been directly proportional with the surface of the particular sphere they occupied, and since the surfaces of a series of concentric spheres are directly proportional with the squares of their distances from the centre, the radiating force in the several discharges was directly proportional with the squares of the distances to which the several atomic showers were driven.

On the consummation of this secondary creative act, as the diffusion may be called, there occurred, says Poe, a recoil, a striving of the atoms each to each in order to regain their primitive condition; and this tendency, which is now being satisfied, is expressed in gravitation, the mutual attraction of atoms with a force inversely proportional with the squares of the distances. In other words, the law of gravitation is found to be the converse of the law of radiation, as would be the case if the former energy were the reaction of the latter as is claimed; furthermore, the distribution of the atoms in space is seen to be such as would result from the mode of diffusion described. The return of the atoms into their source, however, would take place too rapidly, adds Poe, and without accomplishing the Deity's design of developing out of the original homogeneous particle the utmost heterogeneity, were it not that God, in this case a true *Deus ex machina*, has interposed by introducing a repelling force which began to be generated at the very inception of the universal reaction, and ever becomes greater as the latter proceeds. Poe names this force electricity, while at the same time he suggests that light, heat, and magnetism are among its phases, and ascribes to it all vital and mental phenomena; but of the principle itself he makes a mystery, since he is intuitively convinced that it belongs to that spiritual essence which lies beyond the limits of human inquiry. In the grand reaction, then, the universe is through attraction becoming more condensed, and through repulsion more heterogeneous. Attraction and repulsion taken together constitute our notion of matter; the former is the physical element, the Body, the latter is the spiritual element, the Soul. Incidentally it should be remarked that since in a divine design, being perfect, no one part exists for the sake of others more than the others for its sake, it is indifferent whether repulsion be considered, as hitherto, an expedient to retard the attractive force, or, on the other hand, the attractive force as an expedient to develop repulsion; in other words, it is indifferent whether the physical be regarded as subordinate to the spiritual element, or *vice versa*. To return to the main thread, Poe affirms that repulsion will not increase indefinitely as the condensation of the mass proceeds, but when in the process of time it has fulfilled its purpose — the evolution of heterogeneity — it will cease, and the attractive force, being unresisted, will draw the atoms back into the primordial particle in which, as it has no parts, attraction will also cease; now, attraction and repulsion constituting our notion of matter, the cessation of these two forces is the same thing with the annihilation of matter, or, in other words, the universe, at the end of the reaction which has been mentally followed out, will sink into the nihility out of which it arose. In conclusion Poe makes one last affirmation, to wit, that the diffusion and ingathering of the universe is the diffusion and ingathering of Deity itself, which has no existence apart from the constitution of things.

It is difficult to treat this hypothesis, taken as a metaphysical speculation, with respect. To examine it for the purpose of demolition would be a tedious, though an easy task; but fortunately there is no need to do more than point out a few of its confusions in order to illustrate the worthlessness of Poe's thought in this field, and to indicate the depth of the delusion under which he labored in believing himself a discoverer of new truth. For this purpose it will be best to take the most rudimentary metaphysical ideas involved. The primordial particle is declared to be unconditioned — "my particle proper is absolute Irrelation," — or in other words it is the Absolute; but this is incompatible with its being willed into being by Deity, to which it would then necessarily stand related as an effect to its cause; on the contrary, it must itself, being the Absolute, be Deity with which Poe at last identifies it. In other words, when Poe has reached the conception of the primordial particle as first defined by him, he is just where he started, that is, at the conception of Deity, and at that point, as has been seen, he had to end. The difficulty which bars inquiry — the inconceivability of creation — remains as insuperable as ever, although Poe may have cheated himself into believing it overcome by the legerdemain of a phrase from physics; in the attempt to describe the generation of the phenomenal universe out of the unknowable, he has been foiled by the old obstacles — the impossibility of making an equation between nothing and something, of effecting a transformation of the absolute into the conditioned. If the primordial particle be material, it is only the scientific equivalent of the old turtle of the Hindoos, on which the elephant stands to support the globe; if it be immaterial, it is the void beneath.

Such a criticism as the above belongs to the primer of thought in this science; but objections as obvious, brief, and fatal may be urged against every main point of the argument. Without entering on such a discussion it is sufficient to observe, as characteristic illustrations of the density of Poe's ignorance in this department of knowledge, that he regards space not as created but as given, explains the condensation of the universe as being a physical reaction upon the immaterial will of God (for the original radiating force cannot be discriminated from and is expressly identified with the divine volition, just as the primordial particle cannot be discriminated from and is expressly identified with the divine essence), and lastly so confuses such simple notions as final and efficient causes that he contradistinguishes the force of repulsion from that of attraction as arising and disappearing in obedience to the former instead of the later sort. In a word, Poe's theory belongs to the infancy of speculation, to the period before physics was separated from ontology; in this sense, and in no other, Kennedy's remark that Poe wrote like "an old Greek philosopher," was just.

What Poe himself most prized in this hypothesis was its pantheistic portion. The sentence of Baron Bielfeld, — "nous ne connaissons rien de la nature ou de l'essence de Dieu; — pour savoir ce qu'il est, il faut être Dieu même," — had made a deep impression on his mind early in life; it is one of the half-dozen French quotations that he introduces at every opportunity into his compositions; in "Eureka" he translates it, "We know absolutely *nothing* of the nature or essence of God; in order to comprehend what he is, we should have to be God ourselves," — and he immediately adds, "I nevertheless venture to demand if this our present ignorance of the Deity is an ignorance to which the soul is *everlastingly* condemned."[1] Now after reflection he boldly took the only road to such knowledge that was left open by the apothegm, and affirmed that he was God, being persuaded thereto by his memories of an ante-natal and his aspiration for an immortal existence, and in particular by his pride. "My whole nature utterly *revolts*," he exclaimed, "at the idea that there is any Being in the Universe superior to *myself!*"[2] On reading so violent an expression of belief one involuntarily examines the matter more closely and pushes home the question whether Poe did actually so fool himself to the top of his bent; and after some little investigation one finds that, if he was his own dupe, the reason is not far to seek. It is necessary here to summarize the speculations which were put forth elsewhere by Poe, especially in the metaphysical tales, and either led up to or supplemented the views of "Eureka."

[1] *Works*, ix, 26.

[2] Ingram, ii, 144.

According to these other statements, the Universe is made up of gross matter sensibly perceived and of fine matter so minutely divided that the atoms coalesce (this is, of course, a contradiction in terms) and form an unparticled substance which permeates and impels all things. This unparticled substance or imperceptible coalescent matter is the universal mind (into such unintelligible phraseology is the keen analyst forced); its being is Deity; its motion, regarded on the material or energetic side, is the divine volition, or, regarded on the mental or conscious side, is the creative thought. Deity and its activity, being such in its universal existence, is individualized, by means of gross matter made for that end, into particular creatures, among which are men; the human being, in other words, is a specialization of the universal, or is God incarnate, as is every other creature whatsoever. It is superfluous to follow Poe in his fantastic conception of the universe as the abode of countless rudimentary incarnations of the Deity, each a divine thought and therefore irrevocable; the peculiar form of his pantheism would not be more defined thereby. At the first glance one sees that his theory is built out of Cartesian notions, crudely apprehended, and rendered ridiculous by the effort to yoke them with thoroughly materialistic ideas. In fact, Poe's scraps of speculative philosophy came from such opposite quarters that when his mind began to work on such contradictory information he could not well help falling into inextricable confusion. On the one hand he had derived, early in life, from obscure disciples of the French *philosophes*, the first truth that a materialist ever learns, — the origin of all knowledge in experience, and the consequent limitation of the mind to phenomena; on the other hand he had at a later period gleaned some of the conceptions of transcendentalism from Coleridge, Schlegel, and other secondary sources; from the union of such principles the issue was naturally monstrous, two-natured, like the Centaur. Essentially Poe was a materialist; whether, by gradually refining and subdividing matter, he reaches the unparticled substance, or by reversing the evolution of nature he arrives at the fiery mist and the primordial particle, he seeks to find out God by searching matter; and even in adopting the radically spiritual idea of pantheism, he is continually endeavoring to give it a materialistic form. He persuadėd himself, as it is easy for ignorance to do; subtle as his mind was, well furnished for metaphysical thought both by his powers of abstraction and of reasoning, he wrote the jargon that belongs to the babbling days of philosophy because he did not take the pains to know the results of past inquiry and to train himself in modern methods. By his quick perception and adroit use of analogies, and especially by his tireless imagination, he gave his confused dogmatism the semblance of a reasoned system; but in fact his metaphysics exhibit only the shallowness of his learning and the self-delusion of an arrogant mind.

It is probable that few readers of "Eureka" ever seriously tried to understand its metaphysics. Its power—other than the fascination which some readers feel in whatever makes of their countenances "a foolish face of wonder" — lies in its exposition of Laplace's nebular theory and its vivid and popular presentation of astronomical phenomena. In this physical portion of the essay it has been fancied that Poe anticipated some of the results of later science; but this view cannot be sustained with candor. His own position that matter came from nihility and consisted of centres of force had been put forth as a scientific theory by Boscovich in 1758–59, had been widely discussed, and had found its way into American text-books. The same theory in a modified form had just been revived and brought to the notice of scientists by Faraday in his lecture in 1844. It has not, however, occupied the attention of first-class scientific men since that time. There may be, in the claim that "the recent progress of scientific thought runs in Poe's lines," some reference to Sir William Thomson's vortex theory of the constitution of atoms, but its resemblance to Poe's theory of vortices is only superficial, for what he puts forth was merely a revival of one of the earliest attempts to explain the Newtonian law, long since abandoned by science. It is true that in several particulars, such as the doctrine of the evolution of the universe from the simple to the complex, Poe's line of thought has now been followed out in detail; these suggestions, however, were not at the time peculiar to Poe, were not orignated or developed by him, but on the contrary were common scientific property, for he appropriated ideas, just as he paraphrased statements of fact, from the books he read. He was no more a forerunner of Spencer, Faraday, and Darwin than scores of others, and he did nothing to make their investigations easier.

Poe's purely scientific speculations are mainly

contained in the *Addenda*[1] to a report of his lecture on "The Universe" sent to a correspondent, and consist either of mathematical explanations of Kepler's first and third laws; or of statements, "that the sun was condensed at once (not gradually according to the supposition of Laplace) into his smallest size," and afterwards "sent into space his substance in the form of a vapor" from which Neptune was made; or of similar theories. They exhibit once more Poe's tenacity of mind, the sleuth-hound persistence of his intellectual pursuit; but, like his metaphysics, they represent a waste of power. They are, moreover, characterized by extraordinary errors. Some of the data are quite imaginary, it being impossible to determine what are the facts; some of them are quite wrong. The density of Jupiter, for example, in a long and important calculation, is constantly reckoned as two and one half, whereas it is only something more than one fifth, and the densities of the planets are described as being inversely as their rotary periods, whereas in any table of the elements of the solar system some wide departures from this rule are observable. Again, it is stated that Kepler's first

[1] Addenda MS. enclosed in a letter to G. W. Eveleth, February 29, 1848, and first published, *Works*, ix, 293 *et seq.*

and third laws "cannot be explained upon the principle of Newton's theory"; but, in fact, they follow by mathematical deduction from it. Poe's own explanation of them is merely a play upon figures. A striking instance of fundamental ignorance of astronomical science is his statement at various places that the planets rotate (on their own axes) in elliptical orbits, and the reference he frequently makes to the *breadth* of their orbits (the breadth of their paths through space) agreeably to this supposition. Such a theory is incompatible with the Newtonian law of gravitation, according to which any revolution in an elliptical orbit implies a source of attraction at the focus of the ellipse. Examples of bodies which have breadth of orbit in Poe's sense are found in the satellites of all the planets, each of which, however, has its primary as a source of attraction to keep it in its elliptical orbit; the primary by its revolution round the sun gives then the satellite a breadth of orbit. But to make the proper rotation of the planets themselves take place about a focus, which would be merely a point moving in an elliptical orbit about the sun, would be to give them an arbitrary motion with no force to produce it.

So far was Poe from being a seer of science,

that he was fundamentally in error with regard to the generalizations which were of prime importance to his speculations. The one grand assumption of his whole speculation is the universality of the law of inverse squares as applied to attraction and repulsion, whereas it has been known since the beginning of study regarding them that that law does not explain all the forces involved, as, for example, molecular forces; and for this Boscovich himself had provided. Again, to illustrate his scientific foresight, he reproaches Herschel for his reluctance to doubt the stability of the universe, and himself boldly affirms, consistently with his theory, that it is in a state of ever swifter collapse; than this nothing could be more at variance with the great law of the conservation of energy. Undoubtedly Poe had talents for scientific investigation, had he been willing to devote himself to such work; but, so far as appears from this essay, he had not advanced further in science than the elements of physics, mathematics, and astronomy, as he had learned them at school or from popular works, such as Dr. Nichol's "Architecture of the Heavens," or from generalizations, such as the less technical chapters of Auguste Comte's "Philosophie Positive." Out of such a limited stock of knowledge Poe could not by mere reflection generate any Newtonian truth; that he thought he had done so, measures his folly. In a word, for this criticism must be brought to a close, "Eureka" affords one of the most striking instances in literature of a naturally strong intellect tempted by overweening pride to an Icarian flight and betrayed, notwithstanding its merely specious knowledge, into an ignoble exposure of its own presumption and ignorance. The facts are not to be obscured by the smooth profession of Poe that he wished this work to be looked on only as a poem; for, though he perceived that his argument was too fragmentary and involved to receive credence, he was himself profoundly convinced that he had revealed the secret of eternity. Nor, were "Eureka" to be judged as a poem, that is to say, as a fictitious cosmogony, would the decision be more favorable; even then so far as it is obscure to the reader it must be pronounced defective; so far as it is understood, involving as it does in its primary conceptions incessant contradictions of the necessary laws of thought, it must be pronounced meaningless. Poe believed himself to be that extinct being, a universal genius of the highest order; and he wrote this essay to prove his powers in philosophy and in science. To the correspondent to whom he sent the *addenda* he declared, "As to the lecture, I am very quiet about it — but if you have ever dealt with such topics, you will recognize the novelty and *moment* of my views. What I have propounded will (in good time) revolutionize the world of Physical and Metaphysical science. I say this calmly, but I say it."[1]

Besides "Eureka," Poe's publications for the first half year were of the slightest, consisting only of "Marginalia," in January and February, and "Fifty Suggestions," a paper of the same character, in May and June, in "Graham's," and "An Enigma," an anagrammatic poem to Sarah Anna Lewis, commonly called "Estelle," in the "Union," in March.

The principal events of his private life, while "Eureka" was being published, were the beginning of his courtship of Mrs. Helen Whitman and the termination of his intercourse with Mrs. Shew. Since the death of Virginia, Mrs. Shew had maintained her intimacy with the family, and had actively befriended him in his literary projects. In the earlier part of the year she had asked him to furnish the music room and library of a new house which she was to

[1] Poe to Eveleth. Ingram, ii, 141.

occupy, and she made him at home when he visited her. One such visit is especially of interest, since to it has been ascribed the first suggestion of Poe's second great popular poem, "The Bells." It was early in the summer that he one day called and complained that he had to write a poem, but felt no inspiration. Mrs. Shew persuaded him to drink some tea in a conservatory whose open windows admitted the sound of church-bells, and gave him some paper, which he declined, saying, "I so dislike the noise of bells to-night, I cannot write. I have no subject — I am exhausted." Mrs. Shew then wrote, "The Bells, by E. A. Poe," and added, "The Bells, the little silver bells"; on the poet's finishing the stanza thus suggested, she again wrote, "The heavy iron bells," and this idea also Poe elaborated, and then copying off the two stanzas, headed it, "By Mrs. M. L. Shew," and called it her poem.

Such, nearly in Mr. Ingram's own words, is the story which he derived from Mrs. Shew's diary. But although the incident is, without doubt, truly related, it may be questioned whether this was the original genesis of the poem. It will be remembered that Poe derived several suggestions from Chateaubriand at the

[*Facsimile of a portion of original MS.*
By courtesy of J. Pierpont Morgan, Esq.]

The Bells.

By Edgar A. Poe.

1.

Hear the sledges with the bells —
Silver bells!
What a world of merriment their melody foretells
How they tinkle, tinkle, tinkle,
In the icy air of night!
While the stars that oversprinkle
All the Heavens, seem to twinkle
With a crystalline delight;
Keeping time, time, time,
In a sort of Runic rhyme,
To the tintinabulation that so musically wells:

From the jingling and the tinkling of the bells.

2

Hear the mellow wedding bells—
Golden bells!
What a world of happiness their harmony foretells!
Through the balmy air of night
How they ring out their delight!—
From the molten-golden notes
And all in tune,
What a liquid ditty floats
To the turtle-dove that listens while she gloats
On the moon!
Oh, from out the sounding cells
What a gush of euphony voluminously wells!

4.

Hear the tolling of the bells —
Iron bells!
What a world of solemn thought their monody compels!
In the silence of the night
How we shiver with affright
At the melancholy ~~meaning~~ menace of their tone!
For every sound that floats
From ~~out their ghostly~~ the rust within their throats
Is a groan.
And the people — ah, the people
~~Who live~~ They that sleep up in the steeple
All alone,
And who, tolling, tolling, tolling,

On the human heart a stone —
They are neither man nor woman —
They are neither brute nor human,
But are pestilential carcases disparted from their souls —
Called Ghouls: —
And their king it is who tolls: —
And he rolls, rolls, rolls, rolls
A Paan from the bells!
And his merry bosom swells
With the Paan of the bells:
And he dances and he yells;
Keeping time, time, time,
In a sort of Runic rhyme,
To the Paan of the bells —
Of the bells: —

very beginning of his career. The parallelism that exists between the completed poem of "The Bells" and a brief chapter of the "Génie du Christianisme"[1] in which he suggests a poem on the same subject and similarly treated, is not likely to be a fortuitous coincidence. In view of Poe's known habits of composition, this poetic suggestion in a work to which he was in early years under considerable obligations, may have been one of the ideas that haunted him for years, and this is sustained by his frequent reference to the magical sounds of bells throughout his literary life. It may well be that this is the poem referred to in Griswold's memoir as the subject on which he meant to write for the Boston Lyceum — "a subject which he said had haunted his imagination for years."[2] If there be any plausibility in this inference, the likelihood is that Mrs. Shew, who pleads guilty to Poe's reproach that she never read his tales or poems, merely recalled to him thoughts and words which she already knew had been running in his mind.

The events immediately subsequent to this in-

[1] *Gênie du Christianisme.* Par M. le Vicomte de Châteaubriand. Paris: P. Pourrat Frères, 1836, tome ii, 261.

[2] Griswold, xxxviii.

cident also deserve mention. Word was sent to Mrs. Clemm that Poe would remain in the city, and, going to his room, he slept twelve hours, after which he only faintly remembered what he had done. "This showed," says the diary, "that his mind was injured, nearly gone out for want of food and from disappointment. He had not been drinking, and had only been a few hours from home. Evidently his vitality was low and he was nearly insane. While he slept we studied his pulse, and found the same symptoms which I had so often noticed before. I called in Dr. Francis (the old man was odd, but very skillful), who was one of our neighbors. His words were, 'He has heart disease and will die early in life.'"[1] On the next day he was taken home by his friend, but did not seem to understand that he was ill.

It must have been very soon after this that Mrs. Shew, finding that her protégé was too irresponsible and too romantic to be allowed such freedom with her as he had been accustomed to, broke off the acquaintance. The consequence which, although he had foreseen it, must, in his state of health, have been a deprivation, was the sudden and complete cessation of intercourse between the families. In June Mrs. Shew wrote

[1] Ingram, ii, 156.

an explanatory letter to him, and he replied as follows, but they never afterwards met on the old terms: —

Can it be true, Louise, that you have the idea fixed in your mind to desert your unhappy and unfortunate friend and patient? You did not say so, I know, but for months I have known you were deserting me, not willingly, but none the less surely — my destiny —

> "Disaster, following fast and following faster, till his song one
> burden bore —
> Till the dirges of his Hope that melancholy burden bore —
> Of 'Never — nevermore.'"

So I have had premonitions of this for months. I repeat, my good spirit, my loyal heart! must this follow as a sequel to all the benefits and blessings you have so generously bestowed? Are you to vanish like all I love, or desire, from my darkened and "lost soul"? I have read over your letter again and again, and cannot make it possible, with any degree of certainty, that you wrote it in your right mind. (*I know you did not without tears of anguish and regret.*) Is it possible your influence is lost to me? Such tender and true natures are ever loyal until death; but you are not dead, you are full of life and beauty!

Louise, you came in, . . . in your floating white robe — "Good morning, Edgar." There was a touch of conventional coldness in your hurried manner, and your attitude as you opened the kitchen door to find Muddie, is *my last remembrance of you.* There was love, hope, and *sorrow* in your smile, instead of love, hope, and *courage*, as ever before. O Louise, how many sorrows are before you! Your ingenuous and sympathetic nature will be constantly wounded in its contact with the hollow, heartless world; and for me, alas! unless some true and tender, and pure womanly love saves me, I shall hardly last a year longer alive! A few short months will tell how far my strength (physical and moral) will carry me in life here. How can I believe in Providence when *you* look coldly upon me? Was it not you who renewed my hopes and faith in God? . . . and in humanity? Louise, I heard your voice as you passed out of my sight leaving me . . .; but I still listened to your voice. I heard you say with a sob, "Dear Muddie." I heard you greet *my Catarina*, but it was only as a memory . . . nothing escaped *my ear*, and I was convinced it was not your generous self . . . repeating words so foreign to your nature — to your tender heart! I heard you sob out your sense of duty to my mother, and I heard her reply, "Yes, Loui . . . yes," . . . Why turn your soul from its true work for the desolate to the thankless and miserly world? . . . I felt my heart stop, and I was sure I was then to die before your eyes. Louise, it is well — it is fortunate — you looked up with a tear in your dear eyes, and raised the window, and talked of the guava you had brought for my sore throat. Your instincts are better than a *strong man's reason for me* — I trust they may be for *yourself*. Louise, I feel I shall not prevail — a shadow has already fallen upon your soul, and is reflected in your eyes. It is *too late* — you are floating away with the cruel tide . . . it is not a common trial — it is a fearful one to me. Such rare souls as yours so beautify this earth! so relieve it of all that is repulsive and sordid. So brighten its toils and cares, it is hard to lose sight of them even for a short time . . . but you must know and *be assured* of my regret and sorrow if aught I have ever written has hurt you. *My heart never wronged you.* I place you in *my esteem* — in *all solemnity* — beside the friend of my boyhood — the mother of my school-fellow, of whom I told you, and as I have repeated in the poem . . . as the truest, tenderest of this world's most womanly souls, and an angel to my forlorn and darkened nature. I will not say "lost soul" again, for your sake. I will try to overcome my grief for the sake of your unselfish care of me in the past, and in life or death.

I am ever yours gratefully and devotedly,

EDGAR A. POE.[1]

Poe was sincere in his gratitude, and he wrote very many grateful letters; it is at such moments that he shows some of the qualities that attached him to his own circle of friends; but he was already beginning to weave the best known and most public romance of his life.

[1] Ingram, ii, 157-159.

CHAPTER XIV

HELEN WHITMAN

On his visit to Boston, in the summer of 1845, while passing through Providence Poe had seen a lady among the roses of her garden in the moonlight. He learned she was a poetess, Mrs. Sarah Helen Whitman,[1] and a verbal description of her romantic temperament had further attracted him. No meeting took place, but when three years later they became acquainted, Poe

[1] The story of this chapter has been told by Mrs. Whitman in her *Edgar A. Poe and his Critics*, New York, 1860, and in her correspondence with Poe's biographers, printed in their memoirs of Poe. She furnished to Ingram the correspondence published by him. Her literary executors published new documents and letters, *Poe and Mrs. Whitman* (by James A. Harrison and Charlotte F. Dailey), *The Century*, lxxvii, 3 (January, 1909), and it is there editorially announced that Professor Harrison "has prepared a paper in which Poe's letters are given without omission, garbling, or diversion, and in their proper order and arrangement, instead of as they have hitherto appeared in the version brought out by Mr. Ingram," which latter is described as of "imperfect character." The quotations from Ingram in this chapter must be read subject to this intimation. Mrs. Whitman's verses, several of which relate to Poe, are most accessible in *Poems*, by Sarah Helen Whitman, Boston, Houghton, Osgood & Co., 1879.

described to her the state of his mind during the interval: —

"She [Miss Anna Blackwell] had referred to thoughts, sentiments, traits, *moods*, which I knew to be my own, but which, until that moment, I had believed to be my own solely — unshared by any human being. A profound sympathy took immediate possession of my soul. I cannot better explain to you what I felt than by saying that your unknown heart seemed to pass into my bosom — there to dwell forever — while mine, I thought, was translated into your own. From that hour I loved you. Since that period I have never seen nor heard your name without a shiver, half of delight, half of anxiety. — The impression left upon my mind was that you were still a wife, and it is only within the last few months that I have been undeceived in this respect. For this reason I shunned your presence and even the city in which you lived. You may remember that once when I passed through Providence with Mrs. Osgood I positively refused to accompany her to your house, and even provoked her into a quarrel by the obstinacy and seeming unreasonableness of my refusal. I dared neither go nor say why I could not. I dared not speak of you — much less see you. For years your

SARAH H. WHITMAN

name never passed my lips, while my soul drank in, with a delirious thirst, all that was uttered in my presence respecting you. The merest whisper that concerned you awoke in me a shuddering sixth sense, vaguely compounded of fear, ecstatic happiness, and a wild inexplicable sentiment that resembled nothing so nearly as a consciousness of guilt." [1]

Mrs. Whitman, on her part, had been informed of frequent commendatory allusions to herself made by Poe, and was prevailed upon to address some verses to him for the entertainment of what was termed a valentine party given February 14, 1848, at the house of Anne C. Lynch, in New York, to what appears to have been the entire body of the literati.[2] The two did not meet on this occasion. The verses entitled "The Raven," in Mrs. Whitman's "Poems," were published by Willis, with the characteristic note with which he prefaced his reprints of Poe's poems, in the "Home Journal," March 18, 1848. They had been sent to Poe. He says, in the continuation of the letter just quoted, that he was thrown into a state of ecstasy by this proof of

[1] Poe to Mrs. Whitman, no date. Ingram, ii, 161, 162.

[2] A full account of this party is given in the *Life and Letters of Bayard Taylor*, i, 115, 120. Cf. *Home Journal*, March 4, 1848.

her regard, and, as he could not express his emotion in spontaneous lines, took down a volume of his old poems and read "To Helen," with the result that the identity of name and the aptness of the sentiment, which "to one accustomed to the Calculus of Probabilities" wore "an air of positive miracle," overwhelmed him with the belief that their destinies were conjoined. He sent her the printed lines from his old poems. He was, also, aroused to the point of composition, and replied to her valentine with the lines "To ——," afterwards elaborated into the lines "To Helen," which is supposed to commemorate his first sight of this lady among the roses; he sent these to her anonymously in manuscript, and, in June, to the "Union Magazine" with his name. Whether the legend be true or not, — and there is no reason to doubt it, — the scene of the lines is clearly a mere elaboration of that suggested in the seventh stanza of Mrs. Whitman's "The Raven," in connection with the vista obviously repeated from his lines of the previous year to Mrs. Shew. This poem drew no acknowledgment from its object. On June 19, 1848, he applied to his informant of the previous autumn, Miss Blackwell, who was then at Providence, and, in the course of a letter of literary advice respecting the publication of her poems, begged her to write him something about Mrs. Whitman, and added, "*Keep my secret* — that is to say, let no one know I have asked you to do so." [1] This lady did not answer his note; on the contrary, hearing Miss Maria McIntosh, another literary woman, tell Mrs. Whitman that one evening at Fordham a month previously Poe had talked only of her, Miss Blackwell gave the letter at once to Mrs. Whitman herself, who continued to observe an obstinate silence towards her admirer.[2] This was the month when Mrs. Shew broke off all communication with him, as has been related.

Poe went to Lowell, Massachusetts, the residence of his old correspondent, Mrs. Locke, and lectured July 10 on "The Poetic Principle." There he made acquaintance with a family, the Richmonds, who became his devoted friends. Immediately upon his return to New York, July 13, being furnished with funds for his long-delayed journey in behalf of the "Stylus," derived possibly from this lecture or the two advances made by Wiley & Putnam on "Eureka,"

[1] Ingram, ii, 165.

[2] Cf. Mrs. Whitman to R. H. Stoddard, September 30, 1872. Stoddard, cxxxiv–cxxxix.

he started for Richmond July 16. In that city Mr. John R. Thompson, editor of the "Southern Literary Messenger," found him:—

"I accidentally learned that a person calling himself Edgar A. Poe had been, for a fortnight, in a debauch, in one of the lowest haunts of vice upon the wharves in this City. If you have ever visited Richmond, you may perhaps know that the business portion of the town and the sites occupied by residences exclusively are distant from the shipping by a mile and a half, so that very few persons not actually engaged in commercial affairs ever visit the landing at all. As soon as I heard the name Poe in this connection my worst suspicions were excited, and I at once took a carriage and went to seek him. It was a very warm day in the latter part of May or early in June [July]. When I reached the purlieus of this abandoned quarter, I learned that such a person had indeed been there, drunk, for two weeks, and that he had gone a few hours previous, without hat or coat, to the residence of Mr. John MacKenzie, some three miles distant in the country, alone and on foot. It was Poe. The next day he called on me with Mr. MacKenzie. From that time until his death we were much together and in constant correspondence.

I did all I could to restrain his excesses and to relieve the pressure of his immediate wants (for he was extremely indigent), but no influence was adequate to keep him from the damnable propensity to drink."[1]

Poe made Thompson's office a resort and had bachelor lodgings with Mr. Pleasants, editor of the "Whig." His friends received him kindly, especially the MacKenzies, with whom his sister Rosalie was still living, and in whose home, Duncan Lodge, he himself had always been welcomed like a child of the house. He led a Bohemian life, scenes of which survive in Richmond tradition; there were nights of genius and days of little labor. He passed a pleasant six weeks between his lodgings and Duncan Lodge and visits to his female friends. One of these, Mrs. Clarke, who had been a fellow-boarder with him in the old "Messenger" days, says[2] that he called on her daily and sometimes oftener, and represents him as shar-

[1] Thompson to Patterson, November 9, 1849, *America*, April 11, 1889. This letter, most accessible in *The Virginia Poe*, xvii, 403, gives the frankest account of Poe's life in Richmond. Compare also Thompson's reminiscences, *Harper's New Monthly Magazine* (by R. H. Stoddard), September, 1872.

[2] Mrs. Weiss, p. 159.

ing the sports of the group of young men at the Lodge. In his worst estate, Poe was subject to cheerful moments, just as in the midst of his sentimental passions he could attend soberly enough to business affairs; so now, if he read the "Raven" by daylight in a darkened room by the light of an astral lamp, he also played leap-frog with the young men in the broad alleys of the garden, "skimming over their backs like a bird." One recalls the days after Virginia's death, when he gave the party on winning his libel suit,[1] and the tale of another Southern lady [2] who took pleasure in "romping with him and dancing while his sister Rosalie Poe played waltzes and polkas." It was this vein of social gayety and natural happiness, familiar to him in boyhood, that was renewed in the friendliness he found in his old haunts and the social warmth of that community which was the only one he ever really belonged to; elsewhere he was always an exile, misunderstood, unattached, incomprehensible. He read and recited at friends' houses, and gave one public reading at the Old Exchange Hotel, but it was a failure; only thirteen persons were

[1] *The Curio* (by J. P. Beecher), January–February, 1888.

[2] Reminiscences of Mrs. Mary Andre Phelps, *Newark Courier*, July 19, 1900.

present. Meanwhile he had got into trouble with one of his newspaper friends, Daniels, editor of the "Examiner," with regard to both the two principal causes of duels, — a debt and a lady, — and challenged him. He was at this point, it is said, when he received from the lady, Mrs. Whitman, who had begun to question the propriety of her summer neglect, two stanzas of her poem, "A Night in August," unsigned, and sent, she says, after a lapse of more than two months, in "playful acknowledgment" of his own anonymous lines. In the letter already quoted, Poe represents his state of mind during her silence as a hoping against hope culminating in a spirit far more reckless than despair; and he concludes, referring, as is claimed, to his challenge, which was farcically settled, "Your lines reached me in Richmond on the very day in which I was about to enter on a course which would have borne me far, far away, from *you*, sweet, sweet Helen, and from the divine dream of your love." There had been much brightness and some calm in this checkered visit to the old city; its convivial side was known to his male companions, younger men, some of whom were physicians, but Poe must have felt that he was turning from a kind and hospitable community, however lost was his place in it, when he went back, soon after receiving Mrs. Whitman's anonymous verses, to Fordham. The first step Poe took in prosecuting his suit for Mrs. Whitman was to write in a disguised hand, or cause to be written, a request for her autograph, under the assumed name of Edward S. T. Grey. This note was dated September 8, at New York. A week later, September 15, he obtained a letter of introduction from Miss McIntosh. He found time to write an open letter, September 20, to Mr. C. F. Hoffman of "The Literary World," in reply to a criticism on "Eureka" which had appeared during his absence, and in which he observes that the ground covered by Laplace compares with that covered by his own theory as a bubble with the ocean on which it floats; and on the next day presented himself with his letter of introduction to his poetical correspondent, passed two evenings in her company, and, with a characteristic choice of place, asked her, as they were walking in the cemetery, to marry him. Mrs. Whitman, who had delayed her reply, wrote to him a letter in which, as may be gathered from Poe's indignant protest against confounding so spiritual a love as his with merely mortal matters, she referred to her age, — she had been born on the same day of the month, January 19, as Poe, but six years earlier, and was forty-five, and had been widowed for the past fifteen years, — her personal appearance, and her illness; but such objections could not withstand the sentiment of Poe's vein, and she was forced to acknowledge, though rather by suggestion than confession, the real ground of her refusal, which was the representations of her friends in regard to Poe's character. To this he replied, October 18, with a protestation that "with the exception of occasional follies and excesses which I bitterly lament but to which I have been driven by intolerable sorrow, and which are hourly committed by others without attracting any notice whatever — I can call to mind no act of my life which would bring a blush to my cheek — or to yours." [1] He reminded her of the enemies he had made by his published criticisms, of the result of his libel case, and of her distance from his friends, and concluded with a sketch of the secluded Eden he had fancied for their abode (out of "Landor's Cottage," which he was then writing), and expressions of his sorrow that his dream was not to be realized, of his deep devotion to herself, and his utter hopelessness.

[1] Ingram, ii, 171.

Soon after dispatching this letter, however, being on his way to Lowell to deliver a new lecture, he stopped at Providence, and, calling upon Mrs. Whitman, he again urged her to accept his hand and realize the last and brightest hope that remained to him in life. She promised still to entertain his proposal, and to write to him at Lowell the decision at which she should arrive. Thither he went, and though he did not deliver his lecture, cemented his acquaintance with his new friends the Richmonds, and spent some days at the village of Westford, where he rested, waited, strolled off "to look at the hills," and enjoyed the society of "Annie," Mrs. Richmond, whom he had taken into his confidence, and of her sister. The latter, who was then a school-girl, in her reminiscences of Poe, draws the familiar portrait of him, self-possessed, serious, deferential to all women, distinguished by the large, deep eyes and low baritone voice that charmed so many of them; but she adds nothing of novel interest except a quiet indoor scene, vividly illustrative of the speed with which he established a habit of intimacy with married women.

"My memory photographs him, sitting before an open wood fire, in the early autumn evening, gazing intently into the glowing coal, holding the hand of a dear friend — 'Annie' — while for a long time no one spoke, and the only sound was the ticking of the tall old clock in the corner of the room."[1]

About the 2d of November, having received an indecisive letter from Mrs. Whitman, who seems to have been always struggling between her own inclination and her friends' prudence, and having replied that he would call at her house on Saturday, November 4, he left this pleasant home.

Two weeks later he wrote to his friend at Lowell, referring to what happened after he bade her farewell, as follows: —

"I remember nothing distinctly from that moment until I found myself in Providence. I went to bed and wept through a long, long, hideous night of Despair — When the day broke, I arose and endeavored to quiet my mind by a rapid walk in the cold, keen air — but all *would* not do — the Demon tormented me still. Finally, I procured two ounces of laudanum, and without returning to my hotel, took the cars back to Boston. When I arrived I wrote you a letter, in which I opened my whole heart to you — to

[1] Ingram, ii, 190.

you. . . . I told you how my struggles were more than I could bear. . . . I then reminded you of that holy promise which was the last I exacted from you in parting—the promise that, under all circumstances, you would come to me on my bed of death. I implored you to come *then*, mentioning the place where I should be found in Boston. Having written this letter, I swallowed about half the laudanum, and hurried to the Post Office, intending not to take the rest until I saw you — for, I did not doubt for one moment, that Annie would keep her sacred promise. But I had not calculated on the strength of the laudanum, for, before I reached the Post Office my reason was entirely gone, and the letter was never put in. Let me pass over — my darling *sister* — the awful horrors that succeeded. A friend was at hand, who aided, and (if it can be called saving) saved me, but it is only within the last three days that I have been able to remember what occurred in that dreary interval. It appears that, after the laudanum was rejected from the stomach, I became calm, and to a casual observer, sane — so that I was suffered to go back to Providence." [1]

[1] Poe to "Annie," November 16, 1848. Ingram, ii, 193, 194.

On Tuesday morning, November 7, Poe called at Mrs. Whitman's; but she, having been alarmed, it is said, by his failure to keep his engagement the previous Saturday, which she distinctly ascribes to his having become intoxicated in Boston, refused to see him until noon, despite all the messages that he could invent. In the afternoon he again called, by appointment, and once more implored her to marry him at once and return with him to New York. He excused his excesses in Boston on the ground of his anxiety in respect to her decision, and on that and the following day continued to plead his cause with all his eloquent abandonment of language and manner. The details of the termination of this interview and of its consequences have been narrated by Mrs. Whitman herself with slight variations. The earliest account, so far as is known, is contained in a private letter of March, 1860. In this, after mentioning that Poe "had vehemently urged me to an immediate marriage," she continues as follows: —

"As an additional reason for *delaying* a marriage which, under any circumstances, seemed to all my friends full of ėvil portents, I read to him some passages from a letter which I had recently received from one of his New York associates.

He seemed deeply pained and wounded by the result of our interview, and left me abruptly, saying that if we met again it would be as strangers. He passed the evening in the bar-room of his hotel, and after a night of delirious frenzy, returned the next day to my mother's house in a state of great mental excitement and suffering, declaring that his welfare for time and eternity depended on me. A physician, Dr. O. H. Oakie, was sent for by my mother, who, perceiving indications of brain fever, advised his removal to the house of his friend, W. J. Pabodie, of this city, where he was kindly cared for until his recovery." [1]

Later and possibly more accurate accounts change some of these details and amplify others. In the interview of November 8, according to these, Mrs. Whitman showed Poe several letters, one of which especially moved him; on reading it, further confidential conversation being prevented by visitors, he took leave at once with a look of strange excitement, and made no reply to her invitation, "We shall see you this evening?" He did not, however, return, but sent a note of renunciation. On the next day when Poe called he was so uncontrollable that his passionate ap-

[1] Mrs. Whitman to Eveleth. MS.

peals rang through the house. "Never have I heard anything so awful," records Mrs. Whitman, "awful even to sublimity. It was long before I could nerve myself to see him. My mother was with him more than two hours before I entered the room. He hailed me as an angel sent to save him from perdition. . . . In the afternoon he grew more composed, and my mother sent for Dr. Oakie." [1]

In consequence of this exhibition of Poe's state, and with the hope of helping him in what seemed to be a last struggle for life itself, Mrs. Whitman consented within a few days to a conditional engagement. Forced to be content with this, Poe, having on his side repeated the promise of reform that he had given to every woman whom he had known intimately, returned to New York on November 14, and on the same evening wrote to assure his *fiancée* that he had not dared to break his pledge.

In spite, however, of his success in so difficult and indeed desperate a wooing, he felt little of the happiness of an accepted lover. He arrived at Fordham safely, but so changed in outward appearance by the wear of the last fortnight that Mrs. Clemm declares, in a letter to "Annie,"

[1] Ingram, ii, 176.

written two days later, he was hardly recognizable. All the previous night, according to the same authority, he had raved about this last lady, and the same day, November 16, he also wrote to her a letter which is inexplicable on the theory that he put any faith in the happy issue of his betrothal, since after giving the account, already quoted, of what happened at Boston, he proposes to take a cottage for his mother and himself at Westford, where he might see her family every day and herself often, and concludes with a passionate appeal that she would come on to Fordham at once, if only for a week, saying, "I am so *ill* — so terribly, hopelessly *ill* in body and mind, that I feel I *cannot* live." [1] In his next letter, however, written four days later, to Edward Valentine, the brother of the first Mrs. Allan, sent under cover to Mrs. Weiss, then Miss Talley, and containing merely a request for the loan of $200 to start the "Stylus," he expresses a strong hope of surmounting his difficulties. On November 21, 22, and 24, and presumably on other dates, he wrote to Mrs. Whitman, warning her against his slanderers, particularly the women, begging her to be true to him, as his sole hope was in her love, and drawing golden antici-

[1] Ingram, ii, 194.

pations of their worldly triumph. Meanwhile, on November 23, he had written to "Annie's" sister, already mentioned, in hardly less affectionate terms than to herself or Mrs. Whitman, protesting his love for "Annie" and imploring an answer to his former letter to the latter, containing the Boston episode, with a fervor amply indicated by a single line: "Her silence fills my whole soul with terror."[1]

With such conflicting and exhausting emotions, which happily have not been further disclosed by his confidants, Poe passed another fortnight, when, about December 12, he is said to have visited Providence, but no record of the journey remains; it may be conjectured, however, that it had to do with financial arrangements relating to his marriage. On December 20 he again left Fordham to give the fifth lecture before the Franklin Lyceum of Providence. At the New York station he met Mrs. Hewitt, who said to him, "Mr. Poe, are you going to Providence to be married?" "I am going," he replied, "to deliver a lecture on Poetry." Then he added, after a moment, "That marriage may never take place." Mrs. Whitman's friend, Mr. Pabodie, in describing this interview, states that

[1] Ingram, ii, 196.

"circumstances existed which threatened to postpone the marriage indefinitely, if not altogether to prevent it." [1] On reaching Providence he delivered the lecture, "The Poetic Principle," the fifth in the Franklin Lyceum course, in Howard's Hall, the same evening, December 20, to a large audience, said to have numbered eighteen hundred, and was greatly pleased with his success. He remained in the city, and still pleaded with Mrs. Whitman to be married and to return with him to Fordham. He was stopping at the Earl House, and there occasionally drank at the bar with some young men of the city. On Friday evening, December 22, he called at Mrs. Whitman's, partially intoxicated; but, says Mr. Pabodie, who was present, he was quiet and said little, which perhaps was not surprising, as his business was to affix his signature, as a prospective husband, to a legal instrument transferring all Mrs. Whitman's property to her mother. The next morning he was full of contrition for his intemperance and profuse of promises for the future, and he persuaded Mrs. Whitman to appoint Monday even-

[1] Pabodie to Griswold, June 11, 1852. Gill, 224. The interview with Mrs. Hewitt has been variously related, but the substance of it was a prediction that the marriage would not occur.

ing for the ceremony. He then wrote to Dr. Crocker, engaging him to officiate, and to Mrs. Clemm, advising her to expect himself and his wife on Tuesday at Fordham. In the afternoon, however, Mrs. Whitman received a note from a friend, informing her that Poe had that morning again drunk at the bar of his hotel, and she therefore finally decided to break off the match. When Poe called, says Mrs. Whitman, "no token of the infringement of his promise was visible in his appearance or manner." [1] This circumstance, however, she disregarded, and carried out her predetermined plan. "Gathering together some papers," she says, "which he had intrusted to my keeping, I placed them in his hands without a word of explanation or reproach, and, utterly worn out and exhausted by the mental conflicts and anxieties and responsibilities of the last few days, I drenched my handkerchief with ether and threw myself on a sofa, hoping to lose myself in utter unconsciousness. Sinking on his knees beside me, he entreated me to speak to him, — to speak *one* word, but *one word.* At last I responded, almost inaudibly, 'What can I say?' 'Say that you love me, Helen.' '*I love you.*' These were the last words I ever spoke to

[1] Ingram, ii, 184, 185.

him." [1] She adds, in another account, that her mother, worn out by his long stay, "hastened his departure" by some expressions of her own; "turning to the door, he exclaimed bitterly, 'Mr. Pabodie, you hear how I am insulted.'" The two gentlemen went at once to the station and Poe left for Fordham. It was just three months since he had first left New York to meet Mrs. Whitman. About three weeks later he addressed a last letter to her, in respect to some slanderous misrepresentations of his conduct in this affair, which had been put in circulation; but to this, which he had first sent unsealed to "Annie," Mrs. Whitman made no reply, except, weeks afterward, indirectly by some "Stanzas for Music," published in "The Metropolitan" for February, and now included, in a revised version, in her "Poems" as "The Island of Dreams."

This episode has been narrated in minute detail because gross perversions of the facts were once common; and in the relation it has not been possible to ignore, as one would desire to do, the letters written by Poe, during this period, to Mrs. Whitman, "Annie," and her sister. If Poe's correspondence with other women — with

[1] Ingram, ii, 184, 185.

Mrs. Osgood, for example, who terms his letters "divinely beautiful" — bore any resemblance to that of the last year of his life, fortune has been more than usually kind in destroying it; but all his intimate correspondence with women seems to be of the same tissue. Not one word from these letters ought ever to have been published, but now it is too late to exclude them from the record. Poe had made up his mind to adopt Mrs. Shew's advice, and to try to save himself in what she had declared the only possible way, — marriage. He meant to extricate himself from his poverty by marrying a woman with property. This was his practical plan, wholly aside from his entanglement with any particular woman; but he worked it out under the conditions of his temperament. He had found romantic attachments consistent with his previous marriage, and he did not consider them inconsistent with his wooing. He was irresponsible in all his relations with women, — governed by no manly principle but by what they would permit in endearing language and behavior, and using the power of his fascination to satisfy his own craving. The contact of two such abnormal natures as Poe and Mrs. Whitman was full of danger. Mrs. Whitman herself, notwithstanding her many virtues and admirable qualities of heart, so finely exercised in her lifelong devotion to Poe's memory, was eccentric, susceptible to romantic fancies and mystical moods, one of those strange transcendental women, bred in New England, of whom Emily Dickinson was the latest example. She dressed in white, and is said to have carried the odor of ether wherever she went. She was in particular a believer in occult spiritual influences, and she liked to think herself akin by blood to Poe. She wrote, with reference to this trait of her book on Poe, a short passage to a correspondent who says: —

"The lady addressed me on Jan. 15, 1865, relative to the *spiritual* suggestions in her little volume. She says: 'It is strange that, in no notice of the book, have I ever seen an allusion, the most distant, to this part of the book, which to me is the most significant and important feature in it. Do you remember that I once wrote you a letter, in answer to some enquiries of yours, in which I spoke of the strange spiritual energy or effluence which seemed to surround or ensphere the "Raven," and which acted on those who were *en rapport* with him, enhancing and intensifying the spiritual faculties of insight and intuition? and do you remember that I instanced an impression which suddenly flashed on me of the original identity of the names of *Power*' (her maiden name) 'and *Poe* — an impression which I told you was afterwards corroborated, if not authenticated?'

"The instancing of that impression was, substantially, as follows: 'We were sitting together [in the autumn of 1848], when it all at once flashed upon me that we were blood-relations. I looked up at him. His eyes were fixed intensely upon me. On my naming the thought which had come to me, he said: "Helen, you startle me — thereby hangs a tale." He then gave me an outline of the history of his ancestors, as he reckoned them — of the Powers, the le Poers, the De la Poes.' "[1]

Poe, in his letters to her and in the recorded fragments of their conversation, rhapsodized about these affinities, as if that were the sure chord to respond to his touch. In all this correspondence there is a total and absolute absorption of his mind in his own affairs, — his injuries, distresses, and hopes; indeed, to one familiar with his modes of expression, it seems almost an accident that these letters were addressed to Mrs. Whitman. The language, confi-

[1] G. W. Eveleth to the author, July 9, 1883.

dential and studded with terms of endearment, is such as he habitually used both in written and spoken words to other women who he thought understood him. So far as his need of sympathy, pity, consolation, was concerned, he put more trust in "Annie's" heart, just as he wrote to her with more freedom and besought her aid with more simplicity. Infatuation was at all times characteristic of his acts and words. It was temperamental and took many forms, — intellectual in "Eureka," sentimental in his love affairs, practical in his projects; a striking instance of such obsession is this brief passage: —

"Was I right, dearest Helen, in my first impression of you? — you know I have implicit faith in first impressions — was I right in the impression that you are ambitious? If so, and *if you will have faith in me*, I can and will satisfy your wildest desires. It would be a glorious triumph, Helen, for *us* — for *you and me.* I dare not trust my schemes to a letter — nor indeed have I time even to hint at them here. When I see you I will explain all — as far, at least, as I dare explain *all* my hopes even to you. Would it *not* be 'glorious,' darling, to establish in America, the sole unquestionable aristocracy — that of intellect — to secure its supremacy — to lead and to control it? All this I can do, Helen, and will — if you bid me — and aid me." [1]

Such a wooing fortunately ended in disaster, and this may be ascribed to her friends; but an element of prudence, the cynicism of real life, as it might seem, was also grimly present in the romance on both sides. She divested herself of her worldly goods, and, to use the words of the editor of these letters, "there is reason to think that Poe's common-sense came to his rescue, and saved him from a marriage with a lady all of whose property had just been legally transferred to his future mother-in-law." [2]

On reaching Fordham Poe found Mrs. Clemm, who had never favored the match, overjoyed to see him unaccompanied by a wife, and, were it possible, more devoted to himself. He set to work, and wrote several hours each day; but, in consonance with the view that has been taken, although doubtless bitterly aggrieved, he exhibited no regret at the event which he had always considered likely, and no fidelity to the woman whose loyalty to his memory in after years was almost ideal. On January 11, 1849, he wrote to "Annie" as follows: —

[1] Poe to Mrs. Whitman, November 22, 1848. Ingram, ii, 180, 181.

[2] *The Century*, lxxvii, 3 (January, 1909), p. 446.

"In spite of so many worldly sorrows — in spite of all the trouble and *misrepresentation* (so hard to bear) that Poverty has entailed on me for so long a time — in spite of *all* this — I am *so*, *so* happy. . . . I need not tell you how great a burden is taken off my heart by my rupture with Mrs. W.; for I have fully made up my mind to break the engagement. . . . *Nothing* would have deterred me from the match but — what I tell you." [1]

Two weeks later he enclosed to the same correspondent a last letter to Mrs. Whitman, in which, after referring to the evil reports of him originating at Providence, he declared, "No amount of provocation shall induce me to speak ill of *you* [Mrs. Whitman], even in my own defense," [2] — with directions to read it, seal it with wax, and mail it in Boston; and to this singularly indelicate act, which is excused only by the circumstance that "Annie's" confidence in him had been shaken by these same slanders, he added the dishonor of a hasty expression of his pique in words too violently in contrast with the line just quoted to escape notice.

"Of one thing rest assured, from this day forth I shun the pestilential society of *literary*

[1] Ingram, ii, 202.

[2] Ingram, ii, 185.

women. They are a heartless, unnatural, venomous, dishonorable *set*, with no guiding principle but inordinate self-esteem. Mrs. Osgood is the *only* exception I know."[1]

It is said, on one hand, that Mrs. Whitman's name never afterwards passed his lips, and, on the other, that he stated on his last visit to Richmond that she "made repeated efforts toward a reconciliation, which he refused."[2]

[1] Ingram, ii, 205.

[2] Richmond *Times-Dispatch* (by J. H. Whitty), January 17, 1909.

CHAPTER XV

THE END

On his return to New York Poe set himself diligently to work. In pursuance of his plan to found the "Stylus," he had given lectures, as has been seen, in Lowell and Providence, but his income must have been of the scantiest; he had not yet taken up his literary work as a magazinist in any earnest since his illness, and his poems, except "Ulalume," had been desultory. In the last six months his published work was limited to the "Messenger" and the "Union"; in the former in September a criticism of Mrs. Lewis's poems, and in October and November "The Rationale of Verse," revised from his "Notes on English Verse" in the "Pioneer"; and in the "Union," in November, his lines "To Helen." Late in January, 1849, he wrote to his friend in Lowell:—

" . . . I am *so* busy, now, and feel so full of energy. Engagements to write are pouring in upon me every day. I had two proposals within the last week *from Boston*. I sent yesterday an article to the 'Am. Review,' about 'Critics and Criticism.' Not long ago I sent one to the 'Metropolitan' called 'Landor's Cottage': it has something about 'Annie' in it, and will appear, I suppose, in the March number. To the 'S. L. Messenger' I have sent fifty pages of 'Marginalia,' five pages to appear each month of the current year. I have also made permanent engagements with every magazine in America (except Peterson's 'National') including a Cincinnati magazine, called 'The Gentlemen's.' So you see that I have only to keep up my spirits to get out of all my pecuniary troubles. The *least* price I get is $5 per 'Graham page,' and I can easily average 1½ per day—that is $7½. As soon as 'returns' come in I shall be out of difficulty."[1]

Poe was elated with his immediate prospects; and he had good reason, if there was no exaggeration in these statements. On February 6, according to the same authority, he finished "The Bells," presumably the second draft, and the next day "Hop-Frog," a tale of grotesque humor out of Berner's Froissart. He also mentions "Annabel Lee," one of his most characteristic poems, apparently as recently written, but he may mean (as in the case of "The Bells")

[1] Ingram, ii, 205.

only the latest draft, since a poem of that name is said to have been written three years earlier, according to others. His publications, so far as traced, were the review of Lowell's "Fable for Critics," in the February "Messenger"; "Mellonta Tauta," a revision of the introduction to "Eureka," in "Godey's" for the same month; the lines "For Annie" (reprinted, as usual, at his request, by Willis), the sonnet "To my Mother," and "Hop-Frog," in the "Flag of Our Union," all, as it would seem, in April; and lastly, in "Sartain's Magazine" for March, "A Valentine," the anagrammatic poem to Mrs. Osgood. Perhaps "El Dorado," the only poem of which the first publication is unknown, belongs to this same period.

His correspondence reflects this active state of mind. He wrote to Thomas an old-time letter, and it is pleasant to see that he still commanded a man's style: —

FORDHAM, February 14, 1849.

MY DEAR FRIEND THOMAS, — Your letter, dated November 27, has reached me at a little village of the Empire State, after having taken, at its leisure, a very considerable tour among the Post-Offices — occasioned, I presume, by your indorsement "to forward" wherever I might be

— and the fact is, where I might *not* have been, for the last three months, is the legitimate question. At all events, now that I have your well-known MS. before me, it is most cordially welcome. Indeed, it seems an age since I heard from you, and a decade of ages since I shook you by the hand — although I hear *of* you now and then. Right glad am I to find you once more in a true position — in the field of Letters. Depend upon it, after all, Thomas, Literature is the most noble of professions. In fact, it is about the only one fit for a man. For my own part, there is no seducing me from the path. I shall be a *Littérateur* at least all my life; nor would I abandon the hopes which still lead me on for all the gold in California. Talking of gold, and of the temptations at present held out to "poor-devil authors," did it ever strike you that all which is really valuable to a man of letters — to a poet in especial — is absolutely unpurchasable? Love, fame, the dominion of intellect, the consciousness of power, the thrilling sense of beauty, the free air of Heaven, exercise of body and mind, with the physical and moral health which result — these and such as these are really all that a poet cares for: then answer me this — *why* should he go to California? Like Brutus, "I pause for a reply" —

which, like F. W. Thomas, I take it for granted you have no intention of giving me. I have read the Prospectus of the "Chronicle," and like it much, especially the part where you talk about letting go the finger of that conceited booby, the East, which is by no means the East out of which came the wise men mentioned in Scripture. I wish you would come down on the Frogpondians. They are getting worse and worse, and pretend not to be aware that there *are* any literary people out of Boston. The worst and most disgusting part of the matter is that the Bostonians are really, as a race, far inferior in point of *anything beyond mere talent* to any other *set* upon the continent of North America. They are decidedly the most servile imitators of the English it is possible to conceive. I always get into a passion when I think about [it]. It would be the easiest thing in the world to use them up *en masse*. One really well-written satire would accomplish the business: but it must not be such a dish of skimmed-milk-and-water as Lowell's. I suppose you have seen that affair—the "Fable for Critics," I mean. Miss Fuller, that detestable old maid, told him once that he was "so wretched a poet as to be disgusting even to his best friends." This set him off at a tangent and he has never been quite right since — so he took to writing satire against mankind in general, with Margaret Fuller and her *protégé*, Cornelius Mathews, in particular. It is miserably weak upon the whole, but has one or two good but by no means *original* things, — oh, there is "*nothing* new under the sun," and Solomon is right — for once. I sent a review of the "Fable" to the "S. L. Messenger," a day or two ago, and I only hope Thompson will print it. Lowell is a ranting abolitionist, and *deserves* a good using up. It is a pity that he is a poet. I have not seen your paper yet, and hope you will mail me one — regularly if you can spare it. I will send you something whenever I get a chance. With your coeditor, Mr. [name crossed out], I am not acquainted personally, but he is well known to me by reputation. Eames, I think, was talking to me about him in Washington once, and spoke very highly of him in many respects, so upon the whole you are in luck. The rock on which most new enterprises in the paper way split is namby-pambyism. It never did do and never will. No yea-nay journal *ever* succeeded. But I know there is little danger of your making the "Chronicle" a yea-nay one. I have been quite out of the literary world for the last three years, and have *said* little or nothing, but, like the owl, I have "taken it out in thinking." By and by I mean to come out of the bush, and then I *have* some old scores to settle. I fancy I see some of my *friends* already stepping up to the Captain's office. The fact is, Thomas, living buried in the country makes a man savage — wolfish. I am just in the humor for a fight. You will be pleased to hear that I am in better health than I ever knew myself to be — full of energy, and bent upon success. You shall hear of me again shortly — and it is not improbable that I may soon pay you a visit in Louisville. If I can do anything for you in New York, let me know. Mrs. Clemm sends her best respects, and begs to be remembered to your mother's family if they are with you. You would oblige me very especially if you could squeeze in what follows, editorially. The lady [Mrs. Lewis] spoken of is a most particular friend of mine, and deserves *all* I have said of her. I will reciprocate the favor I ask, whenever you say the word, and show me how. Address me at New York City as usual, and if you insert the following, please cut it out and enclose it in your letter.

Truly your friend, EDGAR A. POE.[1]

[1] Griswold MSS.

A letter to Duyckinck three weeks later also shows his natural vein: —

FORDHAM, March 8 [1849].

DEAR SIR, — If you have looked over the Von Kempelen article which I left with your brother, you will have fully perceived its drift. I mean it as a kind of "exercise," or experiment, in the plausible or verisimilar style. Of course, there is *not one* word of truth in it from beginning to end. I thought that such a style, applied to the gold-excitement, could not fail of effect. My sincere opinion is that nine persons out of ten (even among the best-informed) will *believe* the quiz (provided the design does not leak out before publication) and that thus, acting as a sudden, although of course a very temporary, *check* to the gold-fever, it will create a *stir* to some purpose.

I had prepared the hoax for a Boston weekly called "The Flag," where it will be quite thrown away. The proprietor will give me $15 for it on presentation to his agent here; and my object in referring the article to you is simply to see if you could not venture to take it for the "World." If so, I am willing to take for it $10 — or, in fact, whatever you think you can afford.

I believe the quiz is the first deliberate literary attempt of the kind on record. In the story of Mrs. Veal, we are permitted, now and then, to perceive a tone of *banter*. In "Robinson Crusoe" the design was far more to please, or excite, than to deceive by verisimilitude, in which particular merely, Sir Ed. Seaward's narrative is the more skilful book. In my "Valdemar Case" (which *was* credited by many) I had not the slightest idea that any person should credit it as anything more than a "Magazine-paper" — but here the whole strength is laid out in verisimilitude.

I am *very* much obliged to you for your reprint of "Ulalume."

Truly yours, EDGAR A. POE.[1]

P. S. If you feel the least *shy* about the article, make no hesitation in returning it, of course: — for I willingly admit that it is not a paper which every editor would like to "take the responsibility" of printing — although merely as a contribution with a known name: — but if you decline the quiz, please *do not let out the secret*.

EVERT A. DUYCKINCK, Esq.

[1] Poe to Duyckinck, *loc. cit.* pp. 10–11.

These various writings probably represent Poe's literary activity for time past as well as present, and this is certainly the case with the noticeable pieces among them, — "The Domain of Arnheim," and "Landor's Cottage," called its pendant. The latter closed the series of the landscape studies, which make as distinct a group in Poe's imaginative work as the tales of mystery, ratiocination, or conscience, since in these the sensuous element, which was primary in his genius, found its simplest and most unrestrained expression. The series had culminated, however, in "The Domain of Arnheim," in which the brilliancy and flood and glow of pure color are a mere reveling of the æsthetic sense; and so gorgeous is the vision and thrown out in so broad an expanse that, although only a description, the piece is as unique among works of imagination as is "The Black Cat" or "The Fall of the House of Usher." The landscape that the mention of the latter recalls, and much more the spectral woodland and tarn of "Ulalume," serve to measure by momentary contrast with the scenes of faëry in "Arnheim" the range of Poe's fantasy, and at the same time to bring out strongly the extent to which his work is dependent for its effect directly on the senses, however abnormally excited. In fact, the impression made in the present case is solely spectacular. The landscape sketches, too, afford some pleasant relief to the paltrinesses, the miseries, and debasements of his ordinary life. The idyllic sweetness of "Eleonora," the quiet beauty of "The Island of the Fay" and "Morning on the Wissahiccon," opened round Poe, as he was seen in his Philadelphia days, the only prospect beyond the mean walls of the newspaper office and the tenement house. Now in this mythical "Arnheim" he indulged most purely his delight in the contemplation of loveliness for its own sake; his country rambles in the wide theatre of the Palisades still gave him an outlook on the things of beauty, of light and calm and joy.

While Poe was thus engaged a successor to Mrs. Ellet had arisen in the home of his Lowell friends in Mrs. Locke, the lady who had helped to relieve his necessities in 1847. She had some communication with Mrs. Whitman, in discouragement of any renewal of relations with Poe, by whom, Mrs. Whitman reports, "she conceived herself to have been deeply wronged"; but, in regard to her complaints, Mrs. Whitman adds, "I saw that she was too much under the influence of wounded pride to exercise a calm judgment in the matter." She busied herself so successfully as to disturb the minds of the Richmonds, and to alienate, at least partially, the good-will of the head of the house. Poe, on being informed of this, accounted for her hostility by saying that he had left her abruptly in consequence of her disparagement of "Annie," and added that he thought it hard that such a quarrel should prejudice him in the latter's mind. He was so far moved by the attitude assumed by her husband that he gave up a proposed visit to his house and the plan of settling near these new friends permanently, and he even professed to think it necessary that the correspondence should cease. He wrote, "I cannot and *will* not have it on my conscience that I have interfered with the domestic happiness of the only being in the whole world, whom I have loved at the same time with truth and with purity."[1]

Such an abrupt termination to one of the happiest friendships of his life was fortunately avoided. Poe was able to sustain his story, and after a few weeks Mrs. Locke, whose connection with his family seems to have been unbroken, wrote to him that she was about to pub-

[1] Poe to "Annie," February 19, 1849. Ingram, ii, 208.

lish a novel recording their relations in detail in such a way as to make his own character appear noble and generous, and that she would come on to Fordham at once to avail herself of any suggestions from him. What became of this novel,[1] or what reception the lady's proposals met with, is unknown; but as in the sequel, even after Poe's death, she still busied herself in scandal, it is likely that there was no reconciliation.

In literary matters the spring had brought disappointment. The "Columbia" and "Union" failed; the "Whig" and "Democratic" stopped payment; the "Messenger," which was in Poe's debt, remained in arrears; another publication with which he had engaged for ten dollars weekly was forced to decline contributions; with "Godey's" he had quarreled: and so, in his own words, he was "reduced to 'Sartain' and 'Graham,' both very precarious." His many engagements, on which he had built so hopefully a few months before, had dwindled away; the "Metropolitan," whose short career was distinguished by some lines addressed to him by Mrs. Osgood, and also by Mrs. Whitman in indirect acknow-

[1] This should not be confused with a novel, in which Poe figured, *Mary Lyndon*, New York, 1855, published anonymously but afterwards acknowledged by Mrs. Gove-Nichols.

ledgment of his last letter, failed to print "Landor's Cottage"; and to add to his misfortunes he had again been seriously ill. "I thought," wrote Mrs. Clemm to "Annie," "he would die several times. God knows I wish we were both in our graves. It would, I am sure, be far better."[1] A deep gloom settled over his mind. He himself wrote to the same lady, in denying that this arose from his literary disappointments, "My sadness is *unaccountable*, and this makes me the more sad. I am full of dark forebodings. *Nothing* cheers or comforts me. My life seems wasted — the future looks a dreary blank; but I will struggle on and 'hope against hope.'"[2] Meanwhile light had broken on the "Stylus." A new promoter, E. H. N. Patterson, had opened negotiations with him as early as the previous December, but the letter had just reached Poe in April, when he replied favorably; on May 7, Patterson made a definite offer, leaving Poe the entire editorial control, together with the expenses connected with that department; the receipts were to be shared, and the magazine to be printed at Oquawka, Illinois. Poe suggested, in view of the obscurity of Oquawka, that an announcement of simultaneous publication at St. Louis

[1] Ingram, ii, 215. [2] Ingram, ii, 214.

and New York be put on the title-page; and in addition asked fifty dollars as Patterson's share of preliminary expenses, and promised to advance the interests of the project by proceeding on the lecturing tour in the South, which he had in view on his first visit to Richmond, but had then abandoned.[1] After this he visited his friends at Lowell the last week in May, and there wrote the third draft of "The Bells"; he soon returned to New York, with the expectation of going South. He was delayed for some weeks, during which his despondency was marked and habitual. Before leaving Fordham he wrote requests that Griswold would superintend the collection of his works, and that Willis would write such a biographical notice as should be deemed necessary. On June 29, having completed his arrangements for his journey, he went to Brooklyn in company with Mrs. Clemm, to pass the night at the house of Mrs. Lewis, the poetess, whose works he had lately reviewed, and with whom during the past year an intimacy of the old kind had sprung up. "He seemed very sad," wrote this lady, "and retired early. On leaving the next morning, he took my hand in his, and, looking in my face, said, 'Dear Stella, my

[1] Poe to Patterson, May 23, 1849, *America*, April 11, 1889.

much beloved friend. You truly understand and appreciate me — I have a presentiment that I shall never see you again. I must leave to-day for Richmond. If I never return, write my life. You can and will do me justice.'"[1] Mrs. Clemm accompanied him to the steamboat, and on parting he said to her, "God bless you, my own darling mother. Do not fear for Eddy! See how good I will be while I am away from you, and will [*sic*] come back to love and comfort you."[2]

Poe went to Philadelphia, and, apparently after a day or two, entered the office of John Sartain, proprietor of "Sartain's Magazine," his friend for the past nine years, and exclaimed excitedly, "I have come to you for refuge." He was delirious and suffering from what seems to have been an habitual delusion in such attacks, a fear of a conspiracy against him. Sartain, who long remembered the visions about which Poe raved and the persistence with which he besought him for laudanum, reassured him, and cared for him some days, accompanied him when he went out, and brought him back; once Poe escaped and seems to have passed that night in an open field, but Sartain told the story with variations at different times; toward the end

[1] Ingram, ii, 220. [2] Ingram, ii, 221.

two other old friends, George Lippard and Charles Chauncey Burr, cared for him.

Meanwhile Mrs. Clemm, not hearing from him, had grown anxious, and wrote to "Annie," July 9: —

July 9, 1849.

Eddy has been gone ten days, and I have not heard one word from him. Do you wonder that I *am distracted?* I fear everything. . . . Do you wonder that he has so little confidence in any one? Have we not suffered from the blackest treachery? . . . Eddy was obliged to go through Philadelphia, and how much I fear he has got into some trouble there; he promised me *so* sincerely to write thence. I ought to have heard last Monday, and now it is Monday again and not one word . . . Oh, if any evil has befallen *him*, what can comfort me? The day after he left New York, I left Mrs. Lewis and started for home. I called on a rich friend who had made many promises, but never knew our situation. I frankly told her. . . . She proposed to me to leave Eddy, saying he might very well do for himself. . . . Any one to propose to *me* to leave my Eddy — what a cruel insult! No one to console and comfor[illegible]m but me; no one to nurse him and take care of him when he is sick and helpless! Can I ever forget that dear sweet face, so tranquil, so pale, and those dear eyes looking at me so sadly, while she said, "Darling, darling Muddy, you will console and take care of my poor Eddy — you will never, *never* leave him? Promise me, my dear Muddy, and then I can die in peace." And *I did promise*. And when I meet her in heaven, I can say, "I have kept my promise, my darling." . . . If Eddy gets to Richmond safely and can succeed in what he intends doing, we will be relieved of part of our difficulties; but if he comes home in trouble and sick, I know not what is to become of us.[1]

The news she feared was already on its way to her. Poe had written on Saturday, two days before: —

NEW YORK, [?] July 7.

MY DEAR, DEAR MOTHER, — I have been so ill — have had the cholera, or spasms quite as bad, and can now hardly hold the pen.

The very instant you get this come to me. The joy of seeing you will almost compensate for our sorrows. We can but die together. It is of no use to reason with me now; I must die.

[1] Ingram, ii, 222.

I have no desire to live since I have done "Eureka." I could accomplish nothing more. For your sake it would be sweet to live, but we must die together. You have been all in all to me, darling, ever beloved mother, and dearest truest friend.

I was never really insane, except on occasions where my heart was touched.

I have been taken to prison once since I came here for getting drunk; but then I was not. It was about Virginia.[1]

[1] *Character of Edgar A. Poe*, by C. Chauncey Burr, *The Nineteenth Century*, V, i (February, 1852), pp. 19–33. There can be no doubt that the letter should have been dated at Philadelphia. Burr prefaced these letters thus: —

"I feel that I am justified in opening to the public eye this sacred retreat of privacy in the life of Poe, in order to defend his fame from the scandalous falsehoods which malice has heaped upon it. Here we shall find traces of an intense, sincere, fiery, loving heart, full of great extremes and wanderings, alas! but somehow, always returning to the same spot of affection and truth. His affection for Mrs. Clemm, the mother of his wife, and his tender and anxious solicitude for her welfare, even in the midst of the most distracting pain and poverty, opens to our view the agonies of a heart overflowing with kindness, gratitude, and faith, yet cruelly dispossessed of every means of the blessing it would bestow. I am greatly indebted to this kind lady for the privilege of making such extracts from her son's letters to her as I may find important for my purpose, and I have taken the liberty to quote only parts of letters, for to

It may fairly be suggested that Poe's reference to being taken to prison was a lingering hallucination. Sartain says: "He said he had been thrown into Moyamensing Prison for forging a check, and while there a white female form had appeared on the battlements and addressed him in whispers. 'If I had not heard what she said,' he declared, 'it would have been the end of me,'"[1] and he went on in the same strain with delirious fancies. Sartain adds elsewhere: "When his turn came in the group before Mayor Gilpin, it was remarked, 'Why, this is Poe, the poet,' and he was dismissed without the customary fine."[2]

He left Philadelphia Friday in season to take the night-boat at Baltimore and arrived in Richmond on Saturday night. The story is told by himself.

NEAR RICHMOND. [Saturday, July 14, 1849.]

The weather is awfully hot, and besides all this, I am so homesick I don't know what to do. I never wanted to see any one half so bad as I want to see my own darling mother. It seems

do more than this would swell my paper beyond the limits of a magazine article."

[1] *Philadelphia Record* (no date).

[2] *Lippincott's*, March, 1889.

to me that I would make any sacrifice to hold you by the hand once more, and get you to cheer me up, for I am terribly depressed. I do not think that any circumstances will ever tempt me to leave you again. When I am with you I can bear anything, but when I am away from you I am too miserable to live.

RICHMOND, Saturday Night. [July 14, 1849.]

Oh, my darling mother, it is now more than three [two] weeks since I saw you, and in all that time your poor Eddy has scarcely drawn a breath except of intense agony. Perhaps you are sick or gone from Fordham in despair, or dead. If you are but alive, and if I but see you again, all the rest is nothing. I love you better than ten thousand lives — so much so that it is cruel in you to let me leave you: nothing but sorrow ever comes of it.

Oh, Mother, I am so ill while I write — but I resolved that come what would, I would not sleep again without easing your dear heart as far as I could.

My valise was lost for ten days. At last I found it at the depot in Philadelphia, but (you will scarcely credit it) they had opened it and stolen both lectures. Oh, Mother, think of the blow to me this evening, when on examining the valise, these lectures were gone. All my object here is over unless I can recover them or rewrite one of them.

I am indebted for more than life itself to B[urr]. Never forget him Mother while you live. When all failed me, he stood my friend, got me money, and saw me off in the cars for Richmond.

I got here with two dollars over — of which I enclose you one. Oh God, my Mother, shall we ever meet again? If possible, oh COME! My clothes are so horrible and I am so ill. Oh, if you could come to me, my mother. Write instantly — Oh do not fail. God forever bless you. EDDY.

RICHMOND, Thursday, July 19.

MY OWN BELOVED MOTHER,—You will see at once by the handwriting of this letter, that I am better — much better — in health and spirits. Oh if you only knew how your dear letter comforted me! It acted like magic. Most of my sufferings arose from that terrible idea which I could not get rid of — the idea that you were dead. For more than ten days I was totally deranged, although I was not drinking one drop;

and during this interval I imagined the most horrible calamities.

All was hallucination, arising from an attack which I had never before experienced — an attack of mania-á-potu. May Heaven grant that it prove a warning to me for the rest of my days. If so I shall not regret even the horrible unspeakable torments I have endured.

To L[ippard] and to C[hauncey] B[urr] (and in some measure, also to Mr. S[artain]) I am indebted for more than life. They remained with me (L[ippard] and B[urr]) all day on Friday last, comforted me and aided me in coming to my senses. L[ippard] saw G[raham], who said everything kind of me, and sent me five dollars; and P[eterson] sent another five. B[urr] procured me a ticket as far as Baltimore and the passage from there to Richmond was seven dollars. I have not drank anything since Friday morning, and then only a little Port wine. If possible, dearest Mother, I will extricate myself from this difficulty for your dear, dear sake. So keep up heart.

All is not lost yet, and "the darkest hour is just before daylight." Keep up heart, my own beloved mother — all may yet go well. I will put forth all my energies. When I get my mind a little more composed, I will try to write something. Oh, give my dearest, fondest love to Mrs. L[ewis]. Tell her that never while I live, will I forget her kindness to my darling mother.[1]

On the same day Poe wrote a brief note [2] to Patterson, with regard to the "Stylus," acknowledging the receipt of fifty dollars; he says he "was arrested in Philadelphia by the Cholera, from which I barely escaped with life," and promises to write in full as soon as he should "gather a little strength." He settled at the old Swan Tavern, in Broad Street, a decayed hotel, where he had stayed before, and was cared for kindly by his old friends.

He was received more cordially and with more distinction than on his previous visit. He divided his time between Duncan Lodge, the residence of the MacKenzies, at one end of the town, and Church Hill, the residence of Mrs. Shelton, at the other; he was made at home at both places; and at Robert Sully's, the artist whom he had befriended in boyhood, and at Talavera, the seat of the Talleys, he passed many of these hours which he said were the happiest he had known

[1] *The Nineteenth Century, loc. cit.*

[2] Poe to Patterson, July 19, *America, loc. cit.*

for years. Mrs. Shelton was his boyish flame, Miss Royster, and he offered her marriage.

There is no room to doubt that in this he obeyed worldly motives; for though there had been romantic passages between them in school-days, there is no likelihood that these would have prevailed on Poe to unite himself with a woman who is described as of plain manners, older than himself, and with no attraction except wealth. Poe attributed his ill-success in the world solely to his poverty; in later years especially this had become so settled a conviction in his mind that, in his letters to "Annie," "I must get rich, get rich," is a refrain so constant as to seem the purpose he had most at heart; he needed money to secure his shattered health against the necessities of hard labor for a support precarious at best, and especially to establish the "Stylus," the scheme he pursued as a phantom. Mrs. Clemm believed that his motive was to provide a home and friends for herself. To her Mrs. Whitman wrote: "I think I can understand all the motives that influenced Edgar in those last days and can see how the desire to provide a home and friends for you swayed him in *all*."[1] His engagement to Mrs.

[1] Mrs. Whitman to Mrs. Clemm, April 17, 1859. MS.

SARAH E. SHELTON

Shelton was announced and is said to have been mentioned in the papers, greatly to his displeasure; and although Mrs. Shelton denied that a formal agreement existed, and acknowledged only a partial understanding, she plainly meant to marry Poe. Toward the end of August an obstacle arose in Mrs. Shelton's determination to retain control of her income (she seems to have held only a life-interest in the estate) and in her lack of sympathy with Poe's plans for the "Stylus," and he therefore broke the engagement. Mrs. Shelton demanded her letters, and, Poe refusing unless his own should be first returned, she held a consultation with the MacKenzies in regard to the difficulty.[1]

As the season went on, Poe was lionized and social attention widely shown him. He gave a public lecture, Friday, August 17, — that on "The Poetic Principle," — in the Exchange Hotel, and, both before and after the performance, the press complimented and praised him. The financial success was not great, however; the audience was less than one hundred persons,[2]

[1] Mrs. Weiss, p. 196, makes these statements with much positiveness, relying on Poe's confidential communications to Dr. Mackenzie, who, she says, had originally, in 1848, suggested Poe's first visit to Richmond to make the marriage.

[2] There is much confusion, in the many Richmond reminis-

and it is plain that he cleared little, but he was encouraged to try again. It was at this time that he is said to have broken with Mrs. Shelton, and at the lecture he ignored her presence and joined the Talley party immediately on its conclusion.

In respect to his other practical interest, the "Stylus," he had written meanwhile to Patterson, August 7,[1] apologizing for his delay by saying that he had "suffered worse than death — not so much from the Cholera as from its long-continued consequences in debility and congestion of the brain — the latter, possibly, attributable to the calomel taken," and saying that he was still "too feeble to travel." He suggested that the price be put at five dollars instead of three, and the publication postponed till July 1, 1850. Patterson consented to this, and hoped for a conference in St. Louis in October. The correspondence ended here, and John R. Thompson responded to Patterson's later inquiries about Poe. He said that for the last three weeks in Richmond Poe was sober, and had

cences of Poe, of the events of the first with those of the second visit with regard to his lectures, his courtship, and his habits. The second visit had a different social character and personal color from the first.

[1] Poe to Patterson, *America*, *loc. cit.*

joined the Sons of Temperance;[1] but he adds, "no confidence could be placed in him in any relation of life," and congratulated his correspondent on not having embarked in the enterprise; "for," he writes, "a more unreliable person than he could hardly be found."[2]

Poe had joined the Sons of Temperance, and a report of this found its way to a Philadelphia paper, and was there commented on. He had arrived in Richmond in a state requiring medical attendance, and it may be presumed that some part of his physician's reminiscences are to be referred to that occasion. The evidence is very direct, nevertheless, to his repeated illness in the earlier part of his stay. On one occasion he seems to have been attended, in delirium, by Dr. George Rawlins,[3] but his physician in 1849

[1] The gentleman who administered the oath on this occasion, writing December 4, 1900, states that Poe was initiated about the first of July, and that for the "next three months or more there was not the least intimation that he had failed to live up to his obligation." *The Virginia Poe*, i, 321. Thompson's statement made within seven weeks of the time, and being from a kindly friend and constant associate, should take precedence as evidence.

[2] Thompson to Patterson, November, 9, 1849, *America*, *loc. cit.*

[3] *The Virginia Poe*, i, 311.

was Dr. William Gibbon Carter.[1] The most specific account of his health is given by Mrs. Weiss when writing of his intemperate habits in her first reminiscences: —

"The knowledge of this weakness was by his own request concealed from me. All that I knew of the matter was when a friend informed me that 'Mr. Poe was too unwell to see us that evening.' A day or two after this he sent a message by his sister requesting some flowers, in return for which came a dainty note of thanks, written in a tremulous hand. He again wrote, inclosing a little anonymous poem which he had found in some newspaper and admired; and on the day following he made his appearance among us, but so pale, tremulous, and apparently subdued as to convince me that he had been seriously ill. On this occasion he had been at his rooms at the 'Old Swan,' where he was carefully tended by Mrs. Mackenzie's family, but on a second and more serious relapse he was taken by Dr. Mackenzie and Dr. Gibbon Carter to Duncan Lodge, where during some days his life was in

[1] Dr. John Carter to the author, June 16, 1884, MS. "My brother, *who attended* (*sic*) Poe, has on occasion defended him through the press from the charge of dram-drinking; he was not a steady drinker, but had his sprees."

imminent danger. Assiduous attention saved him, but it was the opinion of the physicians that another such attack would prove fatal. This they told him, warning him seriously of the danger. His reply was that if people would not tempt him he would not fall. Dr. Carter relates how, on this occasion, he had a long conversation with him, in which Poe expressed the most earnest desire to break from the thralldom of his besetting sin, and told of his many unavailing struggles to do so. He was moved even to tears, and finally declared, in the most solemn manner, that this time he *would* restrain himself — *would* withstand any temptation." [1] It would appear that it was subsequent to this that he joined the Sons of Temperance; from the first of September he was in better health, and no sign of illness occurs until his departure.

Meanwhile Mrs. Clemm at Fordham was destitute, and applied to Griswold for relief. The letter is significant of the relations of the family with him at the time when he was designated by Poe as literary executor: —

NEW YORK, August 27, 1849.

DEAR MR. GRISWOLD, — I feel you will pardon the liberty I take in addressing you, but the ex-

[1] *Scribner's Magazine*, xv, 5 (March, 1878).

treme urgency of my situation compels me to do so. Mr. Poe has been absent from home for some weeks; he is now in Richmond and has been very ill, and unable to send me any money since he left, and is much distressed for fear of my suffering. Indeed I *have suffered.* I have been very sick, and entirely unable to make the least exertion. I have been without the necessaries of life for many days, and would not apply to any one, in hopes that I would soon receive some aid from my poor Eddy. He writes me that he is getting better, and hopes he will be soon able to attend to business. I confide in you, dear sir, and beg you to loan me a small sum until I can receive some from him. I have not the means to go to the city, but a note addressed to Mrs. Maria Clemm, care of E. A. Poe, New York, will reach me. A gentleman in the neighborhood asks every day for me at the post-office. You have no idea how distressing it is to my feelings to make this request, but I think you will feel for my situation.

Respectfully,

MARIA CLEMM.[1]

She addressed him again a week later: —

[1] Griswold MSS.

New York, September 4, 1849.

Dear Mr. Griswold, — I have tried so long to see you without success, that I have taken the liberty of addressing this note to you. I understand from Mrs. Lewis you received the package [a review of her poems to be inserted in Griswold's forthcoming new edition of his "Female Poets of America"] Mr. Poe left at her house for you. I wish you to publish it exactly as he has written it. If you will do so I will promise you a favorable review of your books as they appear — you know the influence I have with Mr. Poe. Not that I think he will need any urging to advance your interest. I have just heard from him; he writes in fine spirits and says his prospects are excellent. Will you be so kind as to let me know if you receive this? Please direct to me at New York, care of E. A. Poe.

Respectfully,

Maria Clemm.[1]

I will call on Saturday at ten o'clock at your room if you will please meet me there.

Poe wrote again to Mrs. Clemm with a glowing account of his success, and it will be observed

[1] Griswold MSS.

that the breach with Mrs. Shelton must have been of brief continuance, if, as is said, it took place in August: —

RICHMOND, September [5], 1849.

[First sheet missing.] . . . possible. Everybody says that if I lecture again and put the tickets at fifty cents, I will clear $100. I *never* was received with so much enthusiasm. The papers have done nothing but praise me before the lecture and since. I inclose one of the notices, the only one in which the slightest word of disparagement appears. It is written by Daniel, the man whom I challenged when I was here last year. I have been invited out a great deal, but could seldom go, on account of not having a dress-coat. To-night Rose [his sister] and I are to spend the evening at Elmira's [Mrs. Shelton]. Last night I was at Poitiaux's; the night before at Strobia's, where I saw my dear friend Eliza Lambert, Gen. Lambert's sister. She was ill in her bedroom, but insisted upon our coming up, and we stayed until nearly one o'clock. In a word, I have received nothing but kindness since I have been here, and could have been quite happy but for my dreadful anxiety about you. Since the report of my intended marriage the

McKenzies have overwhelmed me with attentions. Their house is so crowded that they *could* not ask me to stay. And now, my own precious Muddy, the very moment I get a definite answer about everything I will write again and tell you what to do. Elmira talks about visiting Fordham, but I do not know whether that would do. I think, perhaps, it would be best for you to give up everything there and come on here in the Packet. Write immediately and give me your advice about it, for you know best. Could we be happier in Richmond or Lowell? for I suppose we could never be happy at Fordham, and, Muddy, I *must* be somewhere where I can see Annie. Did Mrs. L[ewis] get the "Western Quarterly Review"? Thompson is constantly urging me to write for the "Messenger," but I am so anxious that I cannot. Mr. Loud, the husband of Mrs. St. Leon Loud, the poetess of Philadelphia, called on me the other day and offered me $100 to edit his wife's poems. Of course I accepted the offer. The whole labor will not occupy me three days. I am to have them ready by Christmas. I have seen Bernard often. Eliza is expected, but has not come. When I repeat my lecture here, I will then go to Petersburg and Norfolk. A Mr. Taverner lectured here on Shakespeare, a few nights after me, and had eight persons, including myself and the doorkeeper. I think upon the whole, dear Muddy, it will be better for you to say that I am ill or something of that kind, and break up at Fordham, so that you may come on here. Let me know immediately what you think best. You know we could easily pay off what we owe at Fordham, and the place is a beautiful one, but I want to live *near Annie*. And now, dear Muddy, there is one thing I wish you to pay particular attention to. I told Elmira when I first came here, that I had one of the pencil-sketches of her, that I took a long while ago in Richmond; and I told her that I would write to you about it. So when you write, just copy the following words in your letter: —

"I have looked again for the pencil-sketch of Mrs. S. but cannot find it anywhere. I took down all the books and shook them one by one, and, unless Eliza White has it, I do not [know] what has become of it. She was looking at it the last time I saw it. The one you spoilt with Indian Ink ought to be somewhere about the house. I will do my best to find it."

I got a sneaking letter to-day from Chivers. Do not tell me anything about Annie — I can-

[*Facsimile of original MS.*
By courtesy of Mrs. W. M. Griswold]

To ———.

I heed not that my earthly lot
Hath —— little of Earth in it —
That years of love have been forgot
In the hatred of a minute: —
I mourn not that the desolate
Are happier, sweet, than I,
But that _you_ sorrow for _my_ fate
Who am a passer by.

E. A. P

not bear to hear it now — unless you can tell me that Mr. —— [her husband] is dead. I have got the wedding ring, and shall have no difficulty, I think, in getting a dress-coat.[1]

Wednesday Night.

. . . [torn out] also the letter. *Return the letter when you write.*

A few days later, on Sunday, September 9, he was at Old Point, near Norfolk, with a Virginia party, one of whom in her old age described the scene, which is too characteristic to be neglected: —

"That Sunday evening in early September at Old Point stands out like a lovely picture. I cannot describe it fitly. There was more in it than may be expressed in mere words. There were several of us girls, all friends, and all of us knew Mr. Poe. I can see just how we looked sitting about there in our white dresses. There was a young collegian, too, who was my particular friend. He is gone long years since, and all the others in that little group have passed away except Sister and myself.

"Mr. Poe sat there in that quiet way of his

[1] Griswold MSS.

which made you feel his presence. After a while my aunt, who was nearer his age, said: 'This seems to be just the time and place for poetry, Mr. Poe.'

"And it was. We all felt it. The old Hygeia stood some distance from the water, but with nothing between it and the ocean. It was moonlight and the light shone over everything with that undimmed light that it has in the South. There were many persons on the long verandas that surrounded the hotel, but they seemed remote and far away. Our little party was absolutely cut off from everything except that lovely view of the water shining in the moonlight and its gentle music borne to us on the soft breeze. Poe felt the influence. How could a poet help it? And when we seconded the request that he recite for us he agreed readily.

"He recited the 'Raven,' 'Annabel Lee,' and last of all 'Ulalume,' with the last stanza, of which he remarked that he feared it might not be intelligible to us, as it was scarcely clear to himself, and for that reason it had not been published."

The next day he sent a copy of "Ulalume" with a letter to this young friend: —

Monday Evening.

I have transcribed "Ulalume" with much pleasure, Dear Miss Ingram — as I am sure I would do anything else at your bidding — but I fear you will find the verses scarcely more intelligible to-day in my manuscript than last night in my recitation. I would endeavor to explain to you what I really meant — or what I fancied I meant, by the poem, if it were not that I remembered Dr. Johnson's bitter and rather just remarks about the folly of explaining what, if worth explanation, would explain itself. He has a happy witticism, too, about some book, which he calls "as obscure as an explanatory note." Leaving "Ulalume" to its fate, therefore, and in good hands, I am, yours truly,

EDGAR A. POE.

"We went from Old Point Comfort," the writer continues, "to our home near Norfolk, Va., and he called on us there, and again I had the pleasure of talking with him. Although I was only a slip of a girl and he what then seemed to me quite an old man, and a great literary one at that, we got on together beautifully. He was one of the most courteous gentlemen I have ever seen, and that gave a great charm to his manner. None of his pictures that I have ever seen look like the picture of Poe that I keep in my memory. Of course they look like him, so that any one seeing them could have recognized him from them, but there was something in his face that is in none of them. Perhaps it was in the eyes, perhaps in the mouth, I do not know, but any one who ever met him would understand what I mean.

"There were no indications of dissipation apparent when we saw Poe in Virginia at that time. I think he had not been drinking for a long time. If I had not heard or read what had been said about his intemperance I should never have had any idea of it from what I saw in Poe. To me, he seemed a good man, as well as a charming one, very sensitive and very high-minded."

She closes her reminiscences with a pleasant touch of Poe's boyhood.

"I remember one little instance that illustrates how loyal he was to the memory of those that had been kind to him. I was fond of orris root and always had the odor of it about my clothes. One day when we were walking together he spoke of it. 'I like it, too,' he said. 'Do you know what it makes me think of? My adopted mother. Whenever the bureau drawers in her room were opened there came from them a whiff of orris root, and ever since when I smell it I go back to the time when I was a little boy, and it brings back thoughts of my mother.'" [1]

On the following Friday, September 14, Poe lectured in the Norfolk Academy on "The Poetic Principle," and was handsomely noticed in the local press,[2] and he was entertained in the city at the best houses. He returned to Richmond, and wrote immediately to Mrs. Clemm. It will be observed that the pseudonym he gives to her is the same as that used in his first note to Mrs. Whitman.

[RICHMOND, VA.
Tuesday, September 18, '49.

MY OWN DARLING MUDDY, — On arriving here last night from Norfolk I received both your letters, including Mrs. Lewis's. I cannot tell you the joy they gave me to learn at least that you are well and hopeful. May God forever bless you, my *dear*, *dear* Muddy. — Elmira has just got home from the country. I spent last

[1] New York *Herald* (by Miss Susan Ingram), February 19, 1905.

[2] The Norfolk *American Beacon*, September 13, 14, 17, 1849.

evening with her. I think she loves me more devotedly than any one I ever knew and I cannot help loving her in return. Nothing is as yet definitely settled —] and it will not do to hurry matters. I lectured at Norfolk on Monday and cleared enough to settle my bill here at the Madison House with $2 over. I had a highly fashionable audience, but Norfolk is a small place and there were two exhibitions the same night. Next Monday I lecture again here and expect to have a large audience. On Tuesday I start for Philadelphia to attend to Mrs. Loud's poems — and *possibly* on Thursday I may start for New York. If I do I will go straight over to Mrs. Lewis's and send for you. It will be better for me not to go to Fordham — don't you think so? Write immediately in reply and direct to Philadelphia. For fear I should not get the letter sign no name and address it to *E. S. T. Grey, Esqre*. *If possible* I will get married before I start, but there is no telling. Give my dearest love to Mrs. L. My poor, poor Muddy, I am still unable to send you even one dollar, — but keep [up heart — I hope that our troubles are nearly over. I saw John Beatty in Norfolk.

God bless and protect you, my own darling Muddy. I showed your letter to Elmira, and she says "it is such a darling precious letter that she loves you for it already."

YOUR OWN EDDY.

Don't forget to write immediately to Philadelphia so that your letter will be there when I arrive.

The papers here are praising me to death — and I have been received everywhere with enthusiasm. Be sure and preserve all the printed scraps I have] sent you and keep up my file of the "Literary World." [1]

On Saturday, September 22, Mrs. Shelton, at Poe's request, wrote her first letter to Mrs. Clemm, which proves her engagement on her part. She says, "I have just spent a very happy evening with your dear Edgar, and I know it will be gratifying to you to know that he is all that you could desire him to be, sober, temperate, moral, & much beloved." [2]

Poe repeated his lecture on "The Poetic Principle" on Monday, September 24, in the

[1] Poe to Mrs. Clemm, MS.; where bracketed, MS. copy. A portion of this letter was published by Burr, *loc. cit.*

[2] Mrs. Shelton to Mrs. Clemm, MS. The letter, which was of an intimate character and therefore suppressed in the former biography, when Mrs. Shelton was still alive, has been partially published in *The Virginia Poe*, xvii, 396.

Exchange Hotel, to a good audience, and was well noticed by the press.

To Mrs. Weiss, who then looked on Poe with the romantic interest of a young poetess as well as with a woman's sympathy with sadness so confessed as his, is due the most lifelike and detailed portrait of him that exists and the most vivid account of him in these last Richmond days. Erect in stature, cold, impassive, almost haughty in manner, soberly and fastidiously clad in black, to a stranger's eye he wore a look of distinction rather than beauty; on nearer approach one was more struck by the strongly marked head, with the broad brow, the black curly hair brushed back, the pallid, careworn, and in repose the somewhat haggard features, while beneath the concealment of a short black mustache one saw the slight habitual contraction of the mouth and occasionally the quick, almost imperceptible curl of the upper lip in scorn — a sneer, it is said, that was easily excited; but the physical fascination of the man was felt, at last, to lie in his eyes, large, jet-black, with a steel-gray iris, clear as crystal, restless, ever expanding and contracting as, responsive with intelligence and emotion, they bent their full, open, steady, unshrinking gaze from under the long black lashes that shaded them. He visited the houses where he was intimate, but was also seen in general society. His sister, Rosalie, who adored her distinguished brother, was greatly pleased to see him made much of, and shadowed him as he went about, sometimes inconveniently. She lived to be old, and the Civil War having broken up the home of the MacKenzies, she wandered about among charitable homes and was at last received into the Epiphany Church Home at Washington, where she died June 14, 1874. This last summer with Poe, of whom she was so proud, was the happiest of her life, as she saw him in their common circle into which both had been adopted in childhood. The old, familiar society and ways of living were scarcely less grateful to Poe; on meeting his friends his face would brighten with pleasure, his features lost the worn look and his reserve its coldness; to men he was cordial, to women he showed deference; and in society with the young he forgot his melancholy, listened with amusement, or joined in their repartees with evident pleasure, though he would soon leave them for a seat in the portico, or a walk in the grounds with a single friend. To the eyes of his young girlish friend, Miss Talley, he seemed invariably cheerful, and often even playful in mood. Once only was he noticeably cast down; it was when visiting the old deserted Mayo place, called The Hermitage, where he used to go frequently in his youth, and the scene was so picturesque that it is worth giving at length: —

"On reaching the place our party separated, and Poe and myself strolled slowly about the grounds. I observed that he was unusually silent and preoccupied, and, attributing it to the influence of memories associated with the place, forbore to interrupt him. He passed slowly by the mossy bench called the 'lovers' seat,' beneath two aged trees, and remarked, as we turned toward the garden, 'There used to be white violets here.' Searching amid the tangled wilderness of shrubs, we found a few late blossoms, some of which he placed carefully between the leaves of a note-book. Entering the deserted house, he passed from room to room with a grave, abstracted look, and removed his hat, as if involuntarily, on entering the saloon, where in old times many a brilliant company had assembled. Seated in one of the deep windows, over which now grew masses of ivy, his memory must have borne him back to former scenes, for he repeated the familiar lines of Moore: —

"'I feel like one
Who treads alone
Some banquet hall deserted,'

and paused, with the first expression of real sadness that I had ever seen on his face. The light of the setting sun shone through the drooping ivy-boughs into the ghostly room, and the tattered and mildewed paper-hangings, with their faded tracery of rose-garlands, waved fitfully in the autumn breeze. An inexpressibly eerie feeling came over me, which I can even now recall, and as I stood there, my old childish idea of the poet as a spirit of mingled light and darkness recurred strongly to my imagination." [1]

Poe talked with his young friend about his plans and hopes; about the restrictions on criticism which are imposed by personal friendship and editorial prepossessions, and from which even he could not wholly free himself; about his New York friends, the misconstructions his nature suffered under even among those who knew him, and other confidential topics that the charm of his listener and his own readiness to indulge in female intimacies beguiled him into. In particular it should be noticed that he showed her a letter from Griswold, accepting his commis-

[1] *Scribner's Magazine*, xv, 5, p. 712 (March, 1878).

sion to edit his works in case of his sudden death.

In order to wind up his affairs in New York and to bring Mrs. Clemm to Richmond, as preliminaries of his marriage, Poe decided to go North. Poe is said to have himself written to Mrs. Clemm that the ceremony was fixed for October 17.[1] He told his friends at Richmond that he would return within two weeks, and expressed his intention to reside thereafter in that city, where there was some talk of his joining the staff of the "Examiner." On the day before leaving, Tuesday, September 25, he passed the evening at Mrs. Talley's, where he had a long conversation with her daughter, in which he spoke of his future, "seeming to anticipate it with eager delight, like that of youth," and, Mrs. Weiss adds, "he declared that the last few weeks in the society of his old and new friends had been the happiest that he had known for many years, and that when he again left New York he should there leave behind all the trouble and vexation of his past life." [2] That night he spent with his friends at Duncan Lodge, and sat late at his window, smoking and silent. The next day he passed in the city with some

[1] Didier, 110. [2] *Scribner's Magazine, loc. cit.*

male friends, sent a note by Rosalie for Mrs. Weiss, enclosing the poem "For Annie," and spent the evening with Mrs. Shelton. She says, writing October 11, "He came up to my house on the evening of the 26th Sept. to take leave of me. He was very sad, and complained of being quite sick. I felt his pulse, and found he had considerable fever, and did not think it probable he would be able to start the next morning (Thursday) as he anticipated. I felt so wretched about him all that night, that I went up early the next morning to inquire after him, when, much to my regret, he had left in the boat for Baltimore."[1] On his walk back from Mrs. Shelton's he stopped at Dr. John Carter's office, as was his custom, and, without mentioning his intention of leaving for Baltimore that night, took his friend's Malacca cane and went to take a late supper across the street, at Sadler's restaurant. There he met some acquaintances, who kept company with him until very late and then accompanied him to the boat, where, as is said, they left him sober and cheerful. He, however, had left his trunk and baggage at the hotel, and

[1] Mrs. Shelton to Mrs. Clemm. *The Poe-Chivers Papers, loc. cit.* This letter, written two weeks after the facts, settles the date on which Poe left Richmond.

from all the circumstances it would seem that his decision to go to Baltimore that night was suddenly executed. The boat left at four o'clock the next morning, September 27, and arrived at Baltimore about twenty-four hours later, early on Friday, the 28th.

Poe wandered in Baltimore or its neighborhood for five days. It is known that he called on his old Baltimore friend, Dr. N. C. Brooks, partially intoxicated, and not finding him at home went away. It is said that he was invited to a birthday party and could not refuse a pledge to his hostess.[1] It is said that he dined with some old military friends. It is said that he took the train to Philadelphia, but either because he was in a wrong car or because the river was in flood, he was brought back from Havre de Grace in a state of stupor. It is said that he was captured by an election gang, drugged, and made to vote at several places. The basis of these statements is lost; in view of the tragic consequences, it was natural that any who shared in his last days should keep silence, and there is no decisive direct evidence to any of these reports, which may be correctly described as rumors. It is plain enough what happened; there is no mystery

[1] *The Virginia Poe*, i, 319.

about it. Just as when in the summer of 1847 at Philadelphia[1] he was saved by a friend, just as when in the summer of 1848 at Boston he was saved by a friend, just as when in the summer of 1849 he was saved by Burr, he had experienced one of those repeated attacks, worse at each return, and of whose fatal issue he had been often warned, and he had found no friend by to save him. On the sixth day, Wednesday, October 3, he was picked up unconscious near one of the rumshops used for voting, Ryan's Fourth Ward Polls. The absence of his baggage, the state of his clothes, his entire condition were a repetition of his experience in Philadelphia. It is a trifling but interesting detail that the Malacca cane had stuck to him through all his adventures; had he been drugged and made to vote in any violent manner, as was represented, it could hardly have failed to be separated from him. A printer recognized him and sent the following note to his old friend, Dr. Snodgrass: —

[1] Poe to —— (the editor of *Graham's*), August 10, 1847. *The Virginia Poe*, i, 270. "Without your aid at the precise moment and in the precise manner in which you rendered it, it is more than probable that I should not now be alive to write you this letter."

BALTIMORE CITY, October 3, 1849.

There is a gentleman, rather the worse for wear, at Ryan's Fourth Ward Polls, who goes under the cognomen of Edgar A. Poe, and who appears in great distress. He says he is acquainted with you, and I assure you he is in need of immediate assistance.

JOSEPH W. WILSON.[1]

To DR. J. E. SNODGRASS.

Dr. Snodgrass called at Ryan's, and Mr. Herring, Poe's relative, who had also been summoned, came to the scene. Between them they put Poe, with the cane, into a carriage, and he was taken to the Washington Hospital, where he was admitted, still unconscious, at 5 P. M. Neilson Poe was also notified, visited the hospital, and sent whatever was necessary. Poe remained in an alarming delirium, with such intervals of apparent sanity as he had shown in his ravings with Sartain. Mrs. Moran, the wife of the resident physician, in his last hours read to him, she says, "the fourteenth

[1] New York *Herald*, March 27, 1881. Cf. *The Virginia Poe*, i, 328 *et seq.*,where a summary with extracts is given from *The Facts of Poe's Death and Burial* (by Snodgrass), *Beadle's Monthly*, 1867, and the examination of this by Mr. Spencer, in the *Herald*.

chapter of St. John's Gospel, gave him a quieting draught, wiped the beads of perspiration from his face, smoothed his pillow, and left him."[1] It is the only mention of religion in his entire life. This was on Sunday, October 7. Shortly after, about five o'clock, he died.

The story of the last days, taken from contemporary documents, is as follows. Dr. Moran wrote: —

BALTIMORE CITY MARINE HOSPITAL,
November 15, '49.

MRS. CLEMM:

My dear Madam, — I take the earliest opportunity of responding to yours of the 9th inst., which came to hand by yesterday's mail. . . .

But now for the required intelligence. Presuming you are already aware of the malady of which Mr. Poe died, I need only state concisely the particulars of his circumstances from his entrance until his decease.

When brought to the hospital he was unconscious of his condition — who brought him or with whom he had been associating. He remained in this condition from five o'clock in the afternoon — the hour of his admission — until three next morning. This was on the 3d October.

[1] *The Virginia Poe*, i, 337.

To this state succeeded tremor of the limbs, and at first a busy but not violent or active delirium — constant talking — and vacant converse with spectral and imaginary objects on the walls. His face was pale and his whole person drenched in perspiration. We were unable to induce tranquillity before the second day after his admission.

Having left orders with the nurses to that effect, I was summoned to his bedside so soon as consciousness supervened, and questioned him in reference to his family, place of residence, relatives, etc. But his answers were incoherent and unsatisfactory. He told me, however, he had a wife in Richmond (which I have since learned was not the fact), that he did not know when he left that city or what had become of his trunk of clothing. Wishing to rally and sustain his now fast sinking hopes, I told him I hoped that in a few days he would be able to enjoy the society of his friends here and I would be most happy to contribute in every possible way to his ease and comfort. At this he broke out with much energy, and said the best thing his best friend could do would be to blow out his brains with a pistol — that when he beheld his degradation he was ready to sink into the earth, etc. Shortly after giving expression to these words Mr. Poe seemed to doze, and I left him for a short time. When I returned I found him in a violent delirium, resisting the efforts of two nurses to keep him in bed. This state continued until Saturday evening (he was admitted on Wednesday), when he commenced calling for one "Reynolds," which he did through the night until *three* on Sunday morning. At this time a very decided change began to affect him. Having become enfeebled from exertion, he became quiet and seemed to rest for a short time; then gently moving his head, he said, "*Lord help my poor soul*," and expired!

This, Madam, is as faithful an account as I am able to furnish from the Record of his case. . . .

His remains were visited by some of the first individuals of the city, many of them anxious to have a lock of his hair. . . .

Respectfully yours,

J. J. MORAN, *Res. Phys.*[1]

[1] Moran to Mrs. Clemm, MS. The omitted portions are of no interest. The different dates and additional circumstances given many years afterward by Dr. Moran in the press, and in *A Defense of Edgar Allan Poe: Life, Character, and Dying Declarations of the Poet: An Official Account of his Death by his Attending Physician, John J. Moran, M. D.*, Washington,

The undistinguished funeral took place on Monday, October 8, and three days later Neilson Poe wrote to Mrs. Clemm:—

BALTIMORE, October 11, 1849.

MY DEAR MADAM, — . . . He died on Sunday morning, about five o'clock, at the Washington Medical College, where he had been since the Wednesday preceding. At what time he arrived in this city, where he spent the time he was here, or under what circumstances, I have been unable to ascertain. It appears that on Wednesday he was seen and recognized at one of the places of election in old town, and that his condition was such as to render it necessary to send him to the College, where he was tenderly nursed until the time of his death. As soon as I heard that he was at the College I went over; but his physician did not think it advisable that I should see him, as he was very excitable. The next day I called, and sent him changes of linen, etc., and was gratified to learn that he was much better, and I was never so much shocked, in my life, as when, on Sunday morning, notice was sent me that he was dead. Mr. Herring and myself im-

D. C., 1885, must give way to the statements here made when the event was fresh in his memory.

mediately took the necessary steps for his funeral, which took place on Monday afternoon at four o'clock. . . . The body was followed to the grave by Mr. Herring, Dr. Snodgrass, Mr. Z. Collins Lee (an old classmate), and myself. The service was performed by the Rev. William T. D. Clemm, a son of James S. Clemm. Mr. Herring and myself have sought, in vain, for the trunk and clothes of Edgar — there is reason to believe that he was robbed of them, whilst in such a condition as to render him insensible of his loss. . . .

Truly your friend and servant,

NEILSON POE.[1]

MRS. MARIA CLEMM.

Three days after Poe's death, Kennedy, who was on the ground, his earliest friend and life-long well-wisher, wrote in his diary the passage from which some brief extracts have already been made: —

Wednesday, Oct. 10, 1849.

On Sunday last Edgar A. Poe died in town here at the hospital from the effects of a debauch. He had been to Richmond, was return-

[1] Neilson Poe to Mrs. Clemm, MS. The omitted portions are of no interest.

ing to New York, where he lived, and, I understand, was soon to be married to a lady in Richmond of quite good fortune. He fell in with some companions here who seduced him to the bottle, which it was said he had renounced some time ago. The consequence was fever, delirium, and madness, and in a few days a termination of his sad career in the hospital. Poor Poe! He was an original and exquisite poet, and one of the best prose writers in this country. His works are amongst the very best of their kind. His taste was replete with classical flavor, and he wrote in the spirit of an old Greek philosopher.

It is many years ago — I think perhaps as early as 1833 or 4 — that I found him in Baltimore in a state of starvation. I gave him clothing, free access to my table, and the use of a horse for exercise whenever he chose — in fact brought him up from the very verge of despair.

I then got him employment with Mr. White in one department of the editorship of the "Southern Literary Messenger" at Richmond. His talent made that periodical quite brilliant whilst he was connected with it. But he was irregular, eccentric, and querulous, and soon gave up his place for other employments of the same character in Philadelphia and New York. His destiny in these places was as sad and fickle as in Richmond.

He always remembered my kindness with gratitude, as his many letters to me testify. He is gone. A bright but unsteady light has been awfully quenched.[1]

Shortly after, Poe's remaining writings were published by the editors or friends who had copies. To mention only the first issue in each case, "Annabel Lee," the simplest and sweetest of his ballads, appeared in the New York "Tribune"; "The Bells," that wonderful onomatopoetic experiment, in "Sartain's" for November; an essay "On Critics and Criticism," in "Graham's" for January, 1850; and in October following, "The Poetic Principle," in "Sartain's."

Meanwhile words, like Kennedy's for kindness, were spoken to the world by Poe's friends and associates over the still recent grave. Graham wrote of him as seen in the editorial office and spoke with most authority of the professional side of his career: "For three or four years I knew him intimately, and for eighteen months

[1] Kennedy MSS.

saw him almost daily, much of the time writing or conversing at the same desk, knowing all his hopes, his fears, and little annoyances of life as well as his high-hearted struggle with adverse fate; yet he was always the same polished gentleman, the quiet, unobtrusive, thoughtful scholar, the devoted husband, frugal in his personal expenses, punctual and unwearied in his industry, *and the soul of honor* in all his transactions. This, of course, was in his better days, and by them *we* judge the man. But even after his habits had changed, there was no literary man to whom I would more readily advance money for labor to be done. . . . The very natural question, 'Why did he not work and thrive?' is easily answered. It will not be *asked* by the many who know the precarious tenure by which literary men hold a mere living in this country. The avenues through which they can profitably reach the country are few, and crowded with aspirants for bread, as well as fame. The unfortunate tendency to cheapen every literary work to the lowest point of beggarly flimsiness in price and profit prevents even the well-disposed from extending anything like an adequate support to even a part of the great throng which genius, talent, education, and even misfortune, force

Facsimile of original MS.
By courtesy of Mrs. Isaac M. Dyckman

Annabel Lee.

By Edgar A. Poe.

It was many and many a year ago,
In a kingdom by the sea,
That a maiden there lived whom you may know
By the name of Annabel Lee; —
And this maiden she lived with no other thought
Than to love and be loved by me.

She was a child and I was a child,
In this kingdom by the sea,
But we loved with a love that was more than love —
I and my Annabel Lee —
With a love that the wingéd seraphs of Heaven
Coveted her and me.

And this was the reason that, long ago,
In this kingdom by the sea,
A wind blew out of a cloud by night
Chilling my Annabel Lee;
So that her high-born kinsmen came
And bore her away from me,
To shut her up, in a sepulchre
In this kingdom by the sea.

The angels, not half so happy in Heaven,
Went envying her and me: —
Yes! that was the reason (as all men know,
In this kingdom by the sea)
That the wind came out of the cloud, chilling
And killing my Annabel Lee.

But our love it was stronger by far than the love
Of those who were older than we —
Of many far wiser than we —
And neither the angels in Heaven above
Nor the demons down under the sea
Can ever dissever my soul from the soul
Of the beautiful Annabel Lee: —

For the moon never beams without bringing me dreams
Of the beautiful Annabel Lee;
And the stars never rise but I see the bright eyes
Of the beautiful Annabel Lee;
And so, all the night-tide, I lie down by the side
Of my darling, my darling, my life and my bride
In her sepulchre there by the sea —
In her tomb by the side of the sea.

into the struggle. The character of Poe's mind was of such an order as not to be very widely in demand. The class of educated mind which he could readily and profitably address was small — the channels through which he could do so at all were few — and publishers all, or nearly all, contented with such pens as were already engaged, hesitated to incur the expense of his to an extent which would sufficiently remunerate him; hence, when he was fairly at sea, connected permanently with no publication, he suffered all the horrors of prospective destitution, with scarcely the ability of providing for immediate necessities. . . . Let the moralist, who stands upon 'tufted carpet,' and surveys his smoking board, the fruits of his individual toil or mercantile adventure, pause before he let the anathema, trembling upon his lips, fall upon a man like Poe, who, wandering from publisher to publisher, with his fine, print-like manuscript, scrupulously clean and neatly rolled, finds no market for his brain — with despair at heart, misery ahead, for himself and his loved ones, and gaunt famine dogging at his heels, thus sinks by the wayside, before the demon that watches his steps and whispers *oblivion*."[1] Willis, his New York

[1] *Graham's Magazine*, March, 1850.

chief, whose description of their collaboration has already been given, wrote of their later friendly, though never intimate, acquaintance: "He frequently called on us afterwards at our place of business, and we met him often in the street, — invariably the same sad-mannered, winning, and refined gentleman such as we had always known him," and found in his letters to himself — friendly business notes — sufficient evidence of "the very qualities denied to Mr. Poe, — humility, willingness to persevere, belief in another's kindness, and capability of cordial and grateful friendship! Such he assuredly was *when sane*. Such only he has invariably seemed to us, in all we have happened personally to know of him, through a friendship of five or six years. And so much easier is it to believe what we have seen and known than what we *hear of* only, that we remember him but with admiration and respect."[1] Mrs. Osgood, writing on her deathbed, with the same limitation, but brightening memory within the little bound, said: "I have never *seen* him otherwise than gentle, generous, well-bred, and fastidiously refined. To a sensitive and delicately nurtured woman there was a peculiar and irre-

[1] *Home Journal*, October 12, 1849.

sistible charm in the chivalric, graceful, and almost tender reverence with which he invariably approached all women who won his respect. It was this which first commanded and always retained my regard for him."[1] Mrs. Whitman said: "He was essentially and instinctively a gentleman."[2] Mrs. Shelton said: "He was a gentleman in every sense of the word. He was one of the most fascinating and refined men I ever knew. I never saw him under the influence of wine."[3] Burr, who knew him in his worst hours, said, characterizing him: "He was also, in the core of his heart, a grateful, single-minded, loving kind of man. . . . A very gentle, thoughtful, scrupulously refined, and modest kind of man. . . . That he had faults and many weaknesses is, also, too true. But that he had a congregation of virtues which made him loved as well as admired by those who knew him best, is also true."[4] Mrs. Clemm, who lived on charity till past her eightieth year and died in the Church Home at Baltimore, February 16, 1871, so long the faithful guardian of his life, wrote

[1] Griswold, lii.

[2] Mrs. Whitman to Gill, August, 1873.

[3] *Appleton's Journal*, May, 1878.

[4] *The Nineteenth Century*, *loc. cit.*

to Willis in the first moments of her grief: "Say what an affectionate son he was to me, his poor desolate mother." [1] This is the sheaf of memories that was laid upon his grave.

[1] Mrs. Clemm to Willis. *Home Journal*, October 12, 1849.

APPENDIX

APPENDIX A

I. THE HOMES OF POE AT RICHMOND

THOMAS H. ELLIS TO THE AUTHOR

No. 11 Cathedral Street, BALTIMORE, MD.
May 28, 1884.

Dear Sir, — So much delay has taken place in my answering your letter of the 5th instant that I think I ought to make an explanation of it.

At the time of the receipt of your letter I happened to be specially engaged with matters of some urgency; but as soon as I could conveniently do so I looked into the old mercantile books of Ellis & Allan with the view to furnish you the information you desired. Before I was able to give you the result of my examination, however, I was called to Baltimore, where I expect hereafter to reside, and since my arrival in this city my engagements have been such as to prevent my writing such a letter as I had contemplated.

I will now give you, as nearly as I could ascertain, the dates of Mr. Allan's departure for England and his return to Richmond.

On the 17th of June, 1815, John Allan is charged in the Cash Account of Ellis & Allan with £335.10.6 paid him, and on the same day with 2*s.* 3*d.* paid for drayage of his baggage, and on the 21st of June with 12*s.* paid for boatage of his baggage; and on the 1st of July he is credited with £2.11.9 sent back by him in a letter from the Capes. My conclusion from these entries is that he went on board of a ship in James River (with his wife, Mrs. Frances Keeling Allan, his sister-in-law, Miss Anne Moore Valentine, and his adopted son, Edgar Allan Poe) on or about the 17th of June, 1815; and I believe the name of the ship was the Lothair.

From various entries it appears that he furnished his own stores for the voyage, which were in part purchased in Richmond, and in part sent to him from Norfolk, as he passed through Hampton Roads, by the firm of Moses Myers & Sons.

There was a sale of some of his household furniture and effects made before he left Richmond, by the auction and commission house of Moncure, Robinson & Pleasants. Among other small bills and accounts paid for him, and charged to his account after his departure, was one of Fitzwhylsonn & Potter, booksellers, in which I noticed these items: One "Olive Branch," one "Murray's Reader," two "Murray's Spelling Books"; cost for the four books 16*s.* 6*d.*; which I doubt not were intended for Edgar Poe's instruction on the voyage.

The letter book of Ellis & Allan shows letters written for the firm by John Allan, dated in Richmond, August 5, 1820, to John Noble, of London, Ewart, Myers & Co., Liverpool, Charles Denny, Glasgow, and to William Taylor, Thomas S. Coles, and A. Saltmarsh (who were the "Inspectors" of Allan & Ellis), London. The last-mentioned letter contains this passage: "Our Mr. Allan arrived here a few days ago, and we hasten to enclose you Messrs. John & William Gilliat's first of exchange of set No. 1, on Messrs. John Gilliat & Co., London, of this date, at sixty days after sight, for one thousand pounds sterling; which we have no doubt will be duly honoured; being for the General Fund; and we shall remit you at least £4000 more in the course of this month." [Which promise was complied with by further remittances on the 10th, 18th, and 28th days of the same month, and an additional £5000 Stg. sent in October following.]

On the 19th of August, 1820, is a letter, copied in the letter book, from John Allan to Maitland & Coles, London, in which he says, "I arrived at this place" [Richmond] "on the 2d instant"; and on the 22d of August another letter from him, to William Taylor, of London, in which he says, "I arrived at New York on the 21st of July after a passage of thirty-six days." [The ocean, he adds, was very rough during the greater part of their voyage, and Mrs. Allan and Miss Valentine suffered exceedingly from sea-sickness. They all complained of the extreme heat which they found on their arrival in New York.]

After Mr. Allan's return to Richmond, he, his wife, Miss Valentine, and Edgar Poe spent the greater part of the first year with my father at his residence on the southwest corner of Franklin and 2d streets. After that, he occupied a long low frame house with dormer windows, fronting west, on 5th Street, with Bishop Moore, Mr. James Brown, Jr., Dr. James Greenhow, and other well-known gentlemen, as his neighbors. At a later day he occupied a house which in the mean time had been left to him by his uncle, Mr. William Galt [who died March 26, 1823], situated at the northwest corner of 14th Street and Tobacco Alley, fronting what is now the west side of the Exchange Hotel; but the building has been greatly changed of late years, and at present it is remarkable for its unusual height and slender proportions. While living there he bought the house at the intersection of Main and 5th streets, — the southeast corner, — which was built by Mr. David Meade Randolph, bought by Mr. Joseph Gallego, and occupied by the last-named gentleman until his death, in 1818. In 1822 Mr. John Richard became the purchaser of it, at $19,100, but Mr. Richard dying, in 1824, before he had completed his payments for it and before a title had been made to him, it was sold by his executrix, at public auction, and bought by John Allan for the price of $14,950, the conveyance to him being made by Peter Joseph Chevallie, as surviving executor of the last will and testament of Joseph Gallego deceased, and Mary Richard, as executrix of the last will and testament of John Richard deceased, and dated June the 28th, 1825. From the time of Mr. Gallego's death until it was taken possession of by Mr. Allan, it was occupied by Mr. Peter J. Chevallie, whose beautiful, graceful, and most accomplished daughter, Miss Sallie Magee Chevallie, married afterwards Mr. Abraham Warwick, an intimate friend of Mr. Allan.

At the time of Mr. Allan's purchase the house had not much more than one half of its present front; a large addition having been made to it, by the late Mrs. Louisa G. Allan, after the death of her husband, and when her three sons were growing up, with tastes for gay and fashionable society, in which their mother (but always with admirable taste and good judgment) participated with them.

In the old house, the small room on the right as you enter the spacious hall from the front door was the morning-reception and tea room; the large octagon room on that floor, with its entrance fronting the front door, was the dining-room; the octagon room, of the same size, upstairs, was the parlor; Mr. Allan's chamber was on the parlor floor, in the front of the house, over the hall and over the front door, with windows looking into the front yard; on the north side of the house, upstairs, upon the parlor floor, were three chambers — one occupied by Miss Valentine, one by Edgar Poe, and one for guests; Edgar's, if I mistake not, was the one with a window fronting east and another window fronting north: and this was before the Second Baptist Church was built, or any other house on Mr. Allan's square, or any house on the square next below, except Dr. Nelson's and the one adjoining it at the southwest corner of Main and 7th streets, and before Messrs. Fleming and Joseph S. James had built their fine residences on the north side of Main Street between 6th and 7th; so that he had an unobstructed view of the city (including the capitol) lying east of 6th Street, and an extensive view of James River, of Manchester on the south side of the river, and of the country stretching on either side of the river, into both Henrico and Chesterfield counties. On the south side of the house there was an unusually large portico extending the full depth of the house, and into which you easily passed, when downstairs, from both the reception room and the dining-room, and, when upstairs, from both Mr. Allan's chamber and the parlor. This portico was indeed, and is, the grand feature of the house; and was as much used, in all favorable weather, for both family and company purposes, as any portion of the house. It was the delight of all boys and girls, who were either intimate enough to run in at all times, or who were invited to entertainments there; for there was a splendid swing securely fastened to the top of the upper portico, and Mr. Allan, who was fond of astronomy, had brought with him from England a fine telescope, through which his young friends (and no man was fonder of children than he) many a time looked with wondering eyes. The garden below was a double one, being for vegetables on the east side of the house, and for fruits, flowers, and shrubbery on the south side. Mr. Gallego was a native of Andalusia, and being, perhaps, naturally fond of grapes, and the slope of the hill being a favorable exposure for them, and the soil and location also suitable for figs and raspberries, these three fruits I recollect grew there in abundance and to perfection.

At that time there were but few houses in the immediate neighborhood; my father-in-law, Mr. Thomas Taylor (whose oldest daughter, Mary, married Mr. William Galt, Jr., a cousin of Mr. Allan's), lived at the corner immediately in front (the southwest corner of Main and 5th streets), and he owned that entire square; Mr. Joseph Tate, who for thirteen years was mayor of the city of Richmond, lived at the northwest corner; at the northeast corner was the residence of Major James Gibbon, commonly known as "the hero of Stony Point," and who for thirty-six years was collector of the port of Richmond; just below, on 5th Street, at the southeast corner of Cary, was Mr. Joseph Marx's residence, and immediately in front of that, Mr. Thomas Gilliat's. Mr. Marx had built for his son-in-law, Mr. Myer Myers, a house on a part of his garden, fronting on 5th Street, and at the corner below Mr. Myers', on the opposite side of the street, was Mr. William Munford's old residence. Mr. Edmund W. Rootes, at or about the time to which I refer, built the house, fronting east, on 5th Street, between Main and Franklin, in which Mr. John Enders lives; and Mr. (Scotch) James Brown owned and had long lived in the fine old frame house, which has recently been taken down, at the southwest corner of Franklin and 5th streets.

These gentlemen were of the highest social position in Richmond; they were the friends and associates of Chief Justice Marshall, Mr. Wickham, Colonel Ambler, Dr. Brockenbrough, Judge Nicholas, Judge Cabell, Judge Stanard, Mr. Leigh, Mr. Chapman Johnson, Mr. Ritchie, Mr. Lyons, and others who were well known in that community; Mr. Allan's relations to all whom I have named were of the most friendly character; and the habits of hospitality among them — the habit especially of giving dinner and whist parties — was different from anything that I know of at this day.

All of Edgar Poe's early associations were consequently among the most highly educated and agreeable people in that community.

I am very respectfully yours,

THOMAS H. ELLIS.[1]

II. THE POE-DUANE LETTERS

The postscript of Poe's letter to Mrs. Clemm, April 7, 1844, — "Be sure and take home the 'Messenger' to Hirst," — though a matter of the most trifling detail, is worth explanation, since the circumstance to which it relates is yet remembered to Poe's discredit in Philadelphia, while the whole paltry affair furnishes a capital illustration of the mean though natural misconstruction to which he was sometimes exposed. The story is completely told in the following papers. William Duane, to whom the letters are addressed, was at one time Secretary of the Treasury.

[1] Cf. "The Tabernacle Site," "The Home of Poe's Boyhood," *Richmond Despatch*, March 18, 1894; "Historic Homes of Richmond. — The Allan House," by Louisa Allan Mayo, *Richmond News Illustrated Saturday Magazine*, July 28, 1900.

NEW YORK, October 28, '44.

MY DEAR SIR, — Owing to my absence from this city (where I am now residing), I did not receive your letter of the 15th until this morning.

I regret exceedingly that circumstances should have led you to think me negligent, or uncourteous, in not returning the volume of the "Messenger" — for one or the other (perhaps both) you must long since have considered me. The facts are these: Some eight months ago, I believe, I chanced to mention, in Mr. Hirst's hearing, that I wished to look over a particular article in the "Messenger." He immediately volunteered to procure me the desired volume from you. I would much rather have borrowed it personally — but he seemed to make a point of the matter and I consented. Soon afterwards he handed me the book, which I retained a very short time. It is now certainly more than seven months since I returned it to Mr. Hirst, through my mother-in-law (Mrs. Clemm), who informs me that she left it at his office, with one of his brothers. Most probably it was deposited in a book-case, and thus overlooked and forgotten. May I trouble you to send for it.

Very truly yours,

EDGAR ALLAN POE.

WILLIAM DUANE, Esqr.

Endorsed by Duane: N. B. The statement contained in this letter that the volume of "The Southern Literary Messenger" in question was returned to Henry B. Hirst, Esqr. was pronounced by Mr. Hirst to be "a damned lie," and subsequent events showed that Mr. Hirst was right in denying it — Mr. Poe having sold the book — I hope unintentionally — to William A. Leary, the bookseller on Second St.

W. D.

New York, January 28, '45.

Sir, — Richmond is the last place in which I should have hoped to find a copy of either the 1st, 2d, or 3d volumes of the "Messenger." For this reason I did not apply there. I have [been] putting myself, however, to some trouble in endeavoring to collect among my friends here the separate numbers of the missing volume. I am glad that your last letter relieves me from all such trouble in future. I do not choose to recognize you in this matter at all. To the person of whom I borrowed the book, or rather who insisted on forcing it on me, I have sufficient reason to believe that it was returned. Settle your difficulties with him, and insult me with no more of your communications.

Edgar A. Poe.

Mr. Duane.

Endorsed by Duane: Bombastes Furioso Poe. Dated January 28, 1845. Received January 31, 1845. Not to be answered. N. B. The volume of "The Southern Literary Messenger" to which this letter, and that of October 28, 1844, refer, was lent by me to E. A. Poe, through Henry B. Hirst, Esq., and was sold by the said Poe among a lot of books belonging to himself to William A. Leary, a bookseller on North Seventh Street. Mr. Leary sold it to a bookseller in Richmond, Va., who sold it to the publishers of the "Messenger," who sold it to a friend of mine who was visiting Richmond, and whom I had commissioned to purchase me a copy. My name was on the title-page during all these sales.

Poe had the grace to be ashamed of himself, when he heard of the manner in which I had had to repurchase my own book. He remarked to H. B. Hirst, Esqr., "What must Mr. Duane think of me," on hearing of which, I sent him word that I thought he ought to send me the five dollars which the repurchase had cost me. He died without doing so, I suppose from inability.

W. D.[1]

Poe's innocence in the matter seems to be proved by the postscript to Mrs. Clemm, nor is there any reason to believe that the original mistake, by which the volume was included in the sale of Poe's books, was anything but a natural blunder made in the confusion of the removal. The set of the "Messenger" in question, now owned in Richmond, contains Poe's emendations in pencil, and shows that he used the volumes in his work of revision, and also for printing. The leaves of "Hans Phaal" were torn out and passed through the hands of at least three printers and have their "take" marks; they were then skillfully replaced. This fact and other indications point to the use of this volume in the publication of the "Tales of the Arabesque and Grotesque," 1840.

III. LOWELL'S LETTERS TO BRIGGS

"January 16, 1845.

"I received this morning the two numbers of your 'Broadway Journal,' & am in haste to tell you how much I like it. . . . The article upon Miss Barrett is extremely well written, I suppose by Poe. It is a good *telling* article, though I do not agree with it in its conclusion. From a paragraph I saw yesterday in the 'Tribune' I find that

[1] Poe to Duane. MS.

Poe has been at me in the 'Mirror.' He has at least the chief element of a critic — a disregard of persons. He will be a very valuable contributor to you."

"August 8, 1845.

"I am glad to hear that the conduct of Poe and Biscoe about the B. J. was not so bad as I had feared."

"August 21, 1845.

"Poe, I am afraid, is wholly lacking in that element of manhood which, for want of a better name, we call *character*. It is something quite distinct from genius, — though all great geniuses are endowed with it. Hence we always think of Dante Alighieri, of Michael Angelo, of Will Shakespeare, of John Milton — while of such men as Gibbon & Hume we merely recall the works, & think of them as the author of this and that. As I prognosticated, I have made Poe my enemy by doing him a service. In the last B. J. he has accused me of plagiarism, and *misquoted* Wordsworth to sustain his charge. 'Armor *rustling* on the walls, On the blood of Clifford calls,' he quotes, italicizing '*rustling*' as the point of resemblance. The word is really '*rusting*.' You will find the passage in Wordsworth's 'Song sung at Brougham Castle,' &c. My metaphor was drawn from some old Greek or Roman story which was in my mind, and which Poe, who makes such a scholar of himself, ought to have known. There is a similar incident in Chaucer's Knight's Tale, probably from the same source. Any one who had ever read the *whole* of Wordsworth's poem would see that there was no resemblance between the two passages. Poe wishes to kick down the ladder by which he rose. He is welcome. But he does not attack me at a weak point. He probably cannot conceive of anybody's writing for anything but a newspaper reputation, or for posthumous fame, which is but the same thing magnified by distance. I have quite other aims. . . . How can I expect to be understood, much more to have my poetry understood, by such a man as Poe. I cannot understand the meanness of men. They seem to trace everything to selfishness. Why, Brackett ('the sculptor,' as he is called,) actually asked Carter how much Poe paid me for writing my notice of him in 'Graham's Magazine.' Did such baseness ever enter the head of man? Why, it could not get into the head of a *dog*, even if had *three* heads like Cerberus."

"November 25, 1849.

"What a contemptible idea of me Willis must have to think that anything Poe might say of me would make any difference in my feeling pity for his poor mother-in-law. I confess it does not raise my opinion of Willis. I knew before, as well as I know now, that Poe *must* have been abusing me, for he knew that ever since his conduct towards you about the 'Broadway Journal' I had thought meanly of him. My 'pleasant letter' to W. was about ten lines, less rather than more, I fancy, & my 'generous donation' was five dollars! I particularly requested of him that it should be anonymous." [1]

IV. UNPUBLISHED CORRESPONDENCE OF POE

POE TO MINOR

RICHMOND, February 5, 1836.

DEAR SIR, — At Mr. White's request I enclose you the sheets of the "Messenger." In your article on "The Ne-

[1] Lowell MSS. The third letter was published in *Letters of James Russell Lowell*, i, 99 (Harpers, 1894).

cessity of Selection in Reading," you will perceive that the original heading is abbreviated to "Selection in Reading." This was necessary in order to preserve uniformity in the captions throughout — it being impossible to get in what you intended, and what, indeed, would have been most proper, except by making use of smaller type than what is used in other articles.

Very resp^{y}. and truly yours,

EDGAR A. POE.[1]

It was thought better upon consideration to omit all in "Liberian Literature" at which offense could, by any possibility, be taken. We availed ourselves of your consent to do so.

Address: LUCIAN MINOR, Esq., Charlotteville, Va.
Endorsed: EDGAR A. POE. Recd. 16th Feb. 1836.

POE TO CAREY

RICHMOND, July 30, 1836.

D^{R} SIR, — Your article on the "Study of the Learned Languages" was duly received, and is already "set up." I am much in hope that it will please the public generally as much as it had done myself. My object in writing you at present is to beg that you will allow us to alter the *heading* which you have affixed to it, from the words "A Looker-on in Venice, No. 2," to the words "On the Study of the Learned Languages," or some similar caption. I have many reasons for requesting this favor. First, it would accord with all the other captions made use of in our magazine; secondly, it would prevent the necessity of making any explanation in regard to the heading of your last article, — and explanations are always inconvenient; thirdly, your article would then stand by itself uncon-

[1] Poe to Minor. MS.

nected with anything going before or to come; fourthly, it would prevent our having a series of *continued* articles, which you must know by experience are the cause of some trouble; and fifthly, the "Looker-on in Venice" is a caption which has been very frequently been [*sic*] made use of before by essayists. I submit all, however, to your better judgment, merely saying that Mr. White would take it as a personal favor if you would allow us to make the alteration proposed.

I am extremely sorry that the error should have occurred in relation to your "Anthologia" and "The Science of Life." We did not, however, suppose it necessary to put the "Anthologia" as a selection — supposing ing the word Anthologia itself sufficiently significant.

With high respect,

Yr. ob. st.

EDGAR A. POE.[1]

I perceive that your article, "National Ingratitude," has attracted great attention and approbation. The "Charlottesville Jeffersonian" among other papers pay it a merited compliment.

[Addressed] MATHEW CAREY, Esq.
Philadelphia,
Pa.

POE TO MAGRUDER

RICHMOND, January 9, 1837.

MY DEAR SIR, — Your kind letter of Christmas eve was duly received — with the Essay.

I have read it with great pleasure and, I confess, some degree of surprise — never having suspected you of any literary designs. It shall certainly appear, entire, in the

[1] Poe to Carey. MS.

February number of the "Messenger." Any supervision on my part, I perceive, would be altogether superfluous.

I must apologize for not having made you a reply before. Ill health and a weight of various and harassing business will prove, I trust, a sufficient excuse.

With sincere friendship and esteem,

I am yours, &c.,

EDGAR A. POE.[1]

ALLAN B. MAGRUDER, Esq.

POE TO NEILSON POE

NEW YORK, August 8, '45.

MY DEAR SIR, — It gave me sincere pleasure to receive a letter from you — but I fear you will think me very discourteous in not sooner replying. I have deferred my answer, however, from day to day, in hope of procuring some papers relating to my grandfather. In this I have failed. Mrs. C. has no memoranda of the kind you mention, and all of which I have any knowledge are on file at Annapolis.

I thank you for the kind interest you take in my welfare. We all speak very frequently of yourself and family, and regret that hitherto we have seen and known so little of each other. Virginia, in especial, is much pained at the total separation from her sisters. She has been, and is still, in precarious health. About four years ago she ruptured a blood vessel, in singing, and has never recovered from the accident. I fear that she never will. Mrs. Clemm is quite well: — both beg to be kindly remembered.

I regret that I had no opportunity of seeing you during my last visit to Baltimore. Virginia and myself, however, will very probably spend a few weeks in your city during

[1] Poe to Magruder. MS.

the fall, when we hope to be with you frequently. When you see any of Mr. Herring's family, will you say that we are anxious to hear from them?

I rejoice to learn that you prosper at all points. I hear of you often. "The B. Journal" flourishes — but in January I shall establish a Magazine.

Very cordially yours,

EDGAR A. POE.[1]

Addressed NEILSON POE, Esqr.
Baltimore,
Md.
Postmarked New York, Aug. 8.

POE TO PERCIVAL

NEW YORK, January 3, '46.
85 Amity St.

CHAS. G. PERCIVAL, Esq.:

Dr Sir, — A few moments of leisure leave me at liberty to look at the cypher which you have done me the honor of submitting to my inspection. It is an illegitimate cryptograph — that is to say, the chances are, that, even *with* the key, it would be insoluble by the authorized correspondent. Upon analysis, however, independent of the key-solution, I find the translation to be the 3 first verses of the 2^{d} chapter of St John.

Very Resp^{y}
Y^{r} Ob. S^{t}

EDGAR A. POE.[2]

I should be happy to hear from you in reply.

POE TO BAYARD TAYLOR

June 15, 1848.

I would feel greatly indebted to you if you could spare time to look over the lines [To Helen] enclosed and

[1] Poe to Neilson Poe. MS.

[2] Poe to Percival. MS.

let me know whether they will be accepted for "the Union" — if so what you can afford to pay for them and when they can appear.

Truly yours,

EDGAR A. POE.[1]

P. S. I feel that I have been guilty of discourtesy in not sooner thanking you for your picturesque and vigorous "Views A-Foot," but when they reached me and long afterwards I was too ill to write, and lately I have been every day hoping to have an opportunity of making your acquaintance and thanking you in person.

CAREY AND LEA TO POE

February 20, 1836.

EDGAR A. POE, Esq., Richmond, Va., — I received your letter this morning, having no knowledge of the MS. mentioned. I applied to Mess. Carey & Hart, who handed over the enclosed which I transmit agreeably to your directions and wish it safe to hand.

November 29, 1836.

MR. EDGAR A. POE, — I have called on Mess. E. L. Carey & A. Hart, who are the publishers of "The Gift," and they have examined among all the MS. and cannot find the story to which you allude. They think it very probable that Miss L. returned it with others but it cannot now be found. Should it be hereafter they will return it.[2]

September 28, 1839.

EDGAR A. POE, ESQ[R]., — As your wish in having your tales printed is not immediately pecuniary we will at our

[1] Poe to Bayard Taylor. MS. [2] Letter Book of Carey & Lea.

own risk & expense print a small edition, say 750 copies. This number if sold will pay but a small profit, which if realized is to be ours. The copyright will remain with you, and when ready a few copies for distribution among your friends will be at your service.

If this is agreeable will you have them prepared and Mr. Haswell will be ready to go in say by Thursday.

They should make 2 vols. of a page like "Isabel," say 240 pages each.

October 30, 1839.

EDGAR A. POE, ESQ[R]., — The printing of a few extra copies of your tales on fine paper would be very troublesome to the printer. But if he is willing we have no objection to *six* copies being printed at your cost.

We designed sending 20 copies of the edition to you on publication for private distribution.

V. POE AND CHIVERS

The renaissance of Thomas Holley Chivers is one of the latest incidents of the Poe legend, which puts forth such curious growths from decade to decade. His fame still lingered here in the seventies, but only as a burlesque survival. At that time Bayard Taylor diverted himself with it in the "Echo Club," recalling what is likely to prove his most immortal stanza: —

"Many mellow Cydonian suckets,
  Sweet apples, anthosmal, divine,
From the ruby-rimmed beryline buckets
  Star-gemmed, lily-shaped, hyaline;
Like the sweet golden goblet found growing
  On the wild emerald cucumber-tree,
Rich, brilliant, like chrysoprase glowing
  Was my beautiful Rosalie Lee."

Swinburne was known, among American friends, to exercise the divine right of inextinguishable laughter over such verses, scores of which he would repeat. The British Museum was fabled to have a complete set of Chivers, which seemed to clench the singularity of the poet, inasmuch as hardly any of his countrymen possessed even a single volume of his works. Collectors found them impossible to buy. Their titles were the most preservative part of them. "Eonchs of Ruby," in particular, was itself antiseptic against time. It fascinated the mind it alarmed, and was eagerly but vainly sought. A few stanzas and lines might be heard quoted in literary small talk; and persons of long memory or deep delvers in our Lilliputian history recalled the fact that Chivers and the friends of Chivers stoutly asserted that he was the original owner from whom Poe conveyed "The Raven"; but the poacher, if trespass there were, seemed to have got safe off with the bird. Mr. Benton, however, strikes beside the mark in saying, "The breadth of his territory of renown among scholars is indicated by the fact that Professor Gierlow, a Danish author, wrote a beautiful poem" on his death. Gierlow was a teacher of language in a school at Macon, Georgia.

Things stood at this pass, with Chivers there in the British Museum, at the last bubble of Lethe, when there came a change, and his name began to brighten and grow frequent again. The fame of Poe had magnetized it, and it gave out new radiant energy. Fresh editions of his rare volumes may now fairly be expected. The late W. M. Griswold, in his edition of his father's correspondence,[1] drew Chivers back from oblivion with a brief account, a

[1] *Passages from the Correspondence and Other Papers of Rufus W. Griswold.* Cambridge, Mass. 1898.

letter to Poe, and a kindly word for his character. Joel Benton followed with a little sheaf of articles, "In the Poe Circle,"[1] and resuscitated the controversy as to who originated "The Raven"; incidentally he reprinted Chivers's more extraordinary poems, and gave some from manuscript that had never seen light before.

"The Virginia Poe" comes last. The editor publishes from the Griswold papers nearly all of Chivers's letters to Poe, and in an appendix he examines Chivers's claims to be the precursor of Poe and decides that Poe was the precursor of Chivers. These letters were in the hands of the present writer when he edited the Griswold papers, but in the absence of Poe's answers it seemed needless to give them at that time. The latter have now come to light, together with companion papers, having survived Sherman's march to the sea and other vicissitudes of the last half century in their nook in Georgia; they afford further illustration of Poe's character and career, and they also allow us to reconstruct somewhat more vividly the interesting figure of Chivers himself.

Dr. Thomas Holley Chivers was born in Wilkes County, Georgia, at Digby Manor, near Washington, in 1807,[2] the eldest of seven children. His father, Robert

[1] The student of Poe should compare, beside the authorities named in the text, the most able defense of Chivers's originality and argument for Poe's indebtedness in a long article by Warfield Creath Richardson of Tuscaloosa, Alabama, "Who was Chivers?" in the *Boston Transcript*, April 24, 1897.

[2] *The Virginia Poe* corrects this date as follows: —

"On page 90 of this volume (1837) he addresses a poem *To my Precious Mother, on the anniversary of my Twenty-fifth Year*, and subscribes it, 'Written at Philadelphia, October 18, 1834.'" The copy of the volume before the writer has a different poem on page 90. On page 89 there is a poem entitled *To my Mother* simply, and no date is subscribed. The phrase "To my Precious Mother"

Chivers, was a cotton-planter, rich in lands and slaves. His grandfather, Thomas H. Chivers, had emigrated from England in the middle of the seventeenth century and settled in Virginia, but afterward removed to Georgia. His mother, whose name was Digby, was of similar emigrant stock, her father having come from England and settled in Pennsylvania before finally transferring the family to Georgia, where she married the poet's father in 1806. He was religiously brought up, all the family being Baptists; and, as appears from his verses, his childhood was happy, his domestic affections were warm and tender, and his love for his mother was devotional. He began to write verse early, and with some mastery of metrical form, to judge by the stanzas entitled "Faith," which belong to his twentieth year, and which he afterward described as "showing that the two angels, Love and Adoration, were the twin Sisters who went hand in hand with him through the Eden of his youth, gathering the purple Violets of Heaven." He adopted medicine as a profession and studied at the Transylvania University, where he took the doctor's degree. He was, however, by his father's kindness, independent of the necessity to practice, and he gave himself up to literary and especially poetical pursuits; later in life he was offered a chair of physiology in the university at Atlanta, which he declined, and this was his nearest approach to a medical or scientific career.

While at the university he had continued to write verse, such as "Georgia Waters," and in 1834 he published a tragedy, "Conrad and Eudora," at Philadelphia; he con-

occurs in the dedication. The copy used by the Virginia editors may belong to a different issue or have manuscript notes. In any case the year 1807 is the accepted family date, and occurs in a sketch of Chivers written apparently by himself late in life.

tributed the next year to the "Southern Literary Messenger" while Poe was editor; and in 1837 he issued his first collection of verse, "Nacoochee; or, The Beautiful Star, with Other Poems," at New York. He spent much of his time at the North in these years, where he had a circle of relatives and friends, and to the end of his life he made long visits there and established connection with writers and scholars of distinction. It is interesting to record also that he was a painter as well as a poet, and that he added to his income as well as his versatility by inventing a machine for unwinding the fibre from silk cocoons.

It was "Nacoochee," the volume of lyrics, which first attracted Poe's public attention to Chivers; but at the age of thirty, when this appeared, Chivers had not developed those characteristics which constitute his originality. The ordinary critic would have found in the verses the metrical form of Moore and Coleridge, and perhaps little else at that time; now other qualities would be more apparent. Though there is no reason to believe that he ever read the poetry of Blake, the Blakeish suggestion in his imagination and diction is occasionally startling; partly because he deals with scriptural allusion and the material imagery of the Bible, his mind having been fed on them, but also because of some similarity in his irregular force of conception and grandiloquent method. In the "Ode to the Mississippi" there are three lines that will serve as an illustration, describing the rivers flowing down to the great "Father of Waters": —

> "Like soldiers enlisted for Freedom to fight!
> Who started their marching ere Adam was born,
> And never shall stop till Eternity's morn."

In the last stanza, too, there is a touch of the same quality and tone: —

"We look on thy bosom, but cannot control
The terror that strikes from the heart to the soul!
We know thee unique in the East or the West,
Who look'st in a calm like a lion at rest!
We give thee the praise — then adieu to the wild
That brought forth a son called Eternity's child."

It is also a noticeable matter now that the new poet must have fed on that Philadelphia reprint of Galignani's edition of Keats, Shelley, and Coleridge in one large volume which first brought the immortal romantic fire to our coast and was for our grandfathers a great altar of the Muse. It was a distinction for a new poet in 1837 to quote "Alastor" and "Rosalind and Helen"; and, in fact, Chivers was one of the first of Americans to be "Shelley-mad." The enthusiasm did not mount to his poetry, but it filled the man. Still a third trait worth pointing out is the fact, disclosed by the preface, that he had the Orphic conception of the nature of poetry and the poet's rôle, though he had not yet reached that Orphic egotism which was to belong to him later. Evidently he had the sensibilities and intuitions that denote the poetic temperament, and he possessed instincts of metre and imagery. It is natural to find him soon that rare thing, a Southern transcendentalist, and soon also a Swedenborgian, and even an "associationist" at a later time. The son of a Southern slaveholder, a devotee of Shelley, a friend of Bostonian vagaries, Chivers had fallen on unlucky times; and as he grew older the unregulated elements in him gradually became most marked, till at last he became, not to speak it profanely, a kind of Southern Alcott.

When in the summer of 1840 Poe endeavored to start the "Penn Magazine" in Philadelphia, Chivers was among those whose support he sought as a writer for magazines and as a collector of subscriptions. Chivers promised his aid, but he found room to remonstrate against Poe's "tomahawk" criticism and to advise a milder method. Chivers appears next to have heard from Poe by an example of that "tomahawk" style, which he had deprecated, applied to himself. In the article "Autography," in "Graham's" for December, 1841, Poe described Chivers in few lines: —

"Dr. Thomas Holley Chivers, of New York, is at the same time one of the best and one of the worst poets in America. His productions affect one as a wild dream — strange, incongruous, full of images of more than arabesque monstrosity, and snatches of sweet unsustained song. Even his worst nonsense (and some of it is horrible) has an indefinite charm of sentiment and melody. We can never be sure that there is *any* meaning in his words, — neither is there any meaning in many of our finest musical airs, — but the effect is very similar in both. His figures of speech are metaphor run mad, and his grammar is often none at all. Yet there are as fine individual passages to be found in the poems of Dr. Chivers as in those of any poet whatsoever."

Chivers wrote in remonstrance against this, and a second time; and Poe replied, June 6, 1842, acknowledging the three unanswered letters and apologizing for the "Autography" squib; and at the same time suggesting that Chivers should join him in the "Penn," which enterprise he was just renewing, and bring financial aid.

Chivers's father had died, and the estate was about to be divided, so it was quite possible that this offer might bear fruit; he wrote a polite and cordial reply, July 12, 1842, in which he explained the situation, but made no promise with regard to the "Penn Magazine" except that he would obtain subscribers for it. Poe wrote again,

September 27, 1842, stating that the sum requisite would be one thousand dollars, and estimating the expenses of the magazine at three thousand dollars, and its profits at ten thousand for each editor, on a list of five thousand subscribers, of whom he felt sure of five hundred at once.

There was, however, to be no result from any of these plans. Chivers lost a little daughter, and went South for the burial. There he received no answers to three letters; but he was a persistent correspondent, and in the spring of 1844 made another attempt, asking whether the "Penn Magazine" was abandoned, and saying that he would receive his part of his father's estate in July and would be glad to join Poe in the enterprise, "provided it would be to my interest to do so." Poe replied to this at once, saying that he still contemplated the "Penn" project, but had changed the name to the "Stylus," and he suggested a conference in New York. This letter contained some metaphysical mysticism. Chivers replied, much delighted with the turn the correspondence had taken, August 6, and again September 24, without receiving any further lucubration from Poe; but correspondence was now to be supplemented by personal acquaintance on the occasion of Chivers's visit to New York in the next summer, 1845, where he brought out his third volume of verse, "The Lost Pleiad." The story of the visit has been told in the text. Chivers's account of his walks and talks with Poe is wild and rambling, but it is not lacking in vividness. He wrote out these reminiscences and impressions, after Poe's death, for a life which he meant to publish in Poe's defense; but the reader must be referred to the magazine in which they were published, if he would know them.

Chivers did not remain long in New York in the memorable summer when he met his idol of genius face to face and consorted with him in so mundane a fashion. "The Lost Pleiad," his last volume of verse, was now safely published. Poe noticed it in the "Broadway Journal," August 2, 1845; he describes the volume as the honest and fervent utterance of an exquisitely sensitive heart which has suffered much and long. "The poems," he goes on, "are numerous, but the thesis is one — *death* — the death of beloved friends. The poet seems to have dwelt among the shadows of tombs, until his very soul has become a shadow. . . . In a word, the volume before us is the work of that *rara avis*, an educated, passionate, yet unaffectedly simple-minded and single-minded man, writing from his own vigorous impulses, — from the necessity of giving utterance to poetic passion, — and thus writing *not* to mankind, but solely to himself. The whole volume has, in fact, the air of a rapt soliloquy." He then gives a long extract from the poem on Shelley, and ends by complimenting the volume as "possessing merit of a very lofty — if not of the very loftiest order."

The correspondence was resumed in August and continued, as usual, with more frequency by Chivers than by Poe, whose main interest seems to have been the hope of obtaining money, of which he was in need for the "Journal." Poe wrote one letter of great biographical interest, July 22, 1846, describing his illness and professing warm friendship, but the correspondence languished after that; Chivers, on his part, offered a home and support to Poe for the rest of his life if he would come South to settle. The later intercourse of the two is obscurely known. Chivers visited New York, it would seem, in the summer of 1847, and certainly in that of 1848. On the last occasion he was invited to Fordham by Poe, but whether the two met is untold. Poe's last reference to his friend, as has been seen, was ungenerous, — one of those words that often escaped him with regard to those with whom he had been intimate; but, by Mrs. Clemm's account, his friendship and admiration had been warm toward his worshiper.

It is apparent that Chivers was filled with an enthusiastic admiration for Poe and worshiped his genius. It is the more striking a tribute because he was of a religious cast of mind and not a sharer in Poe's weaknesses. He was not one of those who drank with Poe; and in spite of what he knew and had seen, he maintained a high respect for his genius and a warm interest in his welfare. Chivers was a hero-worshiper, and he adored the spirit of poetry after that fashion that sees in the poet, whatever he may be humanly, only a great glory. When Poe died, and the trouble arose over Griswold's memoir of him, Chivers, like several others who had known Poe, was desirous to write a life of him and defend his memory. He made some collections for this purpose; his reminiscences are a part of his material. He offered this life to Ticknor, October 27, 1852, as if it were completed; but it seems never to have passed a fragmentary state.

The claim which Chivers here sets up is to an originality in metrical effects independent of Poe's example; he asserts that he practiced these effects before Poe and that Poe borrowed from him, notably in the idea and the rhythm of "The Raven." It is only too obvious that what was styled at the beginning of these articles the "Orphic egotism" was now fully developed in Chivers. He had, in 1849, corresponded with W. E. Channing and proclaimed himself an associationist. He was also in correspondence with Professor George Bush on the candelabrum of the Tabernacle and cognate matters, and devoted somewhat to Hebrew learning. He became, as has been said, a Swedenborgian. His poetic self-sufficiency and illusions were a part of this seething mental state. But if it be thought that his mind had lost its balance in some degree, it is only just to observe that his claim to have developed originality in metrical effects was nothing novel. He maintained his originality in metre from the first. It was not an afterthought.

A poem, "The Lady Alice," seems to me the fairest example of the rhythm which Chivers evolved; and the patient reader may welcome one entire poem from his pen.

THE LADY ALICE

1

The night is serene with pleasure —
    Balmy the air —
For the Moon makes the icy azure
    Argently clear;
And the Stars with their music make measure
    To mine down here —
    My song down here —
    My beautiful song down here.

2

Pale light from her orb is raining
    On earth — the sea;
While I am on earth complaining
    Of one to me
More fair than the Moon now waning —
    More pure than she —
    More fair than she —
    More womanly pure than she.

3

She lives in her golden palace
    Beside the sea;
And her name is the Lady Alice —
    So dear to me!
And she drinks from her crystal Chalice
    Sweet wine so free —

White wine so free —
Because her pure heart is free.

4

She sings while the Angels listen
With pure delight!
And the Stars with new glory glisten,
And laughter bright;
While my heart in its narrow prison
Doth pine to-night —
Pine all the night —
For want of my Moon to-night.

5

She smiles while my soul is sorry
With love divine;
And the Stars hear in Heaven the story
Which makes me pine!
I would give all their crowns of glory
If she were mine —
Were only mine —
Were only forever mine.

6

Oh! come from thy golden palace,
Sweet Lady bright!
And fill up this empty Chalice
With wine to-night! —
I drink to my Lady Alice!
My soul's delight —
Heart — soul's delight —
My ever divine delight!

The likeness to Poe is unmistakable; but in the poem as a whole there is to my ear a Celtic quality in the refrain which Poe never naturalized in his own verse. It may be allowed that, though overlaid with Poe's peculiar myth-names and vocal mystery, Chivers's verse had a music of its own. From the start he had sought the melodic effects of the refrain more markedly than Poe himself, and he had been bred on Coleridge and Shelley, the lyrical masters of sound. He was in parallelism with Poe, so to speak, and was attracted to him till he coalesced. It is no wonder that he himself sincerely regarded his work as the primary one, and Poe's as the derivative, given his egotism. The claim he made in regard to "The Raven" can be defined precisely. He had employed an iambic metre with three feminine rhymes for elegiac verse in the poem "To Allegra Florence in Heaven," and he had developed the idea of the return of the dead woman's soul to her lover in "Uranothen" — a title certainly pre-Poesque. If one chooses the marvelous lines from the first of these to illustrate the kind of metre, it is easy to give the impression of a *reductio ad absurdum*. No account of Chivers would be complete without them.

"As an egg when broken, never can be mended, but must ever
Be the same crushed egg forever, so shall this dark heart of mine
Which, though broken, still is breaking, and shall nevermore cease aching,
For the sleep which has no waking — for the sleep that now is thine!"

But the absurdity of the substance is not one of the arguments, after all, and the rest of the poem is not like this.

It is not too much to grant that in the many atmospheric influences that surrounded the germination of "The Raven" (and their number was a multitude) these two poems, familiar to Poe, and certainly the last of them, "Uranothen," had a place. The two poets were extraordinarily sympathetic, but what was intense and firm in Poe was diffused and liquescent in Chivers, who was in truth a kind of double to him in what seems sometimes a spiritualistic, sometimes a grotesque way. He was, indeed, to Poe not unlike what Alcott was to Emerson, and the comparison helps to clarify the confusion of their mutual relations, while it maintains Poe's mastery unimpaired. Chivers continued to publish new volumes, and reissue the old, until he died in Georgia in 1858.

Unfortunately, in attempting to reconstruct the image of Chivers it is impossible to escape that burlesque effect, though with the kindest intention in the world, which has proved the most enduring element in his works. He did not really change and lose his balance of mind in poetic egotism; the lack of balance was always there, and only declared itself more spectacularly as time went on. The tumultuous vacuity of Blake is found in him from the start and at the finish; it took the form of senseless sonority of diction and mindless rhyme-echo at the end, instead of visible chaotic things of line and color. But at the beginning there was the germ. Here is a stanza from one of his early pieces, entitled "To a China Tree."

> "How gladly I looked through the suckle-gemmed valley,
> The grove where the washwoman filled up her tank —
> And stood by the well, in the green oakey alley,
> And turned down the old cedar bucket and drank.
> But farewell, ye oaks! and the trees of my childhood!
> And all the bright scenes appertaining to joy!
> I think of ye often, away in this wildwood,
> But never shall be as I was when a boy.
> Nor shoot with my cross-bow — my mulberry cross-bow —
> The robins that perched on the boughs near the gate."

This is something that neither Moore, nor Coleridge, nor even Woodworth, would have been capable of; but in it are the imitative catch, the liking for the refrain, the unconscious dips into bathos, that appear also in the later verses. Many poets have felt that Poe escapes these things only by a hair's-breadth, though his material is finer. The difference was that Poe was a genius, while Chivers only thought he was one. Poe, I think, played with Chivers to make something out of him; but there was nothing to be made of him but a friend, and that was not Poe's game. Apart from Poe, Chivers was an interesting illustration of his times: the vast, unfathomable ocean of American crudity was in Chivers, Alcott, Whitman. He was, without regard to his poetry, a most estimable man in his intellectual sympathy, his ideals and labors, and kindly and honorable in all his relations with his fellows.

VI. GRISWOLD'S WORLD[1]

The one distinguishing tribute paid to Rufus Wilmot Griswold, one that establishes his characteristic excellence, was his selection by Poe to be his literary executor just before his death. Poe was a good judge of editorial capacity; and, notwithstanding a history of personal relations that would seem to exclude the possibility of such a choice, Poe showed great sense in regard to his own interests when he engaged the best-known and best-equipped American editor to collect and publish his works. He thus secured, under favorable conditions, a form of publication which he had always failed in accomplishing himself. Griswold was in his day an important person in American literary life. His connection with Poe was incidental. To himself and others he was first of all the one man who had attempted to show the poetic accomplishment of our country in its first half-century, for the honor and encouragement of our literature, and had succeeded in the task, difficult and in many ways ungrateful, of a proper selection and just arrangement of the material. This work con-

[1] *Passages from the Correspondence and other Papers of Rufus W. Griswold.* Cambridge, Mass. W. M. Griswold. 1898.

stitutes his real claim to thankful remembrance; it is, and for students of American literature it must remain, a landmark volume, which for their purposes cannot be displaced. Whatever its demerits of substance may be, they faithfully reflect the time's qualities, and the editorial part is unexceptionable. Griswold was a born compiler, as Greeley saw from the start when he was employing him in the scissors work of journalism: "He [Raymond] has no judgment with regard to selections. There you are unrivaled"; and again, "In literary cooperism you were boss, decidedly." And in his book-work Griswold was putting to use the same ability that he had exercised in newspaper offices. The sort of labor involved and the kind of success he achieved are fairly stated in his own words: —

"There had been published in this country about five hundred volumes of rhythmical compositions of various kinds and degrees of merit, nearly all of which I read with more or less attention. From the mass I chose about one-fifth, as containing writings not unworthy of notice in such an examination of this part of our literature as I proposed to make. I have been censured, perhaps justly, for the wide range of my selections. But I did not consider all the contents of the volume poetry. I aimed merely to show what had been accomplished toward a poetical literature by our writers in verse before the close of the first half century of our national existence. With much of the first order of excellence, more was accepted that was comparatively poor. But I believe nothing was admitted inferior to passages in the most celebrated foreign works of like character. I have also been condemned for omissions. But on this score I have no regrets. I can think of no name not included in the first edition which I would now admit without better credentials than were before me when that edition was printed."

Apart from the merit of his work, his position as the Rhadamanthus of contemporary poetic ambitions, then perhaps more numerous even than now, made him the centre of much correspondence, and resulted in his papers becoming the repository of an unusual amount of literary information about books and their authors, biographical data at first hand, and other matters of transitory nature.

It is true that the world of letters depicted seems to have little to do with Longfellow, Lowell, and Hawthorne; it is the more populous world of the "Literati," the little New Englanders, the little Knickerbockers, and others of the gnomes and elves of Parnassus, if such small people have any abiding-place in the crevices and on the swards of that mystic place. It is the world of the magazines and journals and their brief and flimsy reputations, of coteries and circles in the city and visitants from the Southwest and the Illinois prairies — the world which seems now more malicious and now more humorous, but which was the environment, in taste, feeling, and culture, of the pursuit of letters here for a generation. The talk is "small-talk"; and the names of the speakers come like faint echoes of a "ruined Paradise." A Paradise, in some sort, it seemed to themselves. Here is a peep into it, on July 10, 1842, just after Griswold joined "Graham's": —

"I have been to New York for a few days, and saw all the people — breakfasted with Willis, smoked with Halleck, took tea with Keese, dined with Maria 'del Occidente,' chatted with Hoffman, Balmanno, Mrs. Embury, Seba Smith, Miss Thayer (an old Boston friend of yours, who is one of the greatest of living characters), etc. Touching Maria Brooks — she is a wonderful woman — I have never seen her compeer. She talked as volubly as any woman, but not as women talk; but what I have to say of her must be addressed to Whipple, concerning whom, and Macaulay, we held appreciative converse. You have seen, I doubt not, the new arrangements for the magazine. I had little to do with the July No., as it was nearly all printed before I came hither; but the August is better, and the September will be better still. Cooper, Bryant, Longfellow, all the while! besides Fields and Tuckerman! — of course you will send me something in time for it. Speaking of Longfellow — the MS. of his 'Spanish Student' I shall have bound in green and gold — would you not like to have it? Such autographs are not to be picked up every day."

Thus Griswold to Fields. More remote still — more redolent of the Elysian poppy in the burying-meadows of time — is this advice of Hoffman, December 28, 1844: —

"I certainly would balance the florid style of Bancroft with the directness of Sparks — nor would your book be complete without quotations from Gouverneur Morris, whom the men of his day thought a master of elegant writing. In making my selections, I would choose the passages which are most characteristic of the writer (which in some instances are not the best that might be culled). Timothy Flint's description of Red River, for instance, in his 'Francis Berrien,' is happily the most Flintish as well as the finest passage you could quote from him. Irving's 'Bracebridge Hall' has a passage which is the very tiptoppery of his elegance. In Frisbie's review of Byron there is a passage of rare musical cadence. In Gouverneur Morris you will find a blending of the epigrammatic style of Junius with much of the polished facility of the old

French memoirs — and in John Randolph you have more than the biting sarcasm of Wilkes."

On the next page there is a grave-to-grave poll of the candidates, from the pen of a Cambridge divine. We rub our eyes as if we had reversed the legend of Sleepy Hollow and waked in a world of "lang syne" as unfamiliar, and as disproportioned to our recollection, as Rip Van Winkle's.

But, after all, though humorous surprise will intrude upon the reader, there is a great deal of reality in this literary past. The sight of Longfellow reading the works of John Neal "straight through" is almost educative in the actuality it gives to boredom. Whipple's remark is brief but full as to certain aspects of the matter: "I have no patience with the New York literati. They are all the time quarrelling with each other. Why not kiss and be friends? You have a precious lot of feuds on your own hands. 'A plague on both your houses, say I.'" Boston is sketched out a bit by Fields, who contributes to the volume two familiar epistles in verse to "Rufe," as the great editor is companionably called (or "Gris") throughout by his friends; but no quotation could do sufficient injustice to them — they must be read in order to be properly damned.

The most interesting person who appears is Horace Greeley, whose letters are numerous and such as no other could indite. They are rapid notes, business notes, familiar in the extreme, and all strongly marked with the hard good sense, the activity, the homely directness, the excellent intellectual interests and friendly serviceableness of the restless and various writer. His desire to issue an edition of Praed, and his comments on the poet ("I will get it published somewhere if I have to run in debt for it"), and still more his interest in Shelley's poems ("There is not a copy of them to be had here [New York: 1845], and I presume not in the country. You know they ought to be published"), are curious memoranda of his tastes. In the business of public notices he was sadly unscrupulous: "Get a right notice in the 'Ledger,' if you can. Swain would like to do me a kindness. But pay for it rather than not get a good one." The advice was proof of the mercenary custom of criticism then, as is plain from many a line elsewhere, as where Epes Sargent sends his "little book" with this request: "Please keep the authorship a secret, and if you can get the accompanying notices published, one in the 'North American' and the other in the 'Evening Journal' without betraying it, do so. I shall be much obliged, and will cheerfully reciprocate the favor at any time." Greeley's characterizations are the shrewdest in the volume, often only hints, but effective, and to Griswold himself he sometimes uses a tell-tale frankness: "Now write me a few racy, spicy — not personal, far less malignant [letters] depicting society and life in Philadelphia. *Soon*, mind. . . . About half a column in length, spirited and lively, but not spiteful. Satirize Society and customs if you must, but don't touch individuals." Again, "The only principle I ever found you tenacious of is that of having your pay at least as fast as you earn it." There are several other unfavorable *obiter dicta* from different persons with regard to Griswold, who certainly had unamiable traits and grave defects, concerning which the best statement is Leland's: "He was to his death so uniformly a friend to me and so untiring in his efforts to aid me, that I cannot find words to express his kindness nor the gratitude I feel. . . . To the end of his life I was always with him a privileged character, and could take, if

I chose, the most extraordinary liberties, though he was one of the most irritable and vindictive men I ever met if he fancied he was in any way too familiarly treated." Griswold's personality is thus fully suggested.

It would be an interminable task were one to try to survey all in detail. Strange and wonderful persons abound in the crowd, intellects *manqué* and morals very much in the same deplorable state. Chivers is easily the first — no doubt an excellent man, but in verse the idiot form of Poe. No wonder that Poe abandoned him. Here, too, are the unlaid ghosts of H. W. Herbert and G. G. Foster, to the latter of whom Greeley and Griswold were truly friends at need: and among the female literati, Mrs. E. Oakes Smith, whose life was a remarkable one, and of course the Ellets and Osgoods, the Carys, and many more. George William Curtis's account of himself, ending "*Voilà tout!* and Shelley died when he was no older than I am," is interesting; so is John Neal's. In the way of curious literature, those who remember Poe's "Valentine" to Mrs. Osgood in which he wove her name into the verse, will read the similar effusion she addressed to Griswold with a touch of surprise. It is an illustrative document in regard to the literary group. The italics show the inserted names.

"*F*or one, whose being is to mine a sta*r*,
T*r*embling I weave in lines of love and f*u*n
Wh*a*t Fame before has echoed near and *f*ar.
A so*n*net if you like, — I'll give yo*u* one
To be *c*ross-questioned ere it's truth is *s*olv'd.
Here v*e*iled and hidden in a rhyming *w*reath
A name i*s* turned with mine in cunnin*g* sheath,
And unle*s*s by some marvel ra*r*e evolved,
Forever f*o*lded from all *i*dler eyes
Silent and *s*ecret still it trea*s*ured lies,
Whilst mine *g*oes winding on*w*ard, as a rill

Thro' a deep wo*o*d in unseen j*o*yance dances,
Calling in mel*o*dy's bewi*l*dering thrill
Whilst thro' *d*im leaves its partner *d*reams and glances."

Two things stand out. The first is the mean literary poverty of the time, its atmosphere of impecuniosity, of little pay for the best work, of a log-rolling and subsidized criticism and feeble product; its environment of gossip and scandal, its deficient integrity, its undeniable vulgarity, its Grub-Street and Dunciad populace with the disadvantages of a large female immigration into these purlieus; and the second is the character and position of Griswold as a prince among his peers; but what a princedom and what a peerage! If oblivion could have been the lot of such literary mortality as is here disclosed, it would have been nothing to be sorry for; but we must accept a literary ancestry exposed to the full light that now beats upon the mob as hotly as once upon the throne.

APPENDIX B

FRAGMENTS OF POE'S TALE: THE LIGHT-HOUSE

. . . the three that are usually put in. The duty is a mere nothing; and the printed instructions are as plain as possible. It never would have done to let Orndoff accompany me. I never should have made any way with my book as long as he was within reach of me, with his intolerable gossip — not to mention that everlasting meerschaum. Besides, I wish to be *alone*. . . . It is strange that I never observed, until this moment, how dreary a sound that word has — "alone"! I could half fancy there was some peculiarity in the echo of these cylindrical walls — but oh, no! — this is all nonsense. I do believe I am going to get nervous about my insulation. *That* will never do. I have not forgotten De Grät's prophecy. Now for a scramble to the lantern and a good look around to "see what I can see." . . . To see what I can see indeed! — not very much. The swell is subsiding a little, I think — but the cutter will have a rough passage home, nevertheless. She will hardly get within sight of the Norland before noon to-morrow — and yet it can hardly be more than 190 or 200 miles.

Jan. 2. I have passed this day in a species of ecstasy that I find it impossible to describe. My passion for solitude could scarcely have been more thoroughly gratified. I do not say *satisfied;* for I believe I should never be satiated with such delight as I have experienced to-day. . . . The wind lulled about day-break, and by the afternoon the sea had gone down materially. . . . Nothing to be seen, with the telescope even, but ocean and sky, with an occasional gull.

Jan. 3. A dead calm all day. Towards evening, the sea looked very much like glass. A few sea-weeds came in sight; but besides them absolutely *nothing* all day — not even the slightest speck of cloud. . . . Occupied myself in exploring the light-house. . . . It is a very lofty one — as I find to my cost when I have to ascend its interminable stairs — not quite 160 feet, I should say, from the low-water mark to the top of the lantern. From the bottom *inside* the shaft, however, the distance to the summit is 180 feet at least: — thus the floor is 20 feet below the surface of the sea, even at low-tide. . . . It seems to me that the hollow interior at the bottom should have been filled in with solid masonry. Undoubtedly the whole would have been thus rendered more *safe:* — but what am I thinking about? A structure such as this is safe enough under any circumstances. I should feel myself secure in it during the fiercest hurricane that ever raged — and yet I have heard seamen say that, occasionally, with a wind at South-West, the sea has been known to run higher here than any where with the single exception of the Western opening of the Straits of Magellan. No mere sea, though, could accomplish anything with this solid iron-riveted wall — which, at 50 feet from high-water mark, is four feet thick, if one inch. . . . The basis on which the structure rests seems to me to be chalk. . . .

Jan. 4

[The MS., from the Griswold Papers, is in Poe's hand, very clearly written, without alteration or erasure, on three narrow strips of blue paper such as Poe used in other MSS. of 1845.]

APPENDIX C

BIBLIOGRAPHY OF THE TALES AND POEMS WITH NOTES

I. THE TALES

[The following abbreviations are used: S. L. M., Southern Literary Messenger; A. Mo., American Monthly; G. M., Gentleman's Magazine; Gra. M., Graham's Magazine; S. L. C., Snowden's Lady's Companion; God. L. B., Godey's Lady's Book; A. W. R., American Whig Review; B. J., Broadway Journal; A. M., Arthur's Magazine; C. M., Columbian Magazine. The editions of 1840, 1843, 1845, are indicated by those dates only.]

Poe was careful in composition and solicitous for the printed text of his works. He published nearly all his tales repeatedly, both in periodicals and in volumes; and, on each reissue, he revised the text, except when some particular tale appeared nearly simultaneously in two places. The extent of the revision varied; usually he shortened the tale, and simplified, moderated, and harmonized the language, but in some instances while keeping the incidents, dialogue, and ideas intact, he rewrote the tale verbally. "The Imp of the Perverse" and "The Tell-tale Heart" are examples of such minute correction. He seems never to have regarded any form as final, but made new changes on the margin of the last printed copy. The following list shows the date and place of publication of each tale, so far as known, in chronological order of composition, so far as can be conjectured on safe grounds. The three tales of which in respect to these points there is no certain knowledge were either from manuscript in Griswold's hands, an unlikely hypothesis except in one instance, or from periodicals of which no file exists, such as "The Flag of Our Union," or from obscure publications which have escaped search.

1. MS. Found in a Bottle. Baltimore Saturday Visiter, Oct. 12, 1833; S. L. M., Dec. 1835; The Gift, 1836; 1840; B. J. ii, 14.
2. The Assignation (The Visionary). God. L. B., Jan. 1834; S. L. M., July, 1835; 1840; B. J. i, 23.
3. Berenice. S. L. M., March, 1835; 1840; B. J. i, 14.
4. Morella. S. L. M., April, 1835; 1840; B. J. i, 25.
5. Lionizing. S. L. M., May, 1835; 1840; 1845; B. J. i, 11.
6. Hans Pfaall. S. L. M., June, 1835; 1840.
7. Bon-Bon. S. L. M., Aug. 1835; 1840; B. J. i, 16.
8. Shadow — A Parable (Fable). S. L. M., Sept. 1835; 1840; B. J. i, 22.

9. Loss of Breath. S. L. M., Sept. 1835; 1840; B. J. ii, 26.
10. King Pest. S. L. M., Sept. 1835; 1840; B. J. ii, 15.
11. Metzengerstein. S. L. M., Jan. 1836; 1840.
12. Duc de L'Omelette. S. L. M., Feb. 1836; 1840; B. J. ii, 14.
13. Four Beasts in One (Epimanes). S. L. M., March, 1836; 1840; B. J. ii, 22.
14. A Tale of Jerusalem. S. L. M., April, 1836; 1840; B. J., ii, 11.
15. Mystification (Von Jung). A. Mo., June, 1837; 1840; B. J. ii, 25.
16. Silence — A Fable (Siope). Baltimore Book, 1839; 1840; B. J. ii, 9.

The "Tales of the Folio Club," submitted to the Committee on the Prize Tale for the Baltimore "Saturday Visiter," before Oct. 12, 1833, and sent to Carey & Lea, Philadelphia, before November, 1834, was made up out of the above titles. "Lionizing" and "The Visionary" are stated to have been among the tales submitted to the Committee, in an editorial note (S. L. M., Aug. 1835), and "Siope" and "Epimanes" are mentioned as among the tales in Carey & Lea's hands, Sept. 11, 1835 (Poe to Kennedy).

The note referred to adds, "The 'Tales of the Folio Club' are sixteen in all, and we believe it is the author's intention to publish them in the autumn." The sixteenth tale of the Folio Club is in doubt. Latrobe mentions "A Descent into the Maelström" as among the "Tales of the Folio Club" in 1833, but he probably confused it with "MS. Found in a Bottle." When Carey & Lea returned Poe's manuscript, one tale was missing and seems not to have been found (Carey & Lea to Poe). This may have been the sixteenth tale in question. The most satisfactory hypothesis is that the sixteen titles above made up the "Tales of the Folio Club." A brief introduction to these tales, found among the Griswold MSS., and entitled "The Folio Club," was published in "The Virginia Poe," ii, xxxvi–xxxix. The volume, not being published by Carey & Lee, was offered by Poe to Harper & Brothers through J. K. Paulding, and by them declined through him, March 3, 1836 (Paulding to White), and also directly, June, 1836 (Harper & Brothers to Poe). It was also offered to another New York house, and its London publication considered, but the documents in the case are unpublished.

17. Ligeia. The American Museum, Sept. 1838; 1840; B. J. ii, 12.
18. How to Write a Blackwood Article (The Signora Zenobia). The American Museum, Dec. 1838; 1840; B. J. ii, 1.
19. A Predicament (The Scythe of Time). A Pendant to the preceding tale. The American Museum, Dec. 1838; 1840; B. J. ii, 1.
20. The Devil in the Belfry. The (Philadelphia) Saturday Chronicle and Mirror of the Times, May 8, 1839; 1840; B. J. ii, 18.
21. The Man That Was Used Up. G. M., Aug. 1839; 1840; 1843; B. J. ii, 5.
22. The Fall of the House of Usher. G. M., Sept. 1839; 1840; 1845.
23. William Wilson. G. M., Oct. 1839; The Gift, 1840; 1840; B. J. ii, 8.
24. The Conversation of Eiros and Charmion. G. M., Dec. 1839; 1840; 1845.

25. Why the Little Frenchman Wears his Hand in a Sling. 1840; B. J., ii, 9.

"Tales of the Arabesque and Grotesque," 2 v., Philadelphia, Lea & Blanchard, 1840, was published in Dec. 1839, and included all the above titles.

26. The Business Man (Peter Pendulum). G. M., Feb. 1840; B. J. ii, 4.
27. The Man of the Crowd. G. M., Dec. 1840; 1845.
28. The Murders in the Rue Morgue. Gra. M., April, 1841; 1843; 1845.
29. A Descent into the Maelström. Gra. M., May, 1841; 1845. Cf. *supra*, i, 284, Poe to Snodgrass, where he speaks of the tale as just written.
30. The Island of the Fay. Gra. M., June, 1841; B. J. ii, 13.
31. The Colloquy of Monos and Una. Gra. M., Aug. 1841; 1845.

Poe offered Lea & Blanchard, Aug. 13, 1841, eight later pieces to be added to the "Tales of the Grotesque and Arabesque" in a second edition; "the later pieces will be eight in number, making the entire collection thirty-three" (Poe to Lea & Blanchard). The offer was declined Aug. 16, 1841 (Lea & Blanchard to Poe).

32. Never Bet the Devil your Head. Gra. M., Sept. 1841; B. J. ii, 6.
33. Three Sundays in a Week (A Succession of Sundays). The (Philadelphia) Saturday Evening Post, Nov. 27, 1841; B. J. i, 19.
34. Eleonora. The Gift, 1842; B. J. i, 21.
35. The Oval Portrait (Life in Death). Gra. M., April, 1842; B. J. i, 17.

36. The Masque of the Red Death. Gra. M., May, 1842; B. J. ii, 2.
37. The Landscape Garden. S. L. C., Oct. 1842; B. J. ii, 11. Afterwards incorporated with "The Domain of Arnheim."
38. The Mystery of Marie Rogêt. S. L. C., Nov., Dec., Feb. 1842–43; 1845.
39. The Pit and the Pendulum. The Gift, 1843; B. J. i, 20.
40. The Tell-tale Heart. The Pioneer, Jan. 1843; B. J. ii, 7.

The titles, 26–40, are given in a footnote to Hirst's Life of Poe (Phil. Saturday Museum, March 4, 1843) as a list of the tales written since the publication of the edition of 1840. The article, which was inspired by Poe and reflects his opinion, says: "All the best of Mr. Poe's prose tales have been published since the issue of the volumes," etc.

"The Prose Romances of Edgar A. Poe," No. 1 (pp. 40), paper cover, Philadelphia, George B. Zieber & Co., 1843, was published in the summer, and included 20, 28. The edition is of great rarity.

41. The Gold Bug. The (Philadelphia) Dollar Newspaper, June 21–28, 1843; 1845.
42. The Black Cat. The (Philadelphia) United States Saturday Post, Aug. 19, 1843; 1845.
43. The Elk (Morning on the Wissahiccon). The Opal, 1844.
44. A Tale of the Ragged Mountains. God. L. B., April, 1844; B. J. ii, 21.
45. The Spectacles. (Sent to Horne, April, 1844.) B. J. ii, 20.

46. Diddling Considered as one of the Exact Sciences. B. J. ii, 10.
47. The Balloon Hoax. The (New York) Sun, April 13, 1844.
48. Mesmeric Revelation. C. M., Aug. 1844; 1845.
49. The Premature Burial. The (Philadelphia) —— ——, Aug. 1844; B. J. i, 24.
50. The Oblong Box. God. L. B., Sept. 1844; B. J. ii, 23.
51. The Angel of the Odd. C. M., Oct. 1844.
52. Thou Art the Man. God. L. B., Nov. 1844.
53. The Literary Life of Thingum-Bob. S. L. M., Dec. 1844; B. J. ii, 3.
54. The Purloined Letter. The Gift, 1845; 1845.
55. The System of Dr. Tarr and Prof. Fether. Gra. M., Nov. 1845.

The titles, 41–55, except 47 and 53, are given as the tales written since Hirst's list, and of these 48–50, 52, 54, 55, are marked as unpublished, May 28, 1844 (Poe to Lowell), — "about sixty altogether including the 'Grotesque and Arabesque.'" The titles, 45, 46, were, therefore, published earlier than in the "Broadway Journal" or the failure to mark them as unpublished may have been due, certainly in the case of No. 45, to Poe's having sent them to England. The title, 49, was published not later than Aug. 1844, as extracts from it appeared in the "Rover" at the end of that month, and were introduced by the words, "A writer in one of the Philadelphia papers recently gave," etc. Poe must have had in mind more tales than he mentioned, as by June, 1844, he had prepared a complete collection, which was even larger in number. He then wrote: "Setting aside, for the present, my criticisms, poems, and miscellanies (sufficiently numerous) my tales are, in number, sixty-six. . . . I have them prepared in every respect for the press" (Poe to Anthon). At that date, Poe had published forty-seven tales, 1–47; and, according to this statement, there were then unpublished nineteen tales, of which the titles of eight only, 48–55 are known. The remaining titles are, in all, thirteen only, of which eleven would be required to justify Poe's statement. In other words, unless there were tales that never appeared at all, the statement of Poe to Anthon would involve the conclusion that he wrote only two tales after June, 1844. It is obvious that he included some of his miscellanies under the term, "Tales." The collection was offered to Harper & Brothers through Anthon, and declined Nov. 1844 (Anthon to Poe).

56. The Thousand and Second Tale. God. L. B., Feb. 1845; B. J. ii, 16.

The titles, 26–56, except 46, are given as the tales written since the publication of the edition of 1840, in a footnote to Lowell's biography of Poe, Graham's Magazine, Feb. 1845.

"Tales," New York, Wiley & Putnam, 1845, appeared about July of that year, and included 5, 22, 24, 27, 28, 29, 31, 38, 41, 42, 48, 54. Poe wrote, Aug. 9, 1846, "The last selection of my tales was made from about seventy by Wiley & Putnam's reader, Duyckinck" (Poe to Cooke). It appears that the selection was made from the Anthon list, or else in the two years the number had not much increased. A reviewer of this volume, however, evidently inspired by Poe, says, — "To our own knowledge he has published at least seventy-five or eighty tales."

57. Some Words with a Mummy. A. W. R., April, 1845; B. J. ii, 17.

The title, 57, was mentioned in the "Columbian Magazine," January, 1845: "Notice to Correspondents. The following articles are accepted. . . . Some Words with a Mummy."

58. The Power of Words. Democratic Review, June, 1845; B. J. ii, 16.
59. The Imp of the Perverse. Gra. M., July, 1845; Mayflower, 1846.
60. The Case of M. Valdemar. A. W. R., Dec. 1845; B. J. ii, 24.
61. The Sphinx. A. M., Jan. 1846.
62. The Cask of Amontillado. God. L. B., Nov. 1846.
63. The Domain of Arnheim. C. M., March, 1847. The tale embodies and develops "The Landscape Garden."
64. Mellonta Tauta. God. L. B., Feb. 1849.
65. Hop-Frog. The Flag of Our Union, 1849.
66. X-ing a Paragrab. Unknown.
67. Landor's Cottage. Unknown. Sent to the Metropolitan toward the end of 1848.
68. Von Kempelen and His Discovery. Unknown. Sent to Duyckinck about March 1, 1849.

Notwithstanding the discrepancy between the number of tales mentioned by Poe in his letters to Lowell, Anthon, and Cooke, and the number that can be traced as existing at the dates on which he wrote, there is little reason to believe that this is not well-nigh a complete list. The fragment entitled "The Light-house," given above in Appendix B, was the only manuscript relating to the tales, beside the Introduction to the Folio Club, found in the

Griswold MSS. The absence of any title, other than those included above, in his correspondence or the publications of the time, discredits the hypothesis that any important compositions were lost among his manuscripts, and it is incredible that any editor suppressed such manuscripts after his death, though unpublished matter exists in some collections. He probably included in his calculation all the tales he had written or was engaged upon, and possibly some of his miscellanies. It is clear that he found publication difficult and often long-delayed, and also that his productivity in this kind of composition almost ceased in the last four years of his life, as at other times it had shown a low degree of vitality. The average number of tales written each year, from 1833 to 1846, is between four and five, but it was higher at both the beginning and the end of the period, and from 1837 to 1841 fell to two, which is nearly as low as from 1846 to 1849; in the first of these periods Poe was otherwise occupied in book-making and editing, and in the second in criticism and lecturing.

Of these tales, the following were reprinted abroad in Poe's lifetime: "The Fall of the House of Usher," in "Bentley's Miscellany"; "The Purloined Letter," in Chambers' "Edinburgh Journal"; "Mesmeric Revelation," in the "Popular Record of Modern Science," London; "The Case of M. Valdemar," in the same, and in "Mesmerism 'In Articulo Mortis'" (paper"), London, 1846; and "The Murders in the Rue Morgue" and other tales, translated in *La Commerce* and *La Quotidienne* and collected in *Les Contes d'Edgar Poe*, 1846.

Of Poe's original contribution to foreign periodicals no trace has been found. He was from the first anxious to publish in England; after the Harpers had declined the

"Tales of the Folio Club," he corresponded with a New York house, having a London agency, with respect to the issue of the book in both countries. The letters have not been shown to me, but I am allowed to say that such is their contents. In 1842, at Philadelphia, he enlisted the interest of Dickens in finding an English publisher for a volume of Tales (*supra*, i, 328), but without avail. Wiley & Putnam, by an arrangement with the Harpers presumably, issued "Arthur Gordon Pym" with a London imprint in 1838 and 1841, and a pirated edition appeared in 1844. The same firm, when they became Poe's American publishers, also regularly issued the "Tales," 1845, "The Raven and Other Poems," 1846, and "Eureka," 1848, with a London imprint.

The account of Poe's connection with foreign periodicals is less clear, but interesting, and comes wholly from himself. The first mention is in a letter to Snodgrass, September 11, 1839: "I have made a profitable engagement with 'Blackwood's Mag.,' and my forthcoming Tales are promised a very commendatory Review in that Journal from the pen of Professor Wilson." He returned to the subject, June 17, 1841: "It was only six weeks since that I had the opportunity I wished of sending a copy to Professor Wilson, so as to be sure of its reaching him directly. Of course I must wait some time yet for a notice, — if any there is to be." Meanwhile he mentioned a connection with D'Israeli in a letter to Cooke, September 21, 1839: "You read my most intimate spirit 'like a book,' and with the single exception of D'Israeli I have had communication with no other person who does." He spoke again of the subject of magazine publication in his manuscript memorandum furnished to Griswold, March 29, 1841: "Lately have written articles continuously for two British journals whose names I am not permitted to mention." In Hirst's sketch of him in the "Saturday Museum," March 4, 1843, written from information furnished by Poe, there is a more modified statement of his British connection, with new revelations; "Besides the works mentioned he is the author of . . . a work of fiction in two volumes under a *nom-de-plume*, never acknowledged; also two papers on American topics for a Parisian critical journal, with one or two anonymous articles in a British periodical, and several also anonymous in an American Quarterly." In 1844 he sent one article to Horne, in furtherance of his old ambition (*supra* ii, 50), without success. No article has been identified as by him in any English periodical or journal, but no systematic search has been made; and there is no other indication that he contributed to a journal in Paris.

II. THE POEMS

Poe's revision of the poems was even more persistent and minute than in the case of the tales, and his republication of them more often repeated. He was especially solicitous also to have them copied into newspapers. The following list shows the date and place of publication of each poem, so far as known, in the chronological order of their issue, with notes on the order of composition so far as can be conjectured on reasonable grounds. In several instances revision occurred very late during his life, notably in his marginal correction of the Lorimer-Graham copy of 1845, and also elsewhere; where Griswold's text, 1850, differs from the last publication, known to him, there is no reasonable ground to doubt that he had manuscript authority in every case, among the Poe papers given into his hands as literary executor; on the other hand, there were final printed texts unknown to Griswold. There is no such example in literature of poetic elaboration as is contained in the successive issues of these poems as here listed.

[The following abbreviations are used: Y. L. G., The Yankee and Boston Literary Gazette; B. J., Broadway Journal; G. M., Burton's Gentleman's Magazine; A. C., Atkinson's Philadelphia Casket; S. L. M., Southern Literary Messenger; S. M., Philadelphia Saturday Museum; Gra. M., Graham's Magazine; A. W. R., American Whig Review; Pio., The Pioneer; S. V., Baltimore Saturday Visiter; S. E. P., Philadelphia Saturday Evening Post; God. L. B., Godey's Lady's Book; A. M., Baltimore American Museum; E. M., New York Evening Mirror; M. M., Missionary Memorial; H. J., Home Journal; C. M., Columbian Magazine; U. M., Union Magazine; S. U. M., Sartain's Union Magazine; F. U., Flag of Our Union; N. Y. T., New York Tribune; Gr. 1842, Griswold, "Poets and Poetry of America," 1842. The editions of 1827, 1829, 1831, 1845, are indicated by those dates only.]

1827. 1. Tamerlane. 1827; extracts in Y. L. G., Dec. 1829; 1829; 1831; 1845.

2. Song (I saw thee on thy bridal day). (To ——), 1827, with same title, and 1829; B. J. ii, 11; 1845.

3. Dreams. 1827.

4. Spirits of the Dead. (Visit of the Dead), 1827; 1829; G. M., July, 1839.

5. Evening Star. 1827.

6. A Dream within a Dream. (Imitation), 1827; extract in Y. L. G., Dec. 1829; (To ——), 1829; incorporated in Tamerlane, 1831. The title is Griswold's.

7. Stanzas. (No title), 1827. The title is Stedman's.

8. A Dream. (No title), 1827; 1829; B. J. ii, 6; 1845.

9. "The happiest day, the happiest hour." (No title), 1827.
10. The Lake. To ——. (The Lake), 1827; 1829; incorporated in Tamerlane, 1831, but not in 1845; 1845; M. M., 1846.

The titles, 1–10, represent Poe's work previous to his nineteenth year. The Wilmer MS. is intermediate between 1827 and 1829, and to the same period properly belongs the poem, "Alone," copied into a Baltimore album, March 17, 1829, and first published in "Scribner's Magazine," Sept. 1875; a poem of the same title occurs in the Wilmer MS., but it is half indecipherable, and wholly different in matter, being related to title 15.

1829. 11. To Science. (No title), 1829; A. C., Oct. 1830; 1831; S. L. M., May, 1836; B. J. ii, 4; 1845. The title is, Sonnet — To Science, in all.
12. Al Aaraaf. Extracts in Y. L. G., Dec. 1829; 1829; 1831; extracts in S. M., March 4, 1843; 1845.
13. To ——. (The bowers whereat in dreams I saw.) 1829; B. J. ii, 11; 1845.
14. To the River ——. 1829; G. M., Aug. 1839; S. M., March 4, 1843; B. J. ii, 9; 1845.
15. To ——. (I heed not that my earthly lot.) (To M——), 1829; 1845.
16. Fairyland. Extract in Y. L. G., Sept. 1829; 1829; 1831; G. M., Aug. 1839; B. J. ii, 13; 1845.
17. Romance. (Preface), 1829; (Introduction), 1831; S. M., March 4, 1843; B. J. ii, 8; 1845.

The titles, 11–17, represent Poe's work during his army life and the summer following, that is, from the age of eighteen to that of twenty-one. It may include earlier work not used in 1827, but this is unlikely.

1831. 18. To Helen. 1831; S. L. M., March, 1836; Gra. M., Sept. 1841; S. M., March 4, 1843; 1845.

19. Israfel. 1831; S. L. M., Aug. 1836; Gra. M., Oct. 1841; S. M., March 4, 1843; B. J. ii, 3; 1845.

20. The City in the Sea. (The Doomed City), 1831; (The City of Sin), S. L. M., Aug. 1836; A. W. R. (sub-title, A Prophecy), April, 1845; B. J. ii, 8; 1845.

21. The Sleeper. (Irene), 1831, and with same title, S. L. M., May, 1836; Gr., 1842; S. M., March 4, 1843; B. J. i, 18; 1845.

22. Lenore. (A Pæan), 1831, and with same title, S. L. M., Jan. 1836; Pio., Feb. 1843; S. M., March 4, 1843; B. J. ii, 6; 1845.

23. The Valley of Unrest. (The Valley Nis), 1831, and with same title, S. L. M., Feb. 1836; A. W. R., April, 1845; B. J. ii, 9; 1845.

The titles, 18–23, represent Poe's work from the age of twenty-one to that of twenty-two and a few months; like the titles, 1–17, they are properly *juvenilia*, their present highly finished forms being due to repeated and mature revision.

1833. 24. The Coliseum. S. V., 1833; S. L. M. (with sub-title, A Prize Poem), Aug. 1835; and, also with sub-title, S. E. P. June 12, 1841; (Coliseum), Gr., 1842; S. M., March 4, 1843; B. J. ii, 1; 1845.

1834. 25. To One in Paradise. (No title), God. L. B. (in The Visionary), Jan. 1834, and S. L. M. (in the same), July, 1835; (To Ianthe in Heaven), G. M., July, 1839; Tales (in The Visionary), 1840; S. M., March 4, 1843; B. J. i, 19; B. J. (in The Assignation), i, 23; 1845.

1835. 26. Hymn. (No title), S. L. M. (in Morella), April, 1845, and (in the same tale G. M., Nov. 1839, Tales, 1840, and B. J. i, 25; (Catholic Hymn), B. J. ii, 6, and with same title, 1845.

27. To F——. (To Mary), S. L. M., July, 1835; (To One Departed), Gra. M., March, 1842, and with same title, S. M., March 4, 1843; B. J. i, 17; 1845.

28. To F——s S. O——d. (Lines Written in an Album), S. L. M., Sept. 1835; (To ——), G. M., Aug. 1839; (To F——), B. J. ii, 10; 1845.

1836. 29. Scenes from Politian. (Scenes from an Unpublished Drama), S. L. M., Dec. 1835–Jan. 1836; 1845.

1837. 30. Bridal Ballad. S. L. M., Jan. 1837; (Ballad), S. E. P., July 31, 1841; (Song of the Newly-Wedded), S. M., March 4, 1843; B. J. ii, 4; 1845.

31. To Zante. S. L. M., Jan. 1837; S. M., March 4, 1843; B. J. ii, 2; 1845. The title is Sonnet to Zante, in all.

The titles, 24–31, represent Poe's work for six years, up to the time of his going North. The order of composition may be conjectured as follows: 27, probably the same with the "poem of six or eight verses, addressed to Mary ——," his inamorata, in a Baltimore paper, 1833, but it should be noted that the title, To M——, occurs as 15, in 1829; 25, 26, 24, 29, the tales and the drama having been written in Baltimore; 28, the lines having been originally addressed to Eliza White, of Richmond; with 30, 31, uncertain as to date. Both 27 and 28 were later addressed to Mrs. Frances Sargeant Osgood, of New York. The title, 30, seems an expansion of 2, and both were doubtless poetic growths from his early romance with Miss Royster; the poem given in S. L. M., Aug. 1835, as an unpublished Scotch ballad is connected with 30, probably the first draft of the theme, and if this conjecture be accepted, the date of 30 would naturally be later than Aug. 1835, and both 30 and 31 may have been written in Richmond; otherwise, there is nothing from Poe's hand, in poetry, except 28, during the year and a half of his residence there.

1839. 32. The Haunted Palace. A. M., April, 1839; (no title), G. M. (in The Fall of the House of Usher), Sept. 1839, and Tales (in the same), 1840; Gr., 1842; S. M., March 4, 1843; (no title), Tales (as before), 1845; 1845.

1840. 33. Silence. (Silence. A Sonnet), G. M., April, 1840; (Sonnet—Silence), S. M., March 4, 1843, and, with same title, B. J. ii, 3; 1845.

1843. 34. The Conqueror Worm. Gra. M., Jan. 1843; S. M., March 4, 1843; B. J. i, 21; B. J. (in Ligeia), ii, 12; 1845.

1844. 35. Dreamland. Gra. M., June, 1844; B. J. i, 26; 1845.

1845. 36. The Raven. E. M., Jan. 29, 1845; A. W. R., Feb. 1845; B. J. i, 6; S. L. M., March, 1845; 1845.

37. Eulalie. A. W. R. (sub-title, A Song), July, 1845, and also with sub-title, B. J. ii, 5, and 1845.

1847. 38. To M. L. S——. H. J., March 13, 1847. Addressed to Mrs. Mary Louise Shew.

39. Ulalume. A. W. R. (sub-title To —— ——), Dec. 1847; H. J., Jan. 1, 1848. The text is Griswold, 1850.

1848. 40. To —— ——. (To ——), C. M., March, 1848. Addressed to Mrs. Shew. The text is Griswold, 1850.

41. An Enigma. (Sonnet.) U. M., March, 1848. Sent to Mrs. Sarah Anna Lewis, Nov. 27, 1847.

42. To Helen. (To —— —— ——), U. M., Nov. 1848. Addressed to Mrs. Helen Whitman. Sent to Bayard Taylor, June 15, 1848. The text is Griswold, 1850.

1849. 43. A Valentine. S. U. M., March, 1849; F. U., 1849. Addressed to Mrs. Frances Sargeant Osgood. MS. dated Feb. 14, 1846.

44. For Annie. F. U., April, 1849; H. J., April 28, 1849; sent to Mrs. Richmond, March 23, 1849. The text is Griswold, 1850.

45. To my Mother. F. U., 1849. Mentioned May, 1849. The text is Griswold, 1850.

46. Annabel Lee. N. Y. T., Oct. 9, 1849; S. L. M., Nov. 1849; S. U. M., Jan. 1850.

47. The Bells. S. U. M., Nov. 1849.

48. Eldorado. Griswold, 1850.

The order of composition of the titles, 38–48, may be conjectured as follows: 43, 39, 38, 40, 41, 42, 47, 44, with

45, 46, 48, uncertain as to date. "Ulalume" is, by conjecture, the poem described by Mrs. Gove-Nichols, in the summer of 1846, but may have been rewritten. The Bells is mentioned in three states; the first draft, left with Sartain, probably in Sept., 1848, on Poe's return from Richmond, and 1848, representing the MS. written at Mrs. Shew's, apparently in the early summer of 1848; the second, mentioned February 8, 1849 (Poe to "Annie"), sent to Sartain about May, 1849; the third, sent to Sartain about Aug. 1849. "Annabel Lee" is first mentioned May, 1849 (Poe to "Annie"), as if then recently written; but Rosalie Poe (Mrs. Weiss, p. 129) professed to have heard it many times at Fordham in 1846, and a gentleman names it ("The Virginia Poe," i, 312) as recited by Poe in Richmond, 1848; Mrs. Osgood believed it commemorated his wife, and Mrs. Whitman that it referred to herself. Poe sent a "perfect copy" to Griswold about June, 1849 (Poe to Griswold). "To my Mother," said (Mrs. Weiss, p. 134) to have been written in 1847, is first mentioned May, 1849 (Poe to "Annie"). "Eldorado" is known only in Griswold's text. The late W. M. Griswold suggested to me that further authentication might be desired, though the copy was doubtless found among Poe's papers. Mrs. Richmond was sure that it did not appear in "The Flag of Our Union," and that Poe never mentioned it to her.

NOTES MAINLY ON OBSCURE OR CONTROVERTED POINTS

VOL. II

Page 4. POE AND HIRST. A sketch of Henry B. Hirst is given by Griswold, "Poets and Poetry of America," 1855, and a biography of him is in preparation by Dr. Matthew Woods. He wrote "The Ante-Diluvians," "Endymion," "The Coming of the Mammoth," "The Penance of Poland," "A Book of Cage-Birds," and, writes Dr. Woods, "much miscellaneous matter in prose and verse, including a couple of novels and some of the book reviews ascribed to Poe. . . . He was a native of Philadelphia, and died here mad in 1874." (Woods to the author, Oct. 14, 1894) Dr. Woods adds (Oct. 29, 1894), "Poe and Hirst became intimate in Philadelphia, so Thomas Dunn English, who told me he introduced them, says. I know also that Mr. Hirst took breakfast with Poe quite frequently Sunday mornings preliminary to their spending the day in country strolls." Theodore F. Wolfe, apparently on the same authority, wrote to the *New York Times*, Feb. 8, 1904: "Poe and Hirst were intimate friends and companions during the greater part of the period of the residence of the former in the Quaker City, and were closely associated not only in the follies and dissipations to which both were more or less addicted, but also in their literary work. Unto his dying day Hirst solemnly affirmed that he and not Poe was the writer of 'The Raven,' and that, at most, Poe had written but one stanza and part of another of the poem, the remainder of that stanza having been plagiarized by Poe from a poem well known to students of poetry. I saw in the hands of Dr.

Matthew Woods of Philadelphia the materials for an as yet unpublished biography of Hirst, in which the doctor expects to substantiate Hirst's claim to the authorship of 'The Raven.' Several of the poems which were published in Hirst's first volume had previously appeared in periodicals of which Poe was editor, and Poe's harsh criticisms of Hirst were subsequent to a quarrel with him and a rupture of the boon relationship which had existed between the two" Poe wrote a notice of Hirst (*Broadway Journal*, July 12, 1845), and during that year had a poem by Hirst accepted for the *Southern Literary Messenger* at the same time that he reprinted "The Raven" there. It seems likely that he may have had some hand in revising Hirst's lines. Mr. J. H. Whitty informs me that "through his [Poe's] efforts poems were published in the *Messenger*, 1843 to 1845, by Anna Marie Hirst, some relative of H. B. Hirst." The cause of the later coolness of the friends, says T. H. Lane, was Hirst's parodying two lines of "The Haunted Palace" thus: —

> "Never nigger shook a shin-bone
> In a dance-house half so fair."

Page 18. The statement of the financial agreement with regard to the *Pioneer* is from the Carter MSS.

Page 31. William Poe, formerly of Augusta, Ga., now resided in Baltimore, but soon removed South.

Page 35. Poe and Reid. The most accessible account of the association of Poe with Mayne Reid is that by Howard Paul (*Munsey's Magazine*, Sept. 1892). Paul was a nephew of T. C. Clarke and saw Poe in his boyhood. The reminiscences contain several curious Poe "legends," such as the detailed narrative of the composition of "Israfel," in less than an hour, for the afternoon paper, on the quotation by Clarke "from the Mohammedan Bible" of the well-known text as a possible subject of "a telling poem." The writer also mentions an elsewhere unknown visit of Poe to the Harvard

Library to consult "Trithemius, Vignere, and Niceron" on cryptography, and says that Poe had but one cryptograph ("a single response") sent to him in answer to his challenge to contributors (cf. ii, 40). The paper is interesting as giving the only picture of Poe at dinner parties, "warmed with wine and in a genial, glowing mood," and of his conversation and manner on such occasions. He describes his appearance at this time (1843): "Poe was a slight, small-boned, delicate looking man, with a well-developed head, which, at a glance, seemed out of proportion to his slender body. His features were regular, his complexion pale; his nose was Grecian and well-moulded, his eyes large and luminous, and when excited, peculiarly vivid and penetrating. He dressed with neatness, and there was a suggestion of hauteur in his manner towards strangers. He was impatient of restraint or contradiction, and when his Southern blood was up, as the saying goes, he could be cuttingly rude and bitterly sarcastic." Mr. Paul also mentions a sketch of a scenario of a tragedy to be worked out with Dr. Bird, of which there is no other hint, and tells an anecdote of Poe and J. B. Booth, father of Edwin Booth, — the twain, on their walk after the theatre, seizing an offended Jew and suspending him "by his breeches on the spikes of a convenient area railing, where they left him kicking and howling while they pursued their torturous way in gladsome mood." Poe's friendship with Booth is not elsewhere mentioned; but he seems to have been a playgoer both in Philadelphia and New York.

Page 37. A Charleston, S C., correspondent of the *New York Times* (no date, 1890?) gives the source of "The Gold Bug" as certain affidavits with regard to the wreck of the brigantine Cid Campeador, Julian de Vega, Commander, in the summer of 1745, off the South Carolina coast, preserved in the Probate Court Records. "It was also discovered," says the writer, "that he [Poe] paid many a visit to the old books in the office of the Probate judge, — certainly he paid one visit, and saw," etc. This was during Poe's soldier-days at Fort Moultrie. The papers were also published in *Frank Leslie's* and elsewhere, but no evidence is alleged except copies of the affidavits of the burying of the treasure.

Page 48. The *Saturday Museum* review was reprinted by Gill.

Page 64. POE IN 1843–44. There is much obscurity in Poe's movements toward the close of his residence in Philadelphia. He seems to have sojourned at times in New York; the only direct evidence, however, is contained in the reminiscences of Gabriel Harrison (*New York Times*, about March 1, 1899). Mr. Harrison was a young actor who had then forsaken the stage for "general merchandise," and was later known as an artist, and was in his shop on Broadway when the acquaintance began: —

"One chilly evening I happened to glance through my window and saw a small man with a large head looking in rather wistfully at some beautiful plugs of tobacco I had displayed. In a moment he entered and asked the price of tobacco. When I had told him he made no move to buy, and after a few general remarks started to leave. I was struck by a certain indefinite something in his manner, by his voice, and by his fine articulation. . . . So I offered the man a piece of tobacco. He accepted, thanked me, and departed. Two or three weeks afterward he came in again."

On the second occasion Poe composed for him a campaign song, of which Mr. Harrison remembered these lines: —

"'See the White Eagle soaring aloft to the sky,
Wakening the broad welkin with his loud battle cry;
Then here's the White Eagle, full daring is he,
As he sails on his pinions o'er valley and sea.'"

Mr. Harrison continues: —

"I was delighted and wanted to pay him something for his trouble, but the only thing he would accept was a bag of my best coffee. As he was going I said that I should like to know his name.

"'Certainly,' he answered, with a faint smile. 'Thaddeus Perley, at your service.'"

On the next occasion Mr. Harrison, after a brief absence with Halleck, found Poe standing by the counter, and he describes the *dénouement:* —

"'Why, good evening, Mr. Perley,' I began. Halleck interrupted me. 'Great heavens, Poe, is this you!' he exclaimed. 'Poe? This is Mr. Perley,' I broke in.

"Poe looked at me and then at Halleck, and after an instant's hesitation said: 'The fact of the matter is, Halleck, I have made this gentleman's acquaintance under the name of Perley; no harm was intended and none done. I knew that the facts would develop themselves. I have walked several miles through the sleet and rain, and, seeing a light in here, thought that perhaps Mr. Harrison would let me warm up somewhat.'

"'Why, of course,' I answered; 'here is the stove behind the tea boxes almost red hot. Take off your coat and dry it. What will you have, some of this old port?' I spread out some crackers, an old English pineapple cheese, and we all nibbled and bent our elbows in homage to his crimson majesty the old port, and talked of pleasant things till my big clock struck the hour of midnight. Poe left with Halleck and stopped at his house that night. He returned to his home in Philadelphia the next day, I believe, but soon afterward came to New York to reside." Cf. Mrs. Weiss (p. 99) in regard to Poe's "sharing the bachelor life and quarters of his associates who were not aware that he was a married man." Du Solle, the informant, seems to be speaking of New York reminiscences of this period.

Mr. Harrison afterward saw Poe habitually in New York, and made a well-known portrait of him. Whether he properly dates the occurrence is uncertain, but the only reason for doubt is that the presidential campaign was in 1844; it may, however, have been a local campaign to which reference is made. Poe had business in Philadelphia in the fall of 1844, when he superintended the issue of the third edition, 1845, of the "Conchologist's First Book," taking his name from the title-page, but signing the prefaces E. A. P. It was this edition which occasioned the charge of plagiarism in the Philadelphia newspapers. The fact of Poe's superintendence of this issue rests on Mr. Whitty's authority, who had the statement from the printers concerned in the work.

Thomas Dunn English refers to the occasion of Poe's leaving Philadelphia as follows ("Reminiscences of Poe," ii, *The Independent*, Oct. 22, 1896): "I happen to know why, and there were several others who knew all about it. They are all, I believe, dead. I am the sole possessor of the scandalous secret, and as its recital would do no good to any one, the whole affair shall be buried with me." The reference appears to be to the Saratoga story, mentioned in the text (ii, 43, 48). Whatever may be the truth as to his motives for leaving, Poe appears to have been making New York connections at this period, and an inquiring and speculative mind might readily find traces of his presence there, or of that of his "double," for example in the literary department of *Brother Jonathan*, 1843, Sept.-Dec. There had been a favorable acquaintance between him and its editor, Park Benjamin, since 1841.

Page 91. It is singular that no record remains of these "whole months" or of shorter periods of rambling. The early rambles at Charlottesville, where his recitations ended at nine o'clock in the morning, his walks with Wilmer at Baltimore and with Hirst at Philadelphia, and his solitary walks at Fordham by night, and his stay at Saratoga, comprise all that is known of these habits, except when he was irresponsible.

Page 100. This letter from Lowell to Poe, as well as all extracts from Stoddard's *Memoir*, is reproduced by the courtesy of G. P. Putnam's Sons (Poe's Works, New York).

Page 114. The story communicated to the *New Orleans Times*, about July 22, 1870, to the effect that "The Raven" was written by one Samuel Fenwick and came to Poe as a contribution which he appropriated on the death of its author, is a plain hoax. It rests, professedly, on an alleged letter of Poe to Daniels, Sept. 29, 1849, which is quoted. Cf. Note on Poe's Death.

Page 138. Mr. Saunders, librarian of the Astor Library, related (*New York Evening Sun*, no date) that he met Poe in Broadway after the publication of "The Raven," and describes him as "effusive" and "maudlin"; he gives a vivid anecdote of Poe's declaration of an intention to read the poem before the Queen, and says that "when he had been drinking, which was of frequent occurrence, he would talk of nothing but himself and his work, and the jealousy of other writers. . . . I knew him quite well in those days," he adds, and describes the next occasion. "The next time I saw him he was very much depressed, and was suffering from a fit of melancholia to which he was subject. He spoke of a conspiracy among the other authors of America to belittle his genius and to smother his work. 'But posterity shall judge,' he said, with a gleam of pride in his eye. 'Future generations will be able to sift the gold from the dross, and then "The Raven" will be beheld, shining above them all, as a diamond of the purest water.'"

Page 144. The reference to "getting up books" is blind; he may refer to the proposed edition of his poems and to the "American Parnassus," which is a natural interpretation. Mr. Whitty, however, whose opinion in this matter is entitled to great weight, writes to me that he believes the reference is to compiling — such books as "The Conchologist's First Book" and Lemonnier's "Natural History" of Philadelphia days; he thinks that Poe learned this art of compiling books with White, at Richmond, and did such hack-work more than has been thought, as a means of income, and some hints of such occupation may be found.

Page 146. Cf. for Poe's conversation on authors the "Poe-Chivers Papers" (*Century*, Aug. 1903). The final expression of Briggs's view of Poe is contained in "The Personality of Poe by the late Charles F. Briggs" (*The Independent*, Dec. 13, 1877): "But his dissipations — which were not intentional, for he was extremely temperate both in his diet and drink, unless he was subjected to strong temptations — were not the repulsive traits of his character. What rendered him so obnoxious to those who knew him intimately were his treachery to his friends, his insincerity, his utter disregard of his moral obligations, and his total lack of loyalty and nobleness of purpose. He aimed at nothing, thought of nothing, and hoped for nothing but literary reputation; and in this respect he gained all he aspired to, and his friends should be satisfied to know that he accomplished all he labored for, and not endeavor to compel the world to award him a character which he never coveted and held in supreme contempt."

Page 152. The comment on Greeley's remarks is a letter from Poe to Greeley, Feb. 21, 1847, on the occasion of some unfavorable notice in the *Tribune*. I know the letter only by the following fragment which is printed in a catalogue (Goodspeed, Boston, 1905): —

"In the printed matter, I have underscored two passages. As regards the first: — it alone would have sufficed to assure me that *you* did not write the article. I owe you money — I have been ill, unfortunate, no doubt weak, and as yet unable to refund the money — but on this ground *you*, Mr. Greeley, could *never* have accused me of being habitually unscrupulous in the fulfillment of my pecuniary engagements. The charge is *horribly false* — I have a hundred times left myself destitute of bread for myself and family that I might discharge debts which the very writer of this infamous accusation (Fuller) would have left undischarged to the day of his death.

"The 2d passage underscored embodies a falsehood — and *therefore you* did not write it. I did *not* 'throw away the quill.' I arose from a sick-bed (although scarcely able to stand or see) and wrote a reply which was published in the Phil. 'Sp. of the Times,' and a copy of which reply I enclose you. The 'columns of the Mirror' were tendered to me — with a proviso that I should forego a suit and omit this passage and that passage, to suit the purposes of Mr. Fuller."

Page 161. Students of the sources of "The Case of M. Valdemar" and "The Imp of the Perverse" may compare "Rambles and Reveries of an Art Student in Europe" by Thomas T. Watts, Philadelphia, pp. 36, 37.

Page 162. The demise of the *Broadway Journal* is narrated in detail by English (*The Independent*, Oct. 15, 1896). He says that Poe applied to him for advice, and that he influenced Lane to join Poe. The agreement between Lane and Poe, drawn by the latter, Dec. 3, 1845, and witnessed by Colton and George Sweet, transferred one half interest to Lane and left Poe in editorial charge. The office was removed to 304 Broadway, where English and Lane occupied adjoining rooms and had one servant in common. After the issue of number 24, Dec. 20, Poe "went off on one of his fits of drunkenness, leaving the material for number 25 partly finished. . . . After vain attempts for several days to get Poe into sobriety, and failing in them, Mr. Lane determined to close the publication with the next number." English furnished two articles, and the last number, 26, was issued Jan. 3, 1846. Mr. Lane certifies to the truth of this account. (Lane to English, *The Independent*, Nov. 5, 1896.)

Page 177. Of the various ladies whose names occur prominently in Poe's life, Miss Lynch (afterwards Mrs. Botta),

Mrs. Hewitt, Mrs. Ellet, Mrs. Osgood, Mrs. Locke, Mrs. Lewis, Mrs. Oakes Smith, Mrs. Gove-Nichols, some account is given by Griswold, "The Female Poets of America," 1854, and by Stoddard in his various articles and reminiscences. English gives (*loc. cit.* Oct. 29, 1896) the characteristic scene: "In the plainly furnished room at one corner stands Miss Lynch with her round cheery face, and Mrs. Ellet, decorous and lady-like, who had ceased their conversation when Poe broke into his lecture. On the sofa on the side of the room I sit with Miss Fuller, afterward the Countess Ossoli, on my right side, and Mrs. Elizabeth Oakes Smith on my left. At my feet little Mrs. Osgood, doing the infantile act, is seated on a footstool, her face upturned to Poe, as it had been previously to Miss Fuller and myself. In the centre stands Poe, giving his opinions in a judicial tone and occasionally reciting passages with telling effect." Cf. Stoddard's review of the "Memoirs of Mrs. Botta," *The Independent*, Feb. 1, 1894.

Page 185. "The Sphinx" appeared in *Arthur's Magazine*, Jan. 1846.

Page 190. Poe and Opium. This account of the source of Poe's ill-health, together with his letters to Snodgrass (i, 254) and to Eveleth (Jan. 4, 1848, Ingram, i, 215), which are the same in substance, makes his own statement of the case. There was always, as here, something enigmatical in the matter. Thus in writing to Chivers (July 22, 1846, "Poe-Chivers Papers," *Century*, Feb. 1903) a declaration of his abandonment of stimulants he expresses his desire to have a long talk some day, and adds, "there is much more in this matter than meets the eye." T. C. Clarke, the anonymous author of "The Late N. P. Willis and Literary Men Forty Years Ago" (*The Northern Monthly*, Jan. 1868), who states Poe was engaged in his office, says: "On this subject [meaning apparently Poe's distress in general] I have some singular revelations which throw a strong light on the causes that darkened the life, and made most unhappy the death, of one of the most remarkable of all our literary men." He does not further indicate the nature of this knowledge.

The earliest published statement, so far as I know, of the use of opium by Poe occurs in William Wallace's reply to John Neal, 1850 (no name nor date), where he uses this expression: "The poison, which, taken alternately with opium, kept him half his days in madness." The only direct testimony is that of Miss Herring (Miss Poe to the author, Aug. 28, 1884): "She told me that she had often seen him decline to take even one glass of wine, but says that, for the most part, his periods of excess were occasioned by a free use of opium." At my request Miss Poe had another interview with Miss Herring, and wrote again, Sept. 13, 1884, with reference to Miss Herring's acquaintance with the family at that time: "In 1840 or '41 her father, Mr. Herring, went to live in Philadelphia, and she was then a widow and lived with him. To her surprise one day she met Mrs. Clemm on Chestnut St., and then for the first time learned that the Poes were living in Philadelphia. After that she frequently went to see them, and had the misfortune to see him often in those sad conditions from the use of opium. . . . During these attacks he was kept entirely quiet, and they did all possible to conceal his faults and failures. After recovery his penitence was genuine, but he made good resolutions only to be broken."

The occasions on which opium is mentioned in his life are in June, 1846, on his return to Fordham, when Rosalie Poe says he "begged for morphine" (Mrs. Weiss, p. 128); in November, 1848, when he wrote Mrs. Richmond that he had taken laudanum in Boston (ii, 277); and in July, 1849, when Sartain says he begged for laudanum when in Philadelphia.

On the other hand, English says (*The Independent*, Oct. 15, 1896): "Had Poe the opium habit when I knew him, I should, both as a physician and a man of observation, have discovered it during his frequent visits to my rooms, my visits at his house, and our meetings elsewhere. I saw no signs of it."

Dr. John Carter also wrote to me, June 16, 1884: "Poe never used opii in any instance that I am aware of, and if it had been an habitual practice, we certainly would have detected it, as he numbered amongst his associates half-dozen physicians. . . . I never heard it hinted at before, and if he had contracted the habit, it would have accompanied him to Richmond." These are all the facts known to me, bearing on the subject.

I may state, in a matter of so leading importance, that I incline to the view that Poe began the use of drugs in Baltimore, that his periods of abstinence from liquor were periods of at least moderate indulgence in opium, and that in 1846–47 under the advice of his physicians he abandoned the habit; that his physical state and mode of life in 1847 are connected with this attempt, and his supposed success in it was the ground of his many statements that the "physical cause" of his fits of intemperance had ceased and the reiterated expressions of the excellence of his health; and that his begging for laudanum after his sprees was a sign of lapsing into an older habit, which he did not take with him to Richmond. This hypothesis seems to me to arrange the facts most harmoniously; but it is only a personal view, and may be erroneous. The student of the psychology of Poe should consult the elaborate work of Émile Lauvrière, "Edgar Poe. Sa Vie et son œuvre. Étude de Psychologie Pathologique." Paris, 1904. It is interesting, also, to observe the effect of this aspect of his hero's life on Baudelaire, "L'Influence d'Edgar Poe sur Charles Baudelaire," par Arthur S. Patterson, Grenoble, 1903.

Page 191. English gave the following account of this incident (*The Independent*, Oct. 29, 1906): —

"Poe came to 304 Broadway . . . and entering Lane's room, adjoining mine, where I was chatting with John H.

Tyler, a nephew of the ex-president, asked of me to lend him a pistol. I told him I had none, but he still insisted; and when asked what he wanted with it said that Colonel Lummis had threatened his life unless he showed him Mrs. Ellet's imprudent letters. I asked him why, if he had such letters, he did not produce them; and he rejoined that he had them, but would n't produce them under compulsion. I told him plainly that he had no such letters in his possession, in my belief, and that the best thing he could do would be to acknowledge that he had used the expression in a moment of irritation, and to make retraction and apology. One word led to another, and he rushed toward me in a menacing manner." The fracas followed, the combatants were separated by Professor Ackerman "from the front room," and Poe was "led away" by him.

On this Lane, in his letter to English, already cited, comments: —

"You had the capacity of being a perfect irritant to Mr. Poe, especially when the poet was lost in the inebriate. When entirely himself . . . he was gentle and respectful to you as to his other acquaintances and friends. How often he had rushed into my room, excitedly exclaiming, — 'Where is English? I want to kill him.' He goes on to speak of Poe's conduct in this instance as 'his maudlin desire to attack you.' English does not state that Poe was intoxicated; but this is implied in Mr. Lane's expressions, and it is agreed that Poe was never subject to such behavior except when so excited."

Mr. Lane writes kindly of Poe, but the expression he uses in giving him the charity of silence is most unfortunate; to profess silence is at best a poor way of keeping silence, and in this case he certainly chose his words ill. He ascribes Poe's failings to his poverty, in similar terms to those used by Graham. English states that Poe's lapses were only occasional. "His offenses against sobriety were commited at irregular intervals. He had not that physical constitution that would permit him to be a regular drinker. . . . He was not even a frequent drunkard when I knew him." He testifies, as to two occasions, "that one glass of liquor would affect him visibly, and the second or third produce intoxication." This statement is repeatedly made by others, and restricted to the effect of one glass. On the other hand, it is accompanied by the equally frequent statement that the effects of drinking were not observable in him after at least some degree of indulgence, and often showed only in his talk. More than one person states that he required to be warmed with wine in order to talk in company, and there are many notices of his wine-drinking without serious results, so far as appears. Thompson tells amazing stories of his capacity to stand a "tumbler-full" of brandy or even (on Poe's word, it is true) a score of juleps before breakfast. It is plain enough that no hard-and-fast limit of "a single glass" will stand examination, further than to sustain the belief that he was easily and immediately exhilarated by wine, and rapidly intoxicated by drams, maintaining a greater or less degree of concealing the fact; and at different times of his life and on different occasions there was considerable variability in the matter.

Page 219. The reminiscences of Mrs. Gove-Nichols ascribed to her, so far as I know, only on internal evidence, afford the only intimate portrait of the cottage at Fordham, and are both in vividness and tone so natural and true that I subjoin from the original the entire article, marking with asterisks the passages used in the text, in which these verbal errors occur owing to my imperfect copy, namely, — read *almost* before *petite*, p. 214; *spread* for *counterpane*, p. 218; *first* before *saw*, p. 219.

(REMINISCENCES OF EDGAR POE (*Sixpenny Magazine*, Feb. 1863).

Some sixteen years ago, I went on a little excursion with two others — one a reviewer, since dead, and the other a person who wrote laudatory notices of books, and borrowed money or favours from their flattered authors afterwards. He was called unscrupulous by some, but he probably considered his method a delicate way of conferring a favour upon an author or of doing him justice without the disagreeable conditions of bargain and sale. It is certain that he lived better and held his head higher than many who did more and better work. The reviewer petted him, and relied upon him, and gave him money when he failed to get it elsewhere.

We made one excursion to Fordham to see Poe. We found him, and his wife, and his wife's mother — who was his aunt — living in a little cottage at the top of a hill. There was an acre or two of greensward, fenced in about the house, as smooth as velvet and as clean as the best kept carpet. There were some grand old cherry-trees in the yard, that threw a massive shade around them. The house had three rooms — a kitchen, a sitting-room, and a bed-chamber over the sitting-room. There was a piazza in front of the house that was a lovely place to sit in in summer, with the shade of cherry-trees before it. There was no cultivation, no flowers — nothing but the smooth greensward and the majestic trees. On the occasion of this my first visit to the poet, I was a good deal plagued — Poe had somehow caught a full-grown bob-o'-link. He had put him in a cage, which he had hung on a nail driven into the trunk of a cherry-tree. The poor bird was as unfit to live in a cage as his captor was to live in the world. He was as restless as his jailer, and sprang continually in a fierce, frightened way, from one side of the cage to the other. I pitied him, but Poe was bent on taming him. There he stood, with his arms crossed before the tormented bird, his sublime trust in attaining the impossible apparent in his whole self. So handsome, so impassive in his wonderful, intellectual beauty, so proud and reserved, and yet so confidentially communicative, so entirely a gentleman on all occasions that I ever saw him — so tasteful, so good a talker was Poe, that he impressed himself and his wishes, even without words, upon those with whom he spoke. However, I remonstrated against the imprisonment of "Robert of Lincoln Green."

"You are wrong," said he, quietly, "in wishing me to free the bird. He is a splendid songster, and as soon as he is tamed he will delight our home with his musical gifts. You should hear him ring out like a chime of joy bells his wonderful song."

Poe's voice was melody itself. He always spoke low, even in a violent discussion, compelling his hearers to listen if they would know his opinion, his facts, fancies, or philosophy, or his weird imaginings. These last usually flowed from his pen, seldom from his tongue. * * * [See ii, 213–215.]

It was very flattering. She told Poe that his "poem of the Raven had awakened a fit of horror in England." This was what he loved to do. To make the flesh creep, to make one shudder and freeze with horror, was more to his relish (I cannot say more to his mind or heart) than to touch the tenderest chords of sympathy or sadness.

On the book-shelf there lay a volume of Poe's poems. He took it down, wrote my name in it, and gave it to me. I think he did this from a feeling of sympathy, for I could not be of advantage to him, as my two companions could. I had sent him an article when he edited the *Broadway Journal*, which had pleased him. It was a sort of wonder article, and he published it without knowing the authorship, and he was pleased to find his anonymous contributor in me. He was at this time greatly depressed. Their extreme poverty, the sickness of his wife, and his own inability to write, sufficiently accounted for this. We spent half an hour in the house, when some more company came, which included ladies, and then we all went to walk.

We strolled away into the woods, and had a very cheerful

time, till some one proposed a game at leaping. I think it must have been Poe, as he was expert in the exercise. Two or three gentlemen agreed to leap with him, and though one of them was tall, and had been a hunter in times past, Poe still distanced them all. But alas! his gaiters, long worn and carefully kept, were both burst in the grand leap that made him victor. I had pitied the poor bob-o'-link in his hard and hopeless imprisonment, but I pitied Poe more now. I was certain he had no other shoes, boots, or gaiters. Who amongst us could offer him money to buy a new pair? Surely not the writer of this, for the few shillings that I paid to go to Fordham must be economized somewhere and somehow, amongst my indispensable disbursements. I should have to wear fewer clean shirts, or eat a less number of oyster stews. In those days I never aspired to a broil. It is well that habit is a grand ameliorator, and that we come to like what we are obliged to get accustomed to. But if any one had money, who had the effrontery to offer it to the poet? When we reached the cottage, I think all felt that we must not go in, to see the shoeless unfortunate sitting or standing in our midst. I had an errand, however — I had left the volume of Poe's poems — and I entered the house to get it. The poor old mother looked at his feet with a dismay that I shall never forget.

"Oh, Eddie!" said she, "how did you burst your gaiters?"

Poe seemed to have come into a semi-torpid state as soon as he saw his mother.

"Do answer Muddie, now," said she, coaxingly.

"Muddie" was her pet name with her children.

I related the cause of the mishap, and she drew me into the kitchen.

"Will you speak to Mr. ——," said she, "about Eddie's last poem?"

Mr. —— was the reviewer.

"If he will only take the poem, Eddie can have a pair of

shoes. He has it — I carried it last week, and Eddie says it is his best. You will speak to him about it, *won't you?*"

We had already read the poem in conclave, and Heaven forgive us, we could not make head or tail to it. It might as well have been in any of the lost languages, for any meaning we could extract from its melodious numbers. I remember saying that I believed it was only a hoax that Poe was passing off for poetry, to see how far his name would go in imposing upon people. But here was a situation. The reviewer had been actively instrumental in the demolition of the gaiters.

"Of course they will publish the poem," said I, "and I will ask C—— to be quick about it."

The poem was paid for at once, and published soon after. I presume it is regarded as genuine poetry in the collected poems of its author, but then it bought the poet a pair of gaiters, and twelve shillings over.

At my next visit Poe grew very confidential with me.

"I write," said he, "from a mental necessity — to satisfy my taste and my love of art. Fame forms no motive power with me. What can I care for the judgment of a multitude, every individual of which I despise?"

"But, Mr. Poe," said I, "there are individuals whose judgment you respect."

"Certainly, and I would choose to have their esteem unmixed with the mean adulation of the mob."

"But the multitude may be honestly and legitimately pleased," said I.

"That may be *possible*," said Poe, musingly, "because they *may* have an honest and legitimate leader, and not a poor man who has been paid a hundred dollars to manufacture opinions for them and fame for an author."

"Do reviewers sell their literary conscience thus unconscionably?" said I.

"A literary critic must be loth to violate his taste, his sense of the fit and the beautiful. To sin against these, and praise an unworthy author, is to him an unpardonable sin. But if he were placed on the rack, or if one he loved better than his own life were writhing there, I can conceive of his forging a note against the Bank of Fame, in favour of some would-be poetess, who is able and willing to buy his poems and opinions."

He turned almost fiercely upon me, his fine eyes piercing me, "Would you blame a man for not allowing his sick wife to starve?" said he.

I changed the subject and he became quiet, and we walked along, noting beauties of flowers and foliage, of hill and dale, till we reached the cottage.

At my next visit, Poe said, as we walked along the brow of the hill, "I can't look out on this loveliness till I have made a confession to you. I said to you when you were last here, that I despised fame."

"I remember," said I.

"It is false," said he. "I love fame — I dote on it — I idolize it — I would drink to the very dregs the glorious intoxication. I would have incense ascend in my honour from every hill and hamlet, from every town and city on this earth. Fame! glory! — they are life-giving breath, and living blood. No man lives, unless he is famous! How bitterly I belied my nature, and my aspirations, when I said I did not desire fame, and that I despised it."

Suggestive that the utterance on both occasions might be true to the mood that suggested them (*sic*). But he declared that there was no truth in his first assertion. I was not as severe with him as he was with himself.

The autumn came, and Mrs. Poe sank rapidly in consumption, and * * * [See ii, 218, 219.]

"My poor child," said Mrs. Clemm, "my blessed and beloved, who has gone before me. Mrs. —— was so good to her. She tended her while she lived, as if she had been her dear sister, and when she was dead she dressed her for the grave in beautiful linen. If it had not been for her, my darling Virginia would have been laid in her grave in cotton. I can never tell my gratitude that my darling was entombed in lovely linen."

It seemed to soothe the mother's sorrow in a wonderful way, that her daughter had been buried in fine linen. How this delicate raiment could add so much to her happiness, I was not able to see, but so it was.

The same generous lady gave the bereaved mother a home for some time after the death of the poet. I think she only left her house to go to her friends in the South.

Soon after Poe's death, I met the aged mother on Broadway. She seized me by both my hands, regardless of the passers by.

"My Eddie is dead," she sobbed, hardly able to speak. "He is gone — gone, and left his poor Muddie all alone."

And then she thought of his fame, and she clung to me, speaking with pathetic and prayerful earnestness. "You will take care of his fame," said she; "you will not let them lie about him. Tell the truth of my Eddie. Oh, tell the truth — tell the world how great and good he was. They will defame him — I know they will. They are wicked and envious; but you will do my poor, dear Eddie justice." She pressed my hands convulsively. "Say that you will take my Eddie's part," said she, almost wildly.

"I can never do him injustice," said I; "I assure you I never will."

"I knew you never would," said she, seeming greatly comforted.

I have said nothing of Poe's genius. His works are before the world. Those who are able to judge of them will do so. There is no need to manufacture fame for the poet now. He cannot be pleased or benefited by it.

Poe has been called a bad man. He was his own enemy, it is true; but he was a gentleman and a scholar. His clear and vivid perception of the beautiful constituted his conscience, and unless bereft of his senses by some poison, it was hard to make him offend his taste.

People may be starved, so that they will eat coarse, disgusting, and unhealthy viands, and a poet has human liabilities. We may be sure if Poe sold his poems, to be printed as the productions of another, or if he eulogized what he despised, that the offence brought with it sufficient punishment. Poor Poe! If the scribblers who have snapped like curs at his remains, had seen him as his friends saw him, in his dire necessity and his great temptation, they would have been worse than they deem him to have written as they have concerning a man of whom they really knew next to nothing.

Requiescat in pace!

The poem which is described above as sold to Colton, editor of the *Whig Review*, and soon published presents a difficulty. No poem was published in the *Whig* until "Ulalume"; the words apply to that poem; but "Ulalume" has hitherto always been referred to a date later than the death of Poe's wife, in 1847. "Ulalume" was, therefore, if these facts be correctly stated, written before the summer of 1846, being a poem, like "The Raven," without reference to a real loss, or else the poem, like "The Bells," was rewritten after this. No other reference to Poe's selling poems to be published under another's name is known. It is plain that the author confuses Mrs. Shew and Mrs. Lewis. Mrs. Clemm lived with the latter at one time after Poe's death.

Other Fordham reminiscences are mainly by the neighbors, brief and simple annals of a poor family in need, and by a priest at Fordham, kindly in recognition of Poe's gentler nature and the pathetic side of his temperament and charitable in mention of his failings; these together with the recollections of the canal-boat boy (a companion piece with those of Poe's office-boy), are given in "Myths about Poe's Habits Refuted" (*New York Press*, April 4, 1897), and "Poe Not a Drunkard," by Appleton Morgan (*New York Commercial Advertiser*, Feb. 11, 1899). Cf. also "Fordham Home of Poe," by T. Waters (*New York Times*, Feb. 14, 1897), and "Edgar Allan Poe" (North Side Board of Trade, Jan. 19, 1909), from which it also appears that Poe was accustomed to row on the East River and swim near the islands south of Blackwell's in 1845–46.

Page 226. POE AND VIRGINIA. The view that the devotion of Poe to Virginia was rather of the nature of family affection than of wedded love was held in his immediate circle and has been much emphasized by Mrs. Weiss; it is, in fact, the substance of her book. Such intellectual sympathy as Poe found in his home, he sought from Mrs. Clemm, to whom he seems to have read his writings habitually in the course of their composition; Virginia, apparently, was not interested in such matters. Mrs. Clemm was credited with having made the marriage to keep the family united. Mrs. Phelps (*Newark Courier*, July 19, 1900) says, sustaining this view, — "Mrs. Clemm, his aunt, was my mother's dear friend . . . I know something about that [the marriage], having heard my mother and Mrs. Clemm discuss it. He did not love his cousin, except as a dear cousin, when he married her, but she was very fondly attached to him and was frail and consumptive. While she lived he devoted himself to her with all the ardor of a lover." Mrs. Osgood expressed (Griswold, liii) her conviction that Poe's wife "was the only woman whom he ever truly loved." His own words to Lowell (ii, 104) should be noted. Yet the impression prevailed among the relatives and family friends that the marriage was originally one of arrangement and had not proved the best.

The story of the accidental preservation of the remains of Virginia by Mr. Gill, when the tomb of the Valentines was abandoned, and of his keeping them in his room in a box, and finally reinterring them in Baltimore by Poe's grave, after a night-visitation from a raven, is a characteristic Poe "legend" which in this case seems to be the truth. (*Boston Herald*, Jan. 20, 1909.)

Page 236. The view of Poe held in New York at the time that he was engaged upon "Eureka" is indicated by two letters published by Eveleth ("Edgar A. Poe," *Portland Transcript*, June, 1849). The first is from the editor of the *New York Weekly Universe* (Aug. 1847): "Mr. Poe, in our estimation, holds a high rank, regarded either as an elegant tale-writer, a poet, or a critic. He will be more fairly judged after his death than during his life. His habits have been shockingly irregular, but what amendment they have undergone within the past six months, we cannot say, for Mr. Poe, during that time, has been in the country. We know him personally — he is a gentleman — a man of fine taste and of warm applause, with a generous heart." The second is from Colton (Oct. 1847): "I hope Mr. Poe has done drinking. I don't think he has drank anything this long time. He is living in a quiet way in the beautiful county of Westchester." Poe, in a letter to Eveleth (Feb. 1848), quoted in the same article, denies any acquaintance with the editor of the *Weekly Universe*, and adds: "My habits are rigorously abstemious, and I omit nothing of the natural regimen necessary for health: i. e. I rise early, eat moderately, drink nothing but water, and take abundant and regular exercise in the open air. But this is my private life — my studious and literary life — and, of course, escapes the eye of the world. The desire for society comes upon me only when I have become excited by drink. Then *only* I go — that is, at these times only I *have been* in the practice of going among my friends; who seldom, or, in fact, never having seen me unless excited, take it for granted that I am always so. Those who *really* know me, know better. But enough of this: the causes which maddened me to the drinking point are no more, and I am done drinking forever. My health is better — best — I was never so well."

Page 258. Another tradition of "The Bells," current several years ago, was revived in "Poe, the Weird Genius" (*Cosmopolitan*, Feb. 1909): —

"On one of these Baltimore visits he wrote the world-famous poem, 'The Bells.' Perhaps Mrs. Houghten had inspired him with the germ of the poem in New York, but the house where it was written in Baltimore still stands, a mute testimony of its Baltimore birth. Tradition treasures this story of 'The Bells': One winter night Poe had been to the public library and was walking home down Saint Paul's Street. It was snowy, and sleigh-bells made merry music. Their lilt and swing got into his brain, and he searched his pockets for pencil and paper. He had none. Stores were closed, and meanwhile exquisite phrases were being lost. He rushed up the steps of Judge A. E. Giles's residence, and rang the bell. The judge himself opened the door, and Poe requested paper and ink. The judge saw that he was a gentleman, invited him into the library, and courteously withdrew. After a time he looked in after his strange guest, only to find him gone; but there, lying on the table, were the first three stanzas of 'The Bells,' which the judge afterward had framed and hung in his office."

Page 273. Some glimpses of Poe's life in "bachelor quarters" are afforded by Col. John H. Montague (Richmond *Times-Despatch*, Jan. 17, 1909), a gentleman some ten or twelve years his junior, who hearing one evening a great noise there near nightfall, entered. He says: —

"I went through the first entrance, and, as the sound came from above, I started up the stairway. I had not gone many steps before I saw Poe standing at the top landing, half dressed, and with a gun in his hand, which he was leveling at me.

"I was almost paralyzed with apprehension, but dared not turn and run back. Being very young and active, I dived under the gun, and embracing him, said: —

" 'Mr. Poe, can you give me a drink?' The question and my expression touched his heart, and he replied: —

" 'Certainly, my boy, come in; we are glad to see you.'

"On another occasion my old schoolmate, John R. Thompson, the poet, suggested a call on Mr. Poe, who was then well known as a sometime contributor to the *Southern Literary Messenger*. He invited us in with politeness, and for a time his conversation was most brilliant and interesting. After a while he lapsed into a wild, unearthly, and wonderful rhapsody, while his great eyes glared and scintillated, and he seemed to be talking more to a peopled atmosphere than to a brace of youngsters."

Mr. John W. Ferguson (*ditto*), the old employee of the *Messenger*, who knew Poe from 1835 in that office, says very succinctly: "Mr. Poe was a fine gentleman when he was sober. He was ever kind and courtly, and at such times every one liked him. But when he was drinking he was about one of the most disagreeable men I have ever met."

The story of the challenge to Daniels is told by J. H. Whitty (Richmond *Times-Despatch*, Jan. 1909), who kindly allows me to reprint the material portion of it: —

"While in Richmond during the summer of 1848, Poe spent most of his time in the company of newspaper writers or about resorts frequented by them. He roomed most of this time with a Richmond newspaper editor. Among others he had met John M. Daniel, of the *Examiner*, and bad blood was shown between them from the start. They had talked about literary matters and did not agree. There also had been a debt transaction, which was a disputed matter. Daniel was also acquainted with some member of the Whitman family and made disparaging allusions to Poe and his intentions toward Mrs. Whitman, which came to the poet's ears.

"He became infuriated and at once sent a challenge to Daniel to fight a duel. Judge Robert W. Hughes, who wrote for the *Examiner* and had a personal acquaintance with Poe, remembered the affair well and told the particulars. The newspaper friends of Poe did not regard the affair as serious, and knew that it would soon blow over. Poe's challenge, written on the letter head of a sheet of one of the Richmond newspaper offices, was taken to Daniel, who also regarded the matter lightly. An arrangement was effected by which Poe was to seek satisfaction from the fiery editor in his sanctum. Poe was informed that Daniel would not meet him on the outside in the usual way, but preferred to settle matters between them alone in the *Examiner* office. While Poe was hardly in any condition to fight a duel, he was induced to go to the *Examiner* office, where Daniel awaited him alone by appointment.

"When he entered and saw Daniel he drew himself up to full height and demanded, in his haughty manner, why he had sent for him. Daniel was sitting near a table on which was displayed two very large, old-fashioned pistols, which the quick glance of Poe soon espied. Daniel in a cool and quiet manner asked Poe to be seated. Then he told him that he did not care to have the matter get to the police authorities, and suggested that instead of the usual formalities of the code they settle the dispute between them then and there. They were alone, the room was large and he pointed to the pistols ready for use. The quietude of the place, Daniel's demeanor, and this strange request tinged something of the grotesque. Poe began to sober up. He asked some questions about their difficulty and soon became convinced that matters were exaggerated.

"Then he told Daniel, in his characteristic way, of the challenge sent by the Maryland poet, Edward Coate Pinkney, to his former early benefactor, John Neal, editor of the *Boston Yankee*, and how the young poet had walked for a week before Neal's office in order to meet him. Daniel evinced much interest in the story, and Poe remarked to him that he hoped that he would not turn matters into ridicule in the next issue of the *Examiner*, like Neal did in his journal.

"Friends who had stood not far away, knowing there was little likelihood of any bloodshed, then broke in upon the scene. Matters were explained in a friendly way, and Poe was called upon by Daniel to finish his story about Pinkney, which he did, and recited as he only could: —

"I fill this cup to one made up
  Of loveliness alone;
A woman, of her gentle sex,
  The seeming paragon;
To whom the better elements
  And kindly stars have given
A form so fair that like the air,
  'T is less of earth than heaven.'

"After this they all repaired to a nearby popular resort, where there were more 'healths.'"

Mr. Whitty maintains that it was to this incident that Poe referred in writing later to Mrs. Whitman that her lines reached him when he was "about to enter upon a course that would have borne me far, far away from *you*, sweet, sweet Helen, and the divine dream of your love," — words that have hitherto been referred to his intention to offer his hand to Mrs. Shelton. It falls in with this view that Mr. Daniels was an acquaintance of the Whitmans, and that Mrs. Shelton in her reminiscences does not speak of meeting Poe before the next year, 1849, and then speaks as if she met him for the first time. It is, nevertheless, proper to observe that the affair with Mrs. Whitman had not gone beyond an anonymous exchange of her valentine and his lines to her privately, though the former had been published by Willis in the *Home Journal;* that it is singular that he should not have met Mrs. Shelton in his stay in the city; that she is said by Mrs. Weiss (on hearsay) to have attended the public reading in the Exchange Hotel, and that the latter states positively that Poe came to Richmond in 1848 to make the match with Mrs. Shelton at the suggestion of Mr. MacKenzie, who told her so. There is, however, except the last statement, nothing first-hand told by Mrs. Weiss, and Poe should have the benefit of any doubt.

Page 293. The only facts that might be held to support Poe's words are the publication by Mrs. Whitman of her poem, "The Island of Dreams," in February, 1848, and of her "Song" ("I bade thee stay") in June, 1849.

Page 316. Of George Lippard and C. Chauncey Burr only brief bibliographical notices have come under my observation. Lippard was the more intimate with Poe; he wrote some novels and a revolutionary history, and contributed to the first number of Burr's *Nineteenth Century* an article, "The Heart Broken," a story of Charles Brockden Brown's career.

Page 325 POE AND MRS. LEWIS. Mrs. Lewis was one of the ladies who relieved Poe in 1847 (Poe to Mrs. Lewis, Nov. 27, 1847), and he gave much attention to noticing her poems in 1848–49. Stoddard writes ("Edgar Allan Poe," 1889), in connection with a curious account of visiting her home while Mrs. Clemm lived there, that Mrs. Lewis "paid him (Poe) one hundred dollars to review one of her books" and that "on his neglecting to do so" she "very naturally complained of him. He did not deny her charges, but simply remarked that if he reviewed her rubbish it would kill him. Nevertheless he did review it in the *Southern Literary Messenger* [Sept. 1848] and in *Graham's Magazine*, sending his notes to Bayard Taylor with the request that he would insert as his own production." Stoddard possessed this note. Taylor, temporary editor of the *Union*, 1848, held only a nominal editorship of *Graham's* for a brief time in the late fall of that year. Besides these notices Poe sent one to Thomas in Louisville, Feb. 14, 1849 (ii, 300), and apparently also to the *Western Quarterly Review* (ii, 327), and one to Griswold (Poe to Griswold, June 28, 1849). With regard to the latter, cf. Mrs. Lewis to Griswold, Sept. 20, (*Century*, Oct. 1894). Stoddard does not specify the source of his information with regard to the alleged payment.

Stoddard was a frequent writer on Poe, and, besides his memoir, originally written for the English edition of Poe's poems (Routledge, 1874) and republished in America (Widdleton, 1874), and the articles already noted in the text, wrote papers in *The Independent* ("Some Myths in the Life of Poe," June 24, 1880: "Ingram *in re* Poe *et al.*," ditto, editorial unsigned), and occasional editorials in the *New York Mail and Express* during his long association with that journal.

Page 342. POE'S DEATH. Griswold, whom later writers have followed, derived his information, obviously incorrect as to dates, probably from Neilson Poe, who, at least, offered it (Neilson Poe to Griswold, Nov. 1, 1849, MS. copy): "The history of the last few days of his life is known to no one so well as to myself, and is of touching and melancholy interest as well as [of] the most admonitory import. I trust that I can demonstrate that he passed, by a *single indulgence*, from a condition of perfect sobriety to one bordering upon the madness usually occasioned only by long continued intoxication, and that he is entitled to a far more favourable judgement upon his last hours than he has received. All this I will make the subject of a deliberate communication."

It is open to conjecture that Poe did not leave Richmond on the boat, as Mrs. Shelton and other friends were told, but this hypothesis has never been put forward, nor is there anything substantial to sustain it. The tale (generally regarded as a hoax) that Poe ascribed the authorship of "The Raven" to Fenwick rests on his alleged letter, which is given, to Daniels, dated Sept. 29, 1849. If there was ever an original for that letter, this date would indicate that he remained in some resort in the vicinity, and wrote the letter under such circumstances.

The only account of Poe's last days not referred to in the text is an interview with "a former Baltimorean recently living in San Francisco" which was widely published in 1889 by Didier and others, in the press. It contains the description of the "widow Meagher's" place, said to have been a resort of Poe, and a detailed narrative of his being drugged and taken from one polling-place to another. It is full of impossible statements of fact. The same interview reappeared in new form and again went the rounds of the press, especially in St. Louis, San Francisco, and the southwestern states. The "Baltimorean" is variously described as residing in Dakota and on the Pacific coast, and is named as Dr. Snodgrass. This interview found its last victim in Mrs. Weiss (p. 205), who takes from it her account of Poe's last days. The Dr. Snodgrass, who was Poe's friend and found him, died long before 1889, and whoever the reminiscent Bohemian may have claimed to be, the story appears merely a fabrication on the basis of the old rumor.

Page 349. POE'S GRAVE. On the occasion of the erection of the Baltimore monument to Poe, in 1875, Mr. Henry Herring wrote to the *Baltimore American* as follows: "He was buried in his grandfather's (David Poe) lot near the centre of the graveyard, wherein were buried his grandmother and several others of the family. I furnished a neat mahogany coffin, and Mr. Nelson Poe the hack and hearse.. Mr. Nelson Poe, Judge Nelson and myself, together with Mr. Charles Suter, the undertaker, were the only persons attending his funeral." A headstone was provided by Neilson Poe, but was broken by accident before it was set up, and the grave remained unmarked except by a fragment of sandstone used for numbering lots, with the figure "80" on it, placed there by the sexton, George W. Spence. This was the only memorial, if it can be called so, for twenty-six years. Mrs. Clemm was buried beside Poe. When the new monument was erected it was necessary to remove the remains to the grave of Mrs. Clemm; the disinterment was made, the bones examined by a curious group, and the coffin enclosed in another and reinterred (*Baltimore American*, Oct. 1, 1875). The new monument was dedicated Nov. 17, 1875.

Page 340. POE AND GRISWOLD. The letters of Poe to Griswold, prefixed to the latter's Memoir of Poe, are the main source of information as to their personal relations. Of these letters two originals only were among the Griswold MSS., and both varied materially from the printed text (cf. "The Virginia Poe," xvii, 200, and 169, 202); but, however garbled the letters, the relations of the two men are plain. The story of these has been told in the text to the time of the breach of their acquaintance in 1843. Poe made advances toward reconciliation in 1845. He desired to be represented in Griswold's new compilation, "Prose Writers of America," and wrote with regard to that subject; their personal relations were renewed, and their correspondence was confined to the business of Poe's texts in Griswold's new work and in his revision of his former work on the American poets, and to a loan of fifty dollars in 1845, when Poe applied in all quarters for money to carry on the *Broadway Journal;* these business communications contain expressions of regard for Griswold's work and apologetic expressions for censure, which may or may not be garbled or interpolated, but which are sustained by Poe's public notices of Griswold in the press. Griswold had great control over literary reputation through his compilations and other publishing connections, and also Poe's pen, critically, was to be feared. The two lived on terms of worldly amity, but each had a private opinion of the other in reserve. Outside of literary affairs, it has been charged that they were rivals in the favor of Mrs. Osgood (cf. *Potter's American Monthly*, July, 1877, in reply to an article by Mrs. M. (Hewitt) Stebbins in the *New York Tribune* of about the same date); but it is plain from the Memoir that the influence of her friendship with Griswold was thrown in defense of Poe, and this intimacy appears to have been of a date somewhat later than 1845. She died May 12, 1850, and was buried at Mt. Auburn. The letters, it should be noted, cease after 1845, with the business of the "Prose Writers" and the *Broadway Journal*, and begin again only in 1849 with the business of the new edition of the "Poets and Poetry of America." There is no mention of any request of Poe to Griswold to serve as his literary executor; but Poe is said to have written to Griswold, and also to have expressed the request verbally through the Lewis family, and Mrs. Weiss says that he showed her a letter in which Griswold accepted the duty. The last letter of Poe to Griswold, June 28, 1849 ("The Virginia Poe," xvii, 362) was printed by Griswold, unless it be regarded as the original of the letter on the same subject given by him, to which it bears the faintest resemblance. Griswold, so far as Poe's judgment was concerned in selecting him as literary executor, was by far the best man in the country for the work.

Horace Greeley, in an editorial note in the *Tribune*, 1850, says: "We learned by telegraph the fact of Poe's death at Baltimore, in the afternoon following its occurrence and soon after, meeting Dr. Griswold, and knowing his acquaintance with Poe, asked him to prepare some account of the deceased for the next morning's paper. He *immediately and hastily wrote in our presence* his two columns or more." This was the obituary notice, signed "Ludwig" (*New York Tribune*, Oct. 9, 1849). Griswold maintained that he did not become the literary executor of Poe until after this was written. He received the papers of Poe from Mrs. Clemm and Neilson Poe. The latter writes (Neilson Poe to Griswold, Nov. 1, 1849, MS. copy), referring to Poe's trunk which had been forwarded from

Richmond by Thompson: "I have opened his trunk and find it to contain very few manuscripts of value. The chief of them is a lecture upon the poetic principle and some paragraphs prepared, apparently, for some literary journal. There are, however, a number of books, his own works, which are full of corrections by his own hand. These ought, undoubtedly, to be placed in your hands." These volumes were the copies of the Tales and Poems, now known as the Lorimer-Graham copies, the copy of "Eureka," now known as Hurst's copy, and possibly others, all afterwards sold with Griswold's library. J. C. Derby, in "Fifty Years Among Authors, Books, and Publishers," 1884, gives the account of the publication: "Dr. Griswold had offered the works to nearly all the leading publishers, who declined to undertake the publication. He finally persuaded Mr. Redfield to try the experiment of issuing two volumes first, which were published and had a fair sale — then the third, and finally the fourth, volume were added to complete the works. The sale reached about fifteen hundred sets every year."

The two volumes appeared early in 1850, with Lowell's article from Graham's, revised, and the obituary notice by Willis from the *Home Journal*, Oct. 13, 1849, as prefatory matter. Willis had quoted in this article from the *Tribune* notice, and remonstrated against it. The *Tribune* notice had been widely reprinted in the press, but Griswold's remarks were first read by Graham, says the latter, in these volumes. Graham addressed an open letter to Willis (*Graham's*, March, 1850) on the subject of Poe's career and Griswold's notice, since often republished as "Graham's Defence of Poe." John Neal wrote a characteristic review of the two volumes, "Edgar A. Poe" (*Portland Daily Advertiser*, April 23, 1850), which, though often referred to, seems seldom to have been seen. It is written in a rambling and vituperative manner, and contains nothing valuable except the account of Neal's early correspondence with Poe. Neal never saw Poe, and claims no direct knowledge of him or his affairs." The following brief paragraphs contain his view of Poe's character and career: "My notion of the poor fellow has been from the first that he was always taken advantage of by others, and therefore he got soured, resentful, and suspicious. I do not mean by this that everybody cheated him, for he was, to my knowledge, handsomely paid for some of his writings; but that he was not discouraged in the very outset by two or three very foolish enterprises, by his friend Graham and others, who knew that he would never be a popular Magazine-writer. . . . I believe that after he had to do with the *Southern Literary Messenger*, and failed in two or three literary adventures, one after another, which as a matter of business, ought never to have been thought of seriously, for a single day, nor ever entered upon, but with a large capital, and a party who would like to spend a few thousands just for the fun o' the thing, his whole outward character changed. . . . I believe, too, that he was by nature, of a just and generous temper, thwarted, baffled, and self-harnessed by his own wilfulness to the most unbecoming drudgery. . . . I believe, too, that he was a very honest fellow, and very sincere, though incapable of doing justice to anybody he might happen to dislike no matter why; or to anybody he thought over-cuddled by the monthlies or over-slobbered by the weeklies. . . . That his natural temper changed before death, and that he saw the world at last, with other eyes than he was born with; and that instead of the unearthly brightness that broke forth, in flashes, every time he lifted the wings of his boyhood, like a seraph, he delighted for the last few years of a weary life, in 'raying darkness' upon the people about him, is clear enough."

William Wallace (cf. i, 336) soon replied to this in an article, "John Neal" (the clipping is without name or date), and had little difficulty in exposing the weak points of Neal's remarks, while he reviewed the connection of Poe and Griswold as evinced by the former's public notices. The controversy was bitter in tone, as was the habit of that day. On the announcement of the third volume of Poe's works, containing "The Literati," a New York correspondent of the *Sentinel of Freedom* thus spoke of Poe as a blackmailer — "a plunderer by profession, — a sort of privateers-man," and he continues with as violent expressions as were ever used of Poe. On the other hand, others, editorially, defended him. It was at this time, probably, that Wilmer also wrote, in Philadelphia, his article, "Edgar A. Poe and His Calumniators," which has not been found, but probably does not differ from Wilmer's later utterances. Such was the atmosphere in which Griswold wrote his Memoir, prefixed to the third volume, signed Sept. 2, 1850, and first published in the *International*, Oct. 1850.

Griswold maintained that he had done a kindly act, in writing the Memoir as he did. Others agreed with him, as, for example, Redfield: "Griswold never received a cent for his labors. Poe named him as his literary executor shortly before he died, although they had quarreled not long before. Griswold's labor was no joke. Few men would have undertaken it with no hope of reward. It is fashionable nowadays to throw mud at him. Knowing, as I did, both of the men, and knowing, also, how assiduously Griswold labored to say everything he could in the biography in Poe's favor, it is very annoying to read these things. The matter of the biography was all read over to me, talked and discussed before printing, and I *know* he did his best to 'set down naught in malice.' He was obliged, as he thought, to state the facts in all cases, and he did state them, favorably as he could to Poe. I *know* he tried to do so Now he is accused everywhere, by people who know nothing about it, of vilely slandering Poe. I had a better opportunity than any one else to know all about it, and I know he did not." (Redfield to Derby, *loc. cit.*)

Charles Godfrey Leland, "Memoirs," 1893, bore precisely the same testimony, and adds this: "One day I found in his [Griswold's] desk, which he had committed to me, a great amount of further material collected to Poe's discredit. I burnt it all up at once, and told the Doctor what I had done, and scolded him well into the bargain. He took it all very amiably." (Cf. Appendix A, "Griswold's World.") Mrs. Clemm stated that she destroyed all letters from women to Poe; and Mrs. Richmond destroyed, before her death, the originals of Poe's letters to her, though copies made apparently without her knowledge may be in existence.

To Griswold's memoir no reply, so far as I know, was made by Poe's friends, except in so far as Burr's article (1852) was a plea in mitigation of judgment, and, long afterwards, Clarke's article (1868) quoted, with cordial endorsement, the testimony of Willis, and added a few words of the writer's own. On the other hand, Thompson, Thomas, and Kennedy, and Mrs. Lewis remained on friendly terms with Griswold; English, Briggs, and Wallace sustained him, Redfield and Leland defended him, and Stoddard wrote often and much to substantiate his statements. It is also just to add that the characterization that Griswold gave, in substance though not in feeling, was the same as that which uniformly prevailed in tradition in the best-informed literary circles in this country. The rebirth of Poe's reputation took place in writers of the next generation.

INDEX

INDEX

The titles of volumes published by Poe are set in small capitals; of his single poems, tales, and other works, in italics; titles of periodicals and of the works of other persons, in roman between quotation marks.

THE END